READER, I MARRIED HIM

Also by Patricia Beer

Autobiography
MRS BEER'S HOUSE

Criticism
AN INTRODUCTION TO THE METAPHYSICAL POETS

Poetry
LOSS OF THE MAGYAR
THE SURVIVORS
JUST LIKE THE RESURRECTION
THE ESTUARY
DRIVING WEST
SELECTED POEMS

READER, I MARRIED HIM

A Study of the Women Characters of
Jane Austen, Charlotte Brontë,
Elizabeth Gaskell and George Eliot

Patricia Beer

First published 1974
Reprinted 1975, 1977
First published in Papermac 1980

Published by
THE MACMILLAN PRESS LTD
London and Basingstoke
Companies and representatives
throughout the world

Printed in Hong Kong

British Library Cataloguing in Publication Data

Beer, Patricia
    Reader, I married him
    1. Women in literature
    2. English fiction — Women authors — History and
    criticism
    3. English fiction — 19th century — History and
    criticism
    I. Title
    823'.7'09352   PR830.W6

    Papermac ISBN 0–333–29326–6

For
Mary Turner

Contents

Preface

The highly important and enjoyable books that have appeared in the last ten years both in England and America on the subject of women's Lib have one shortcoming. Whatever they may claim to do, in fact they treat literature as if it were a collection of tracts into which you dip for illustrations of your own polemic, falsifying and omitting as necessary, your argument being of more moment than the other person's work of art. This rhetorical approach seems a pity as novels and plays are so much more illuminating if they are not used as a means to an end, either by writer or reader. The novel in particular, without benefit of anyone's argument, can show quite precisely how things are or were, in spite of or even through its discrepancies, hesitations and ambiguities, even through the active muddle-headedness of the novelist.

This book sets out to show how women and their situation were depicted in certain English novels of the past. The idea of doing such a book in the first place was suggested to me by Dr Mary Turner, who teaches history. She felt, as I later came to do, that the subject might be of interest to readers who, without being necessarily either students of English literature or supporters of Women's Lib, had a concern in the novel and the cause of female emancipation. I am extremely grateful to her for the suggestion. I have rather limited its scope, I am afraid, by confining myself to a study of only four novelists: Jane Austen, Charlotte Brontë, Elizabeth Gaskell and George Eliot. I hope, however, that what the survey lacks in breadth it will gain in concentration and that the discussion may be given point by the fact that the novelists are all women and that their work spans a period during which the arguments and activities connected with the Woman Question, as it was then beginning to be called, were for the first time occupying a prominent place in English society.

London   P.B.
January 1974

ix

Chapter I

There are probably many women, neither callous nor mercenary, who, presented with the alternatives of inheriting a fortune or marrying Branwell Brontë would unhesitatingly choose the money. Yet Elizabeth Gaskell, in her *Life of Charlotte Brontë*, without checking her facts condemned Mrs Robinson, Branwell's employer, for acting in this way and for having seduced the young tutor in the first place; condemned her so roundly and so noisily that she was threatened with libel action if she did not withdraw her remarks, which in later editions she did. This example of a woman attacking a woman on insufficient evidence, and on the absolute assumption that in any such situation the woman must be at fault, sets the tone of the present discussion.

An examination of the work of four women novelists writing mainly in the nineteenth century – Jane Austen, Charlotte Brontë, Elizabeth Gaskell and George Eliot – reveals a network of discrepancies concerning what came to be known as the Woman Question: between what the novelists thought in real life and the views they set forth or implied in their novels; between what they accepted for themselves and what they accepted for their heroines. Sometimes the novelist was the greater rebel, sometimes the woman. Each was inconsistent in herself and there was little agreement among them. Charlotte Brontë could not see the point of Jane Austen, George Eliot could not see the point of *Jane Eyre*, and Elizabeth Gaskell was distressed that George Eliot was not really Mrs Lewes.

It is only in so far as their work is concerned, of course, that the dissimilarities and inconsistencies of these novelists become truly interesting. Otherwise they are merely the notions of a small sample of intelligent middle-class women with varying degrees of education. With the exception of the first chapter this book deals with the novels, and as novels not as vehicles of opinion. But initially there must be some account of such events and circumstances of the writers'

1

lives as were likely to influence or form their attitudes to the whole question of the status and situation of women in their time.

The looks and destinies of these four novelists, the former affecting the latter and both affecting their creative work, show a wide range. Jane Austen (1775–1817) died a spinster. It is not easy to deduce how she regarded her unmarried state. Claustrophobically as she was situated in her family, with so many close relatives, and particularly her sister Cassandra, to love and take an interest in, it may have given her little pain. Certainly her intense and happy relationship with her sister, threatened at the time of Cassandra's engagement but given a lifelong reprieve by the death of the fiancé, grew with the years and culminated in her dependence on her sister in her last illness. As long as she was able to write letters they expressed her lively positive gratitude to Cassandra, in a tone quite different from the passive acceptance or concealed resentment of most patients.

It was her relatives after her death who spread the tragic story of an admirer to whom she was greatly attracted and who would certainly have proposed had he not died soon after meeting her, but in the absence of firsthand evidence this sounds like a pious fancy especially as they could not agree about such a basic fact as his name. Reports about her appearance are conflicting and inconclusive, and the beady-eyed, puffy-cheeked portraits do not help, but she seems at least not to have been plain to a degree that preys on a woman's mind.

Such of Jane Austen's letters as are preserved are, for the most part, unpenetrating, given up to prattle about muslin gowns, mamalone caps and coquelicot feathers, and riddled with thoughtless flippancies. Occasionally we come across a suspicious piece of bravado about husband-hunting: 'I am prevented from setting my black cap at Mr. Maitland by his having a wife and ten children', but this is nothing to build on. Much more significant are the areas of deep disquiet which the letters taken as a whole seem involuntarily to reveal.

She could not bear to hear about married bliss. It was not that she feared the damping effects of marriage on the brides among her acquaintance, though she did write to her niece Fanny Knight: 'I shall hate you when your delicious play of

Mind is all settled down into conjugal and maternal affections.' It was raptures she could not face, from either bride
or bridegroom.

> I have had a most affectionate letter from Buller; I was
> afraid he would oppress me by his felicity and his love
> for his wife, but this is not the case; he calls her simply
> Anna without any angelic embellishments, for which I
> respect and wish him happy.[1]

> We have heard nothing from Anna. I trust she is very
> comfortable in her new home. Her letters have been very
> sensible and satisfactory, with no *parade* of happiness
> which I liked them the better for. I have often known
> young married women write in a way I did not like in that
> respect.[2]

(Incidentally, the Annas referred to are two quite different
young women.)

The hushed tones and downcast eyes of Jane Austen the
novelist when female sexuality is, unavoidably, somewhere
in the offing, are not matched in the letters, where she can-
vasses the subject with a robustness and a knowing worldli-
ness which do not sit quite easily on her.

> I am proud to say that I have a very good eye at an
> Adultress, for tho' repeatedly assured that another in the
> same party was the *She*, I fixed upon the right one from
> the first.[3]

> She found his manners very pleasing indeed. The little
> flaw of having a Mistress now living with him at Ashdown
> Park, seems to be the only unpleasing circumstance about
> him.[4]

> We plan having a steady Cook, and a young giddy House-
> maid, with a sedate, middle aged Man, who is to under-
> take the double office of Husband to the former and sweet-
> heart to the latter. No children of course to be allowed on
> either side.[5]

[1] Letter to Cassandra Austen, 8 Nov 1800.
[2] Letter to Fanny Knight, 18 Nov 1814.
[3] Letter to Cassandra Austen, 12 May 1801.
[4] Ibid., 8 Jan 1801.   [5] Ibid., 3 Jan 1801.

It was for remarks far milder than these that she condemned Mary Crawford in *Mansfield Park* as being insensitive and coarse. In fact Mary sounds more like Jane Austen herself than any of the heroines do.

Jane Austen had a fear, mounting to an obsession towards the end of her life, about child-bearing. Considering the number of her relatives and friends who died in childbed this was basically a reasonable fear. But it became neurotic. As her own spinsterhood grew more and more inevitable she took to pitying her fertile, nubile nieces, dreading that the 'business of Mothering' would wear them out prematurely. (Ironically, Anna Lefroy and Fanny Knatchbull lived to be nearly a hundred.) When she was in the advanced stages of her last illness the whole concept of pregnancy seemed too much for her and in despair she compared her own condition with that of childbirth.

> Mrs. F. A. has had a much shorter confinement than I have – with a Baby to produce into the bargain. We were put to bed nearly at the same time, and she has been quite recovered this great while.[6]

The letters are full of comments about the dangers and difficulties of having children.

> I believe I never told you that Mrs. Coulthard and Anne, late of Manydown, are both dead, and both died in childbed. We have not regaled Mary with this news.[7]

> Mary does not manage matters in such a way as to make me want to lay in myself. She is not tidy enough in her appearance; she has no dressing-gown to sit up in; her curtains are all too thin; and things are not in that comfort and style about her which are necessary to make such a situation an enviable one.[8]

> Mrs. Tilson's remembrance gratifies me, and I will use her patterns if I can; but poor Woman! how can she be honestly breeding again?[9]

[6] Letter to Anne Sharp, 22 May 1817.
[7] Letter to Cassandra Austen, 17 Nov 1798.
[8] Ibid., 1 Dec 1798.   [9] Ibid., 1 Oct 1808.

Good Mrs. Deedes! I hope she will get the better of this Marianne, and then I would recommend to her and Mr. D. the simple regimen of separate rooms.[10]

Anna has had a bad cold, looks pale, and we fear something else. She has just weaned Julia.[11]

Anna has not a chance of escape; her husband called here the other day, and said she was *pretty* well but not *equal* to so long a walk; she *must come in* her *Donkey Carriage*. Poor Animal, she will be worn out before she is thirty. I am very sorry for her. Mrs Clement too is in that way again. I am quite tired of so many children. Mrs Benn has a 13th ... The Altons dined with us, the last visit of the kind probably, which *she* will be able to pay us for many a month. Very well, to be able to do it so long, for she *expects* much about this day three weeks.[12]

On the day of her arrival at Roe Head School, Charlotte Brontë (1816–55) was told by a fellow-pupil, Mary Taylor, that she was very ugly. Charlotte was fourteen at the time and it seems to have been a definitive experience. Typically, instead of holding it against Mary Taylor or simply avoiding her, Charlotte became a close friend and in later life declared that this piece of truth-telling had done her a great deal of good. Certainly she hugged the idea of her plainness to her, and all the charitable compliments that she received in adult life – about her hair, her voice, her eyes – and her own increasing knowledge that she had the power to win lasting affection, seem never to have loosened this fixed idea.

The two proposals she received in youth did nothing to build up her confidence. One of them was from a most eligible suitor, Henry Nussey, a young clergyman, brother of her friend Ellen. Though acknowledging frankly to Ellen that ten to one she would never have the chance again, she refused, giving two reasons for her refusal, both of them to Ellen, one of them to Henry. To Ellen she explained not only that she felt she could not make Henry happy, but also that

---

[10] Letter to Fanny Knight, 20 Feb 1817.
[11] Ibid., 13 March 1817.
[12] Ibid., 23 March 1817.

though I esteemed, though I had a kindly leaning towards him because he is an amiable and well-disposed man, yet I had not, and could not have, that intense attachment which would make me willing to die for him; and, if ever I marry, it must be in that light of adoration that I will regard my husband.[13]

For Henry, in indicating her own unsuitability, she sketched, with revealing italics, the kind of woman who would really suit him:

The character should not be too marked, ardent and original, her temper should be mild, her piety undoubted, her spirits even and cheerful, and her *personal attractions* sufficient to please your eyes and gratify your just pride.

To him she was equally frank about her future chances, as she saw them:

I scorn deceit, and I will never, for the sake of attaining the distinction of matrimony and escaping the stigma of an old maid, take a worthy man whom I am conscious I cannot render happy.[14]

The second offer came, a few months later, from an Irish curate, Mr Bryce, who declared himself after only one visit to Haworth. In telling Ellen about this proposal and her refusal, for which she appeared to think the reasons self-evident, she concluded, rather perversely in the circumstances:

I am certainly doomed to be an old maid. Never mind, I made up my mind to that fate since I was twelve years old.[15]

Given both Charlotte Brontë's defeatist attitude and her need to adore, her bitterly unhappy experiences in Brussels in 1843 and in the two years after she left it, were inevitable. If M. Heger had not existed she would have had to invent him. It was predictable that the great love of her life would be a teacher, and contemporary accounts agree that, even in an age of pedagogues, Heger was an outstanding teacher.

[13] Letter to Ellen Nussey, 12 March 1839.
[14] Letter to Henry Nussey, 5 March 1839.
[15] Letter to Ellen Nussey, 4 Aug 1839.

Her intellectual temperament, her fierce wish to improve herself and her preference for men, because they were better educated than their wives, all predisposed her to love someone who could teach her. In her youth the Henry Nusseys of the world, whom she might have helped, she rather despised; at any rate, she refused to marry them. Like Mina Laury, the creation of her youth, she had to be able to call a man 'Master'. It was only in later life that she could write:

> Against the teaching of some (even clever) men, one instinctively revolts. They may possess attainments, they may boast varied knowledge of life and the world; but if of the finer perceptions, of the more delicate phases of feeling, they be destitute and incapable, of what avail is the rest? . . . No man ever yet 'by aid of Greek climbed Parnassus' or taught others to climb it.[16]

The other irresistible charm that M. Heger possessed was unavailability. Charlotte Brontë found him in the middle of a close and growing family group. His wife, the former Zoë Parent, was a woman of intelligence and character, who had made a successful career for herself before she married, a sophisticated woman who held enlightened views about such matters as feminism. In other words she excelled in the very qualities that Charlotte could offer and had, by reason of her temperament and circumstances, a great many advantages beside. Although Charlotte Brontë in her novels was to give great importance to the woman who came between the heroine and the man she loved. Mme Heger never acted in this way, except by simply existing; there was no need to.

Miserably back at Haworth, waiting for letters that did not come, Charlotte, 'tamed and broken down' as she described herself, was left only with the support that family life could provide. In the past the company and affection of her sisters had been enough, with only the very minor drawbacks of a certain ganging-up on the part of Emily and Anne, and a certain unacknowledged resentment that Charlotte seems to have felt towards Emily (she stated, for example, that Emily was a much worse linguist than herself, whereas

16 Letter to George Smith, 16 March 1850.

M. Heger's report suggests the opposite). But the consolations of homelife now failed her entirely, even before the sequence of tragedies that came upon her: the increasing blindness and dependence of her father, the complete blighting of her hopes of founding a school, and the deaths of Branwell, Emily and Anne.

Alone, and a famous novelist, her life changed and could have changed more dramatically than it did. The social life of literary London was open to her and she tried it from time to time, but whereas a more robust character could have gained great enjoyment and interest from it, Charlotte Brontë was kept back by her timidity, her headaches, her fits of depression, her lack of what she called 'animal spirits' and her persistent consciousness of her stunted physique and irregular features, a consciousness which was known of or guessed at by others. Years later her publisher, George Smith, wrote:

> There was but little feminine charm about her; and of this fact she was herself uneasily and perpetually conscious ... I believe she would have given all her genius and all her fame to have been beautiful.[17]

However, once away from the world of curates she attracted the attention of a very different kind of man. The same George Smith, whatever he might afterwards say, was sufficiently interested in her to alarm his mother, while James Taylor, third man in Smith Elder & Co., wished to marry her, in which aspiration he had Mr Brontë's all-important vote though unfortunately not Charlotte's. She could not overcome her hesitations about his suitability, though she was naturally tempted; she must have meant physical suitability for in fact he seems to have shared her interests to a far greater degree than did the man she eventually married.

That she should be driven in the end to accept someone so entirely unsuitable as Arthur Bell Nicholls – no responsible marriage bureau would have brought them within miles of each other – proves the extremity of her need, especially as now she was not in the least deluded about her own hopes of happiness or about anyone's.

[17] *Cornhill Magazine*, Dec 1900.

The longer I live the more I suspect exaggeration. I fancy it is sometimes a sort of fashion for each to vie with the other in protestations about their wondrous felicity – and sometimes they – FIB.[18]

Her doubts about her own situation she retained, and indeed imparted to others, up to and beyond the altar. It was as well she made no great parade of romantic attachment, for those who knew her diagnosed her state perfectly well. Thackeray wrote of her, in a letter to an American friend Lucy Baxter, these cruelly penetrating words:

> The poor little woman of genius! the fiery little eager brave tremulous homely-faced creature! I can read a great deal of her life as I fancy her in her book (*Villette*) and see that rather than have fame, rather than any other earthly good or mayhap heavenly one she wants some Tomkins or another to love her and be in love with. But you see she is a little bit of a creature without a pennyworth of good looks, thirty years old I should think, buried in the country, and eating up her own heart there and no Tomkins will come. You girls with pretty faces will get dozens of young fellows fluttering about you – whereas here is one genius, a noble heart longing to mate itself and destined to wither away into old maidenhood with no chance to fulfil the burning desire.

The tone of masculine superiority is so offensive that it is comforting to reflect that on one important point Thackeray was completely wrong. At the time of his writing, spring 1853, Tomkins had already been on the scene for some time, in the person of Mr Brontë's curate, and was just then pressing his suit with considerable vehemence.

Much sweeter and more sensitive is the letter from Catherine Winkworth, a friend of Mrs Gaskell's, who met Charlotte Brontë at Mrs Gaskell's house. The whole letter has great charm and delicacy, but it shows there was little doubt in anyone's mind and certainly not the bride's ('I cannot conceal from myself that he is not intellectual'; 'He is a Puseyite and very stiff') about the reason for marriage.

> I went in on Wednesday. Lily (Mrs. Gaskell) drew me in directly to the room, whispering: 'Say something about

18 Letter to Ellen Nussey, 26 Dec 1854.

her marriage' . . . When she was summoned away I began: 'I was very glad to hear something Mrs. Gaskell told me about you.' 'What was it?' 'That you are not going to be alone any more.' She leant her head on her hand and said very quickly: 'Yes, I am going to be married in June.' 'It will be a great happiness to you to have some one to care for, and make happy.' 'Yes, and it is a great thing to be the first object with anyone.' 'And you must be very sure of that with Mr. Nicholls; he has known you and wished for this so long, I hear.' She stopped and then went on: 'But, Katie, it has cost me a good deal to come to this.'[19]

How the marriage would have eventually turned out we cannot tell. It lasted only nine months. Mrs Gaskell, hopeful and affectionate, speaks lyrically about it:

Henceforward the sacred doors of home are closed upon her married life. We, her loving friends, standing outside, caught occasional glimpses of brightness, and pleasant peaceful murmurs of sound, telling of the gladness within.

Charlotte's own letters support this impression and contain a great deal of the enthusiasm which she deprecated in others. Her honeymoon in Ireland, which introduced her to her new relations, made her much more cheerful about the match she had contracted. It is ironical to see a woman who was as unlike Elizabeth Bennet as could well be, inspired by the sight of her husband's beautiful grounds at Banagher. Back in Haworth, pregnant and ill, she spoke with the deepest feeling of her husband's goodness and care, and on her deathbed declared herself to have been 'so happy'.

Of the four novelists, there is, at this stage of the discussion, least to say about Elizabeth Gaskell née Stevenson (1810–65). She lived what was, according to the conventions of the time, an entirely normal, feminine life – apart from her writing, of course. A very pretty girl, she was married at twenty-two. Her husband was a Unitarian clergyman, of appropriate age, manners and character – and appearance, too: he was a tall, handsome man. She herself had been brought up as a Unitarian and with her humane and socially-conscious disposition was well equipped to be a minister's wife. Indeed with her social and administrative gifts thrown

[19] Letter from Catherine Winkworth to Emma Shaen, 8 May 1854.

in she would have made an excellent Bishop's wife as she said herself, only half-jokingly, 'if the Unitarians ever come uppermost in my day'.

Her marriage was almost certainly a happy one. Some critics, for want of real evidence, have tried to hint into existence terrible rifts and clashes, but in fact the minor annoyances and irritations which occasionally creep into the letters indicate only a realistic, organic relationship. Admittedly, William Gaskell was a self-sufficient man who sometimes liked to go off on holiday by himself, but in the context of a thirty-year marriage this seems not to be such a desperate sign.

Mrs Gaskell lived one of those breathlessly busy Victorian lives which make one feel like taking to the sofa. A great believer in organisation as being half the battle, she ran her household most competently. She was a skilled hostess and nearly always had people staying or dining. Her relationship with her domestic staff was well in advance of the times. Her attitude was maternalistic, it is true, but she treated her dependants as full human beings with human needs and claims which she often went to considerable trouble to gratify. She was popular with both men and women, and was sufficiently secure both emotionally and socially to conduct with perfect propriety a long and sentimental friendship with a man, the American Charles Eliot Norton.

She had six children, four of whom, all daughters, survived. Her warmly maternal disposition caused her to regard the birth of children in general as a signal for rejoicing, and, unlike Jane Austen, she managed to make confinements sound easy, pleasant occasions. On the upbringing of her daughters she brought her full intelligence to bear as well as her full devotion. She studied them closely as individuals, both physically and mentally, and saw them grow up into fine, interesting women.

George Eliot (1819–80), born Mary Ann (or Marian) Evans, decided early in life, though not quite as early as Charlotte Brontë, that 'reciprocated affection' was not to be for her. At the age of twenty-one she wrote to an old school-friend, Martha Jackson:

Every day's experience seems to deepen the voice of foreboding that has long been telling me, 'The bliss of reciprocated affection is not allotted to you under any form. Your heart must be widowed in this manner from the world, or you will never seek a better portion; a consciousness of possessing the fervent love of any human being would soon become your heaven, therefore it would be your curse.'[20]

Like Charlotte Brontë she was obsessed by her lack of beauty, borne in upon her by such presumably well-meant compliments as that of Martha Jackson who, when assigning flower names to her friends, chose for her Clematis or Mental Beauty. At the age of twenty-nine we find her writing to another friend, Sara Sophia Hennell, about her own appearance in a vein of desperate fantasy which is painfully eloquent.

Now over a quarter of a century ago there was a very young sprite who forsooth having turned out some respectable toads and a few indifferent lemurs and marmosets must fain try his hand on a human article and one 22d of November he presented to Dame Nature at her evening levee a rough though unmistakeable sketch of a human baby.

Dame Nature was disgusted.

'A pretty piece of work I should have to patch up this thing into a human soul and body that would hang together! Here', she called to one of her Vishnu-sprites, 'smother it at once to save further harm.'

But the sprite was so distressed at having his work repudiated that his brother genii interceded for him and the monstrous baby was spared, on the condition that a dark-eyed maiden (Sara Hennell, of course) recently created, should be a guardian to the little ogre.

And so Dame Nature heard the intercession and the brother-sprites kept their word. For the poor sketch of a soul was found by the dark-eyed maiden and those other bright and good mortals and they pitied and helped it, so that at last it grew to think and to love.[21]

[20] Letter to Martha Jackson, 20 Oct 1840.
[21] Letter to Sara Hennell, 23 Nov 1848.

The compliment to Sara Hennell – the point of the letter as Sara was touchy and needed a lot of reassurance – is swamped by the fierce self-disgust.

Nearly everyone who knew George Eliot and wrote about her agreed that she was a woman with a longing for love beyond the average and that in spite of her strength of mind and character she was not fitted to stand alone. Her husband John Cross spoke of her 'absolute need of some one who should be all in all to her, and to whom she should be all in all'.[22] This need was not satisfied in her own family. The object of her childhood adoration, her brother Isaac, who comes out of it all as rather a lout, failed her again and again and, at the announcement of her union with George Henry Lewes, not only threw her off himself but persuaded her sister and half-sister to do the same. Even before this, the sisters, though she was fond of them, especially Chrissey, were no real support to her, occupied as they were with their own concerns and far below her intellectually. Her father seems never to have appreciated her till he was on his death-bed. She made attempts at intense friendship with women; at one point she and Sara Hennell were addressing each other as husband and wife. But by the end of her life it became clear that she did not really like women, though as a famous novelist she attracted a great many of them.

Her twenties, though spent mostly in the provinces and in company where she was not likely to be widely appreciated, brought experiences which could have given her some sexual confidence but do not appear to have done so. In 1845 she received a proposal, from a young picture-restorer, which was attractive enough to throw her into a state of considerable agitation and indecision. The previous year her visit to Dr Brabant, a pseudo-scholar and the father of a friend, had resulted in her being shown the door by Mrs Brabant on account of the attention the Doctor paid his young guest. The fact that nobody else thought his attention particularly worth having is irrelevant. At that time George Eliot thought it was and was only too successful in securing it.

In 1851 she went to live in London. Here she was mixing with her peers and a much more adventurous life began. At first the Brabant situation repeated itself, though at a more sophisticated level and with greater complications. John

[22] *George Eliot's Life*, I 15.

Chapman the publisher, at whose house in the Strand she was lodging, raised the ire not only of his wife but of his mistress by the amount of time he spent in George Eliot's room, once being detected holding her hand, 'a little incident' as he called it which led to pitched battle and her enforced departure.

In the same year her close friendship with Herbert Spencer began. The exact course and nature of this relationship are impossible to define. George Eliot at the time spoke of 'delightful cameraderie' and 'calm friendship' while he described her as 'the most admirable woman, mentally' he had ever met; it was Clematis all over again. In much later life Spencer, who survived George Eliot, was suspiciously anxious to assure the public that he had never been in love with her and made a perfect nuisance of himself to John Cross, her widower, trying to dictate to him what to say in his *Life* about the relationship. In Cross, however, he met his match. Spencer never married; he described himself towards the end as a 'melancholy Coelebs' but it seems fairly clear that he would have been a much more melancholy husband, and his offensive hints that George Eliot was not beautiful enough tell us more about him than about her.

What George Eliot really felt about the association, what humiliation or disappointment it may have caused her, are in hindsight all overshadowed by our knowledge of how in 1853 her union with George Henry Lewes began. It lasted till his death in 1878. George Eliot's happiness throughout was open and apparent, in spite of more than average ill-health and anxiety. Her frank expression of her contentment would no doubt have come under Jane Austen's condemnation as a 'parade of happiness', but most people would find both dignified and moving such entries in her Journal as the following:

> The last night of 1857. The dear old year is gone with all its *Weben* and *Streben*. Yet not gone, either; for what I have suffered and enjoyed in it remains to me an everlasting possession while my soul's life remains ... My life has deepened unspeakably during the last year: I feel a greater capacity for moral and intellectual enjoyment, a more acute sense of my deficiencies in the past, a more solemn desire to be faithful to coming duties, than I re-

14

member at any former period of my life. And my happiness has deepened too: the blessedness of a perfect love and union grows daily. I have had some severe suffering this year from anxiety about my sister and what will probably be a final separation from her – there has been no other real trouble. Few women, I fear have had such reasons as I have to think the long sad years of youth were worth living for the sake of middle age.

They could not marry. Agnes Lewes, after eight years of happy marriage and the birth of four sons, had started a liaison with Thornton Hunt which resulted in the birth of four more children. Lewes at first condoned the affair, and this made it impossible for him to get a divorce later when it dawned on even him, with his liberal principles, that the situation was unworkable. By the time he met George Eliot his marriage had quite broken down. But for the rest of his life he continued to give Agnes financial and moral support and to educate and look after his boys with scrupulous care. In all these duties George Eliot joined with great generosity. She was a very good stepmother. How much, if at all, she minded her own childlessness it is impossible to say. It was a deliberate decision on the part of the couple; they practised some form of birth control.

To George Eliot it seemed morally right in the circumstances that she should live with Lewes as his wife. She explained her views to her old friend Cara Bray:

Assuredly if there be one subject on which I feel no levity it is that of marriage and the relation of the sexes – if there is any one action or relation of my life which is and always has been profoundly serious, it is my relation to Mr. Lewes ... Light and easily broken ties are what I neither desire theoretically nor could live for practically. Women who are satisfied with such ties do *not* act as I have done – they obtain what they desire and are still invited to dinner.[23]

This last sentence clearly shows her resentment at the treatment her straightforwardness met with in so many quarters. Sensitive as she was to people's opinions, the degree of ostracism and censure she encountered, often unexpectedly

[23] Letter to Cara Bray, 4 Sep 1855.

as in the case of Harriet Martineau, must have caused her considerable suffering. And it was not only the wider public. Her family, as we have seen, disowned her and even some of her older and most tolerant friends were made uneasy and embarrassed. Cara Bray felt for some time that she could not write to her and though Sara Hennell continued the correspondence the former freedom had gone. Dr Brabant's daughter, Rufa Hennell, came out of it best, as the first to call on the couple and the first to invite them to dinner. Bessie Parkes's support was, to begin with, rather a liability as her feminist principles made her continue to address 'Mrs Lewes' as Miss Evans in spite of George Eliot's natural anxiety to keep in with her landlady.

Eighteen months after Lewes's death, George Eliot, now sixty, married John Cross, aged forty, whom she and Lewes had known for years and called their nephew. Though a marriage of genuine affection it was as much an epilogue to her life as Charlotte Brontë's had been; she died nine months later. The marriage took place at St George's, Hanover Square, and brought about not only a reconciliation with those, like her brother Isaac, who had deplored her illicit union with Lewes but also a breach with her feminist friends who had approved of it.

Three of the four novelists relied on the help of men in getting their work published, and of the three Jane Austen was the least lucky. Her father displayed the lack of persistence in selling which springs from lack of faith in the product. A gap of as long as six years separated one of his attempts from the next. In 1797 he offered *First Impressions* (the original version of *Pride and Prejudice*) to a publisher, and when the very idea of the book was turned down, with offensive speed and firmness, he waited till 1803 before sending *Susan* (the first version of *Northanger Abbey*) to another house. Later, from 1811, the novelist's brother Henry was both more confident and more successful in his negotiations on her behalf, but by then the wagon was beginning to roll, though even so not very fast or noisily.

Elizabeth Gaskell was more fortunate. The story goes that her husband positively encouraged her to write novels in the first place, after the death of her son William, and it is clear that when her work proved to be much more than a pallia-

16

tive hobby and that instead of taking her mind off her troubles it had become a preoccupation in its own right, he readily treated her as a professional with many though not all of a professional's claims. He organised, or at least supervised, the business side of her writing and such practicalities as proof reading.

> Mr. Gaskell consents to a trial of the cheap plan of publication of Cranford... What he wishes to know is what number you would propose to publish in the first instance? and how soon you think the returns on that number are likely to be made?... Mr. Gaskell, in returning one of the proofs, requested you to ask the printer to look whether there was not a repetition.[24]

If Mr Gaskell sounds bossy and interfering we should recall his wife's words: 'I would not trust a mouse to a woman if a man's judgement was to be had.'[25] There is little doubt that she welcomed her husband's management of her money. The much-quoted remark that she had been sent £20 for *Lizzie Leigh* and that William had 'composedly buttoned it up in his pocket'[26] is usually quoted out of context, making her sound aggrieved at this appropriation of her earnings. In fact she was saying that her first reaction to the payment was that it was too good to be true but that William's composure in pocketing it reassured her; that is, she was relying as usual on masculine judgement, and his action indicated not male cupidity but confidence in his wife's powers.

This vivid little scene was re-enacted later with another couple. Marian Evans Lewes thanked John Blackwood 'for the precious cheque which has just been safely deposited in Mr. Lewes's pocket on its way to the bank'.[27] On both occasions one seems to hear the affectionate tones of a strong-minded but not over-confident woman who finds it a relief to be managed. George Henry Lewes, as is well known, managed George Eliot's work as a novelist from the start. She has described in her Journal how the original impetus towards her writing fiction came from him. It had two immensely powerful elements, which put it in quite a different

[24] Letter to Edward Chapman, 25 Apr 1855.
[25] Letter to an unknown correspondent, 31 Oct 1856.
[26] Letter to Eliza Fox, 26 Apr 1850.
[27] Letter to John Blackwood, 25 Sept 1861.

class from Mr Gaskell's encouragement: as a professional himself Lewes was concerned with the artistic not the therapeutic consequence of his advice, and he was realistic, and clever, enough to admit his hesitations on the subject when they coincided with her own doubts and diffidence.

I always thought I was deficient in dramatic power, both of construction and dialogue, but I felt I should be at my ease in the descriptive parts of a novel. My 'introductory chapter' was pure description though there were good materials in it for dramatic presentation. It happened to be among the papers I had with me in Germany, and one evening at Berlin, something lead me to read it to George. He was struck with it as a bit of concrete description, and it suggested to him the possibility of my being able to write a novel, though he distrusted – indeed disbelieved in, my possession of any dramatic power. Still, he began to think that I might as well try, some time, what I could do in fiction.[28]

So she did, with further well-timed prompting by Lewes, and from *Amos Barton* onwards he presided. From first interesting John Blackwood in *Scenes of Clerical Life* and conducting all negotiations on behalf of the anonymous 'friend' whose identity was to cause so much pleasurable, and acrimonious, speculation, he seems to have taken over to the extent that, when at the height of her fame George Eliot decided to publish *Romola* with George Smith, who made a much higher offer for it than Blackwood could, Blackwood did not hesitate, in private, to ascribe her defection to 'the voracity of Lewes'. Certainly Lewes always occupied himself with the technicalities of design, format and production. He also became a sort of honorary research assistant, and the accounts of the help he gave George Eliot with her preparations for *Romola* remind one exactly of the unpaid, second-class secretarial work that the wives of geniuses – Effie Ruskin, for example – were expected gladly to render. He said himself in a letter to Blackwood: 'I am a sort of Italian Jackal, hunting up rare books and vellum bound unreadabilities in all the second hand bookstalls of London.'[29]

Psychologically he cushioned her as few women can ever have been cushioned, trying to protect her from every com-

[28] *Journal*, 6 Dec 1857.   [29] Letter to John Blackwood, 9 Oct 1861.

ment that might undermine her confidence and writing anxious letters to anyone who might be about to say something outspoken or robust, begging them on no account to do so. Whether or not this was necessary, or even good for her, can only be guessed. It is possible that he was compensating for his subsidiary role – though he played it so generously – with fussy over-protectiveness. But however it was, for twenty-four years he brought her great domestic happiness and as hers was clearly not a case where great domestic happiness undermines creativity (she could hardly have written more or better), we can only feel deeply grateful to him.

The forlorn condition of Charlotte Brontë at the beginning of her career as regards male help is well known. Her first attempt at publication, the volume concerned being a selection of poems by herself, Emily and Anne, was, as she said, 'hard work', and in all the practicalities and negotiations she seems to have had little support from her sisters. She set about her task with touching application, buying a book about how to prepare material for the press and diligently working her way through it. Her early letters to Aylott & Jones of Paternoster Row, who agreed to publish the poems, are anxious and careful, not so much from a fear of being deceived or taken advantage of as from a wish to be meticulous and businesslike.

But there was one weapon which a woman struggling alone in a man's world could employ and Charlotte Brontë made full use of it: the male pseudonym. She set out her reasons for doing so in the preface to the 1850 edition of *Wuthering Heights* and *Agnes Grey*:

> Averse to personal publicity, we veiled our own names under those of Currer, Ellis and Acton Bell; the ambiguous choice being dictated by a sort of conscientious scruple at assuming names, positively masculine, while we did not like to declare ourselves women, because – without at the time suspecting that our mode of writing and thinking was not what is called 'feminine' – we had a vague impression that authoresses are liable to be looked on with prejudice.

This perfectly adequate explanation of why the Brontë sisters used men's names – for in spite of Charlotte's jesuitical disclaimers they do sound masculine – conceals something else, the pleasure that Charlotte, if not the others, found in masquerading as a man. There is unmistakable gusto in her allusions to herself as 'he' in the guise of Currer Bell. Her youthful writings had prepared the way – she had often represented herself as a man, called Charles Thunder or Charles Townsend – and so had her identification of herself with Branwell.

In fact a fair amount of teasing along trans-sexual lines went on, rather improbably, at Haworth Parsonage. In the summer of 1840 Charlotte Brontë seems to have been interested in Willie Weightman, the handsome lady-killing curate, and her affection took the form of heavy-handed badinage: because of his curls, his pink cheeks and general charm she called him Celia-Amelia, a nickname which caught on. She seemed quite unable to drop it, even after the joke must long since have become stale, and her allusions to him in a letter to Ellen Nussey have a strangely camp quality. She recalls

> the painting of Miss Celia Amelia Weightman's portrait and that young lady's frequent and agreeable visits. By the bye I inquired into the opinion of that intelligent and interesting young person respecting you – it was a favourable one. She thought you a fine-looking girl and a very good girl into the bargain. Have you received the newspaper which has been dispatched containing a notice of her lecture at Keighley?[30]

Willie Weightman's rather inadequate retort to all this was to call Emily 'the Major'.

To Charlotte, who according to all reports was an essentially 'feminine' woman, the assumption of a masculine name apparently gave a sense of security in general, not only vis-à-vis the critics. The mere presence of men seems to have supported her which, given the characters of her father and brother, represents a triumph of conditioning. It was obviously one of her reasons for marrying Mr Nicholls. At all events to have a man's name herself gave her both pleasure and support.

With regard to her ostensible reason for calling herself Currer Bell, her 'vague impression' that there was prejudice among the critics against women writers was well founded and took solid shape as the years went by. It was not that

[30] Letter to Ellen Nussey, 17 March 1840.

there was open animus towards them but, much more insidious, that there was a double standard. As she wrote to George Henry Lewes on the publication of *Shirley*:

> I wish all reviewers believed 'Currer Bell' to be a man; they would be more just to him. You will, I know, keep measuring me by some standard of what you deem becoming to my sex; where I am not what you consider graceful, you will condemn me.[31]

Mrs Gaskell who quoted this letter in her *Life of Charlotte Brontë* also summarised her friend's view in a way that endorsed them and showed them to be rational rather than paranoid:

> She especially disliked the lowering of the standard by which to judge a work of fiction, if it proceeded from a feminine pen; and praise mingled with pseudo-gallant allusions to her sex, mortified her far more than actual blame.[32]

At the beginning of 1850 Charlotte Brontë's fears were fully realised, as Mrs Gaskell related. (She slightly modified the wording in later editions at George Henry Lewes's request.)

> The January number of the *Edinburgh Review* contained the article on *Shirley*, of which her correspondent, Mr. Lewes, was the writer. I have said that Miss Brontë was especially anxious to be criticised as a writer, without relation to her sex as a woman. Whether right or wrong, her feeling was strong on this point. Now in this review of *Shirley*, the heading of the first two pages ran thus: 'Mental Equality of the Sexes?' 'Female Literature,' and through the whole article the fact of the author's sex is never forgotten.[33]

Charlotte Brontë was furious and wrote to Lewes to say so. He remonstrated with her 'on quarrelling with the severity or frankness of a review, which certainly was dictated by real admiration and real friendship', She tried to make her position clear:

[31] Letter to George Henry Lewes, 1 Nov 1849.
[32] *Life of Charlotte Brontë*, ch. 18.
[33] Ibid., ch. 19.

I will tell you why I was so hurt by that review in the *Edinburgh*; not because its criticism was keen or its blame sometimes severe; not because its praise was stinted (for indeed, I think you gave me quite as much praise as I deserve), but because after I had said earnestly that I wished critics would judge me as an *author*, not as a woman, you so roughly – I even thought so cruelly – handled the question of sex.[34]

Given Lewes's later relationship with a woman novelist and his lifelong admiration and support of her work, this is ironical but less so than the fact that eight years later we find him writing to Blackwood, on the eve of the publication of *Adam Bede*, not only using Charlotte Brontë's argument but alluding to her experiences: 'When *Jane Eyre* was finally known to be a woman's book the tone noticeably changed.'

George Eliot's impression of the prejudice authoresses had to contend with was far from vague. She knew of the difficulties of Harriet Martineau who had to try to make her contributions to the *Edinburgh Review* sound 'like a man's writing' and who with great resourcefulness 'used the mannish way of talking about needlework'. As early as 1844 George Eliot told Cara Bray, only half-jokingly, about her dismay that Strauss, whose *Das Leben Jesu* she had translated, had discovered that the translator was a '*young lady*'.

I am sure he must have some twinges of alarm to think he was dependent on that most contemptible specimen of the human being for his English reputation.[35]

In 1855, just after the publication of an article of hers in the *Westminster Review*, 'Evangelical Teaching: Dr. Cumming', which attacked the religion of her youth, she wrote to Charles Bray:

Since you have found out the 'Cumming', I write by today's post just to say that it *is* mine, but also to beg that you will not mention it as such to anyone likely to transmit the information to London, as we are keeping the authorship a secret. The article appears to have produced a

[34] Letter to George Henry Lewes, 19 Jan 1850.
[35] Letter to Cara Bray, 18 June 1844.

strong impression, and that impression would be a little counteracted if the author were known to be a *woman*.[36]

In fact after she and Lewes had set up house together she had more reason than Charlotte Brontë ever had to cling to her masculine pseudonym. If she were known to be a woman it might soon be discovered which particular woman she was, and the immorality which even charitable readers might see in her situation would not have gone very well with the edifying sentiments of her books. At the time of the publication of *Adam Bede* the Blackwoods certainly had this fear.

But in all these anxieties, exaggerated as literary anxieties always are, and the consequent deceptions thought to be necessary, there was an element of playacting which must have brought some enjoyment with it. George Eliot did not throw herself into the masculine rôle as Charlotte Brontë did, partly because she had less of a taste for fantasy and partly, one suspects, because of an ambiguity in her appearance, which she must have known about and probably regretted. 'She speaks in a soft soprano voice', said Tennyson, 'which almost sounds like a fine falsetto with her strong masculine face.' 'She reminds you continually of a man', said Bret Harte, 'a bright, gentle, lovable, philosophical man', adding idiotically 'without being a bit masculine'. Even so there are signs that she found some relish in the pseudonym. In her Journal she quotes Blackwood's comment on the reception of *Scenes from Clerical Life*:

> The men at the club seem to have mingled their tears and their tumblers together. It will be curious if you should be a member and be hearing your own praises![37]

and goes on, quite conspiratorially: 'There was clearly no suspicion that I was a woman.' The fact that Agnes Lewes was convinced she was 'the father of a family' and 'a man who had seen a great deal of society etc. etc.' presumably amused her for adventitious reasons.

Lewes, who had a wholesome taste for deviousness, clearly enjoyed the whole thing. Whenever he wrote about George Eliot to people not in the know he used the masculine pronoun quite unnecessarily often. He frequently, and again

[36] Letter to Charles Bray, 15 Oct 1855.   [37] *Journal*, 6 Dec 1857.

quite gratuitously, made such remarks as this, in a letter to Blackwood: 'I shall take flight for Jersey and there George Eliot will be with me, engendering new clergymen, I hope.' Deliberately to evoke a fallacious picture of two middle-aged men of letters platonically pottering about together and to use, rather boldly in the circumstances the word 'engender' must have been great fun. So it must have been to say, again to the publisher: 'Last night I saw George Eliot' about the woman he was living with. In fact he continued the masculine pronouns if not the tacit lies long after George Eliot's identity had been revealed to Blackwood.

It is interesting that Dickens was never in the slightest doubt that George Eliot was a woman. Writing to congratulate her on *Scenes of Clerical Life* he said:

> I have observed what seem to me to be such womanly touches, in those moving fictions, that the assurance on the title-page is insufficient to satisfy me, even now. If they originated with no woman, I believe that no man ever before had the art of making himself, mentally, so like a woman, since the world began.[38]

And it was not merely a clever hunch. In a letter to John Blackwood he gave evidence to support his conviction:

> ... all the references to children, and ... such marvels of description as Mrs. Barton sitting up in bed to mend the children's clothes. The selfish young fellow with the heart disease, in 'Mr Gilfil's Love Story,' is plainly taken from a woman's point of view. Indeed I observe all the women in the book are more alive than the men, and more informed from within. As to Janet in the last tale, I know nothing in literature done by a man like the frequent references to her grand form, and her eyes and her height and so forth; whereas I do know innumerable things of that kind in books of imagination by women.[39]

The general experiences, as opposed to the emotional and literary experiences, of these four women compose a short list of the grievances which a woman living in the late eighteenth or nineteenth century might entertain if she were to question her lot at all, and, naturally enough, as the years

[38] Letter to George Eliot, 18 Jan 1858.
[39] Letter to John Blackwood, 27 Jan 1858.

went by and such grievances were increasingly aired she would be more and more likely to question her lot. All four novelists lived in a society based on an apparently unshakeable belief in the superiority of the male, but nevertheless three of them, by their lives or their novels or by both, did manage to shake it, a little.

Jane Austen, as chronology would suggest, was the most conformist of the four. She was in a position to have read Mary Wollstonecraft's *A Vindication of the Rights of Women*, which was published in 1792, but appears neither to have done so nor to have thought at all along the same lines. She not only accepted the limitations of women's scope but seems in her own life to have found happiness within them, being content to see the males of the family winning their way upwards in exciting careers, developing her own talents at odd hours and in secret, taking it for granted that home and devoted ministration to parents and siblings was a woman's portion, staying in brothers' houses as a useful adjunct in times of trouble, and, as spinsterhood clamped down, being patronised by at least one nubile niece: Fanny Knatchbull used to say in later years that her aunt's visits to Godmersham Park improved her beyond recognition.

In spite of her ignorance or dismissal of Mary Wollstonecraft, Jane Austen must have been aware that as far as the status of women was concerned the tide was beginning to turn. The eighteenth-century attitude, exemplified by the tolerant contempt of such writers as Addison towards the 'fair sex', had been greatly modified.[40] Exhortations such as Fordyce's *Sermons to Young Women* (1766) had become a subject that could be joked about. Conduct books such as Lady Sarah Pennington's *An Unfortunate Mother's Advice to her Absent Daughters* (1761), Mrs Chapone's *Letters on the Improvement of the Mind* (1773) and Dr Gregory's *A Father's Legacy to his Daughters* (1774) had been superseded by such manuals as Thomas Gisborne's *An Enquiry into the Duties of the Female Sex* (1797), a work which though far from revolutionary was markedly less reactionary than the other three.

The great causes of the Woman Question were yet to come. Jane Austen had no opportunity to nail such colours

[40] There is an excellent account of the whole situation in Frank Bradbrook's *Jane Austen and her Predecessors* (Cambridge, 1966).

as she might have to any mast or meaningfully to refrain from doing so. It is only from her private attitudes that deductions can be made and there is so much ambiguity of tone in her comments that it is difficult to come to any firm conclusion. How much female solidarity, for example, is to be found in the following remarks about the Princess of Wales's matrimonial troubles?

> I suppose all the World is sitting in judgement upon the Princess of Wales's Letter. Poor woman, I shall support her as long as I can, because she *is* a woman, and because I hate her Husband . . . I do not know what to do about it; but if I must give up the Princess I am resolved at least always to think that she would have been respectable, if the Prince had behaved only tolerably to her at first.[41]

Jane Austen suffered, through no fault of her own, from the ludicrous 'education' thought to be suitable for women in her day but unlike Charlotte Brontë and George Eliot, who made strenuous and more or less successful efforts to supply the deficiencies that society imposed, she endorsed them. If we may judge from her letters, she distrusted intelligence in women and the learning which an intelligent mind can hardly help acquiring, even regarding them as positive handicaps. The letters themselves are relentlessly trivial. She appears wishful to disclaim any pretensions to mind herself, both implicitly and explicitly. In writing to James Stanier Clarke, the Prince Regent's librarian, she describes herself as a woman who 'knows only her mother tongue, and has read very little of that' and adds,

> I think I may boast myself to be, with all possible vanity, the most unlearned and uninformed female who ever dared to be an authoress.[42]

It is difficult to know how to take this. If she really felt a novelist should study English and foreign literature why did she not do so? And she can hardly have thought that general ignorance of one's profession was an advantage; that is more a twentieth-century view. She seems genuinely to be boasting of being a silly little thing. The point of the letter is to turn down a serious though misguided suggestion

[41] Letter to Martha Lloyd, 16 Feb 1813.
[42] Letter to James Stanier Clarke, 11 Dec 1815.

about her future work; there is no need for coy self-depreciation. If the marriage market of the day did a brisk trade in silly women, as was probable, did she feel it necessary to acknowledge the fact and change her image accordingly? Miss Mitford's remark about her having been a 'husband-hunting butterfly' is dismissed by the faithful as spiteful and inaccurate but perhaps there was something in it. She certainly does have a horror of being thought a bluestocking; there are signs of it in the letters, in her habit of dithering when an academic word has to be used, for example in speaking of Southey's *The Poet's Pilgrimage to Waterloo*: 'The opening – the *proem* I believe he calls it – is very beautiful.'[43] She knew perfectly well it was called 'proem', but she had to gulp.

Charlotte Brontë had more occasion than Jane Austen to observe and suffer from the supremacy of men in the domestic situation. Patrick Brontë was undoubtedly a half-crazy tyrant. Even if we are not entirely convinced by Mrs Gaskell's descriptions of how he resented his wife's pregnancies as though he had played no part in them and burnt his children's clothing and hers if he thought it was too showy, we have evidence of his later brutal dismissal of Arthur Bell Nicholls and of his absolute assumption that his daughter, now aged nearly forty, should obey his wishes in the matter.

Then there was Branwell. 'My poor father thought more of his only son than of his daughters',[44] Charlotte wrote after her brother's death as though it was a perfectly natural state of affairs, and indeed since infancy she had lived in a world where it really did seem natural that, to further the career of this hopeless youth, his infinitely more gifted sisters had to go out to the governessing which made wrecks of them. Haworth was a household where men could indulge any caprice or despotism.

Yet Charlotte Brontë loved her home and felt no resentment at being confined to it; on the contrary it was her refuge. Even in the loneliness of her later years she did not often escape from it, though she had many opportunities to lead the fuller life of a famous woman. That was a freedom, denied to so many of her sex, for which she did not

[43] Letter to Alethea Bigg, 24 Jan 1817.
[44] Letter to W. S. Williams, 2 Oct 1848.

hanker. One factor of course was that, even without her writing, she would not have been bored as so many Victorian women were: she took an active part in the housework.

The horror of having to work for a living when for women the only possibility was governessing was experienced by Charlotte Brontë to a full, one sometimes feels to an exaggerated, degree. Her temperament made the very worst of it. More buoyant women suffered much less: Mary Wollstonecraft did pretty well and the Kay-Shuttleworths' governess positively took over. Mrs Gaskell's *Life* vividly conjures up the drawn-out dread that hung over the lives of the Brontë sisters, the nerving of themselves to go out yet once more, the overwork and the humiliation once a post had been secured, and always the financial necessity that would not retreat. She quotes from one of Charlotte's letters to Emily:

> The children are constantly with me. As for correcting them, I quickly found that was out of the question; they are to do as they like. A complaint to the mother only brings black looks on myself, and unjust, partial excuses to shield the children . . . I said in my last letter that Mrs. Sidgwick did not know me. I now begin to find she does not intend to know me; that she cares nothing about me, except to contrive how the greatest quantity of labour may be got out of me; and to that end she overwhelms me with oceans of needlework; yards of cambric to hem, muslin nightcaps to make, and, above all things, dolls to dress . . . I see more clearly than I have ever done before, that a private governess has no existence, is not considered as a living rational being, except as connected with the wearisome duties she has to fulfil.[45]

Of course a woman who ran a school could be an independent and respected member of society, like the Miss Woolers of Roe Head and Mme Heger, and this was for many years what the Brontë sisters aimed at, but it was not easy for anyone, and for them it was not to be.

Sheltered as in most respects Charlotte Brontë's life was, from an early age she learnt enough about what went on in the countryside around her to realise the general injustice with which women were treated in society. Mrs Gaskell relates how Charlotte as a child heard a most harrowing

[45] Letter to Emily Brontë, 8 June 1839.

story of the seduction of a young girl by her brother-in-law when she was a guest at his house while his wife was having a baby. The girl became pregnant and was cast off by her family who, however, 'went on paying visits at their wealthy brother-in-law's house, as if his sin was not a hundred-fold more scarlet than the poor young girl's whose evil-doing had been so hardly resented, and so coarsely hidden'.[46]

In maturity, Charlotte Brontë's views on the Woman Question, as it was brought to her notice over the years, were confused. For one thing her deeply-held belief that adversity does people good was bound to include the notion that for women to be exploited and put upon was not an entirely bad state of affairs. Indeed she suggested this point of view to Mr Williams, her publisher, when he consulted her about careers for his daughters.

> A governess's experience is frequently indeed bitter, but its results are precious; the mind, feeling, temper are there subjected to a discipline equally painful and priceless.[47]

For another thing, like every exponent of every cause under the sun, she was put off by her fellow-exponents.

> I often wish to say something about the 'condition of women' question, but it is one respecting which so much 'cant' has been talked, that one feels a sort of repugnance to approach it.[48]

There were other sources of confusion, particularly a conflict between optimism and pessimism in her thinking. For once she was too sanguine about something: she placed too much reliance on what had already been achieved with regard to the situation of women.

> The girls of this generation have great advantages; it seems to me that they receive much encouragement in the acquisition of knowledge, and the cultivation of their minds; in these days women may be thoughtful and well read, without being universally stigmatised as 'Blues' and 'Pedants'. Men begin to approve and aid, instead of ridiculing or checking them in their efforts to be wise. I must

[46] *Life of Charlotte Brontë*, ch. 3.
[47] Letter to W. S. Williams, 15 June 1848.
[48] Ibid., 12 May 1848.

say that, for my own part, whenever I have been so happy as to share the conversation of a really intellectual man, my feeling has been, not that the little I knew was accounted a superfluity and impertinence, but that I did not satisfy just expectation.[49]

Men begin to regard the position of women in another light than they used to do; and a few men, whose sympathies are fine and whose sense of justice is strong, think and speak of it with a candour that commands my admiration.[50]

Yet at the same time she was deeply gloomy about the efficacy of women's struggles to right the wrongs that remained. She knew that many men – John Stuart Mill was one of them – thought that the situation of women depended largely on themselves, and to an extent she agreed, but she felt that some of the obstacles were insuperable:

Certainly there are evils which our own efforts will best reach; but as certainly there are other evils – deep-rooted in the foundation of the social system – which no efforts of ours can touch: of which we cannot complain; of which it is advisable not too often to think.[51]

Perhaps the real difficulty was that Charlotte Brontë was too soft-centred to found any cause on justice and equity. For her, sentiment was more important than rights. Her reaction to the opinions of John Stuart Mill was illuminating. He was by far the most intelligent champion of women's rights at that time; although in 1851 his greatest pronouncement was still to come, he had published a splendid article on the emancipation of women in the *Westminster Review*. But it would not do for Charlotte Brontë.

Well-argued it is, – clear, logical, – but vast is the hiatus of omission; harsh the consequent jar on every finer chord of the soul. What is this hiatus? I think I know; and knowing, I will venture to say. I think the writer forgets there is such a thing as self-sacrificing love and disinherited devotion. When I first read the paper, I thought it was the

---

[49] Letter to George Smith, 16 March 1850.
[50] Letter to Mrs Gaskell, 27 Aug 1850.
[51] Kate Millett gives a good account of his views in *Sexual Politics*.

30

work of a powerful-minded, clear-headed woman, who had a hard jealous heart, muscles of iron and nerves of bend leather; of a woman who longed for power, and had never felt affection. To many women affection is sweet and power conquered indifferent – though we all like influence won. I believe J. S. Mill would make a hard, dry, dismal world of it; and yet he speaks admirable sense through a great portion of his article – especially when he says, that if there be a natural unfitness in women for men's employment, there is no need to make laws on the subject; leave all careers open; let them try; those who ought to succeed will succeed, or, at least, will have a fair chance – the incapable will fall back into their right place. He likewise disposes of the 'maternity' question very neatly. In short, J. S. Mill's head is, I dare say, very good, but I feel disposed to scorn his heart.[52]

But however confused and timid Charlotte Brontë might be in theory, or rather how unwilling to subscribe to any theory at all, in practice over the years she developed a sort of sensible right-mindedness on the various issues of the Woman Question in so far as they were embodied in the personal concerns of herself and her friends. On the question of marriage, for example: the view that a woman should regard her husband with prostrate adoration – which she had expressed at the time of Henry Nussey's proposal – changed to more dignified notions of mutual respect, with a realistic glance at the extreme vulnerability of a loving woman in the face of her husband's indifference, and to abhorrence of marital tyranny. She challenged the accepted method of educating girls, who might well be capable and strong-minded, to be frail and silly and sheltered while turning boys who might really be frail and silly loose on the world. She argued that an unmarried woman could be as happy and respectable as the matrons.

There was one question on which J. S. Mill could not have helped had he tried, or at least not from experience: a question on which Charlotte Brontë had few predecessors to look to for help – that is, the moral problems besetting a writer who was also a woman. Her soul-searchings on this point were scrupulous and austere; the spirit which in youth led

[52] Letter to Mrs Gaskell, 20 Sep 1851.

her to earnest discussions with women friends about the rights and wrongs of dancing, only a little later carried her through strenuous investigations on this other subject. At the end of 1836 she wrote to Robert Southey, the Poet Laureate, enclosing some of her poems and asking his opinion. He did not reply for some weeks, and when he did, his long, polite, kindly-intentioned letter raised in her doubts of a very different sort from the basic anxiety as to whether or not the poems were any good. She asked for an opinion and got advice.

Literature cannot be the business of a woman's life, and it ought not to be. The more she is engaged in her proper duties, the less leisure will she have for it, even as an accomplishment and a recreation. To those duties you have not yet been called, and when you are you will be less eager for celebrity. You will not seek in imagination for excitement, of which the vicissitudes of this life, and the anxieties from which you must not hope to be exempted, be your state what it may, will bring with them but too much.[53]

Charlotte Brontë accepted Southey's advice, and in her letter of thanks gave a most revealing account of the deceptions which from the beginning a woman who was also a writer found it necessary to practise.

In the evenings, I confess, I do think, but I never trouble any one else with my thoughts. I carefully avoid any appearance of pre-occupation and eccentricity, which might lead those I live amongst to suspect the nature of my pursuits. Following my father's advice – who from my childhood has counselled me just in the wise and friendly tone of your letter – I have endeavored not only attentively to observe all the duties a woman ought to fulfil, but to feel deeply interested in them. I don't always succeed, for sometimes when I'm teaching or sewing I would rather be reading or writing; but I try to deny myself; and my father's approbation amply rewarded me for the privation.[54]

[53] Letter to Charlotte Brontë, 15 March 1837.
[54] Letter to Robert Southey, 16 March 1837.

But however gratefully and humbly Charlotte Brontë received Southey's advice she did not, of course, follow it. She
did to a large extent make literature the business of her life,
but the conflict was never resolved. Her duties, first as a
daughter, and, at the very end, as a wife also, were always
obtruding themselves. Mrs Gaskell, speaking of the months
after the publication of *Jane Eyre*, summed it all up excellently:

> Henceforward Charlotte Brontë's existence becomes divi-
> ded into two parallel currents – her life as Currer Bell, the
> author; her life as Charlotte Brontë, the woman. There
> were separate duties belonging to each character – not
> opposing each other; not impossible but difficult to be
> reconciled. When a man becomes an author, it is probably
> merely a change of employment to him... But no other
> can take up the quiet regular duties of the daughter, the
> wife, or the mother, as well as she whom God has ap-
> pointed to fill that particular place; a woman's principal
> work in life is hardly left to her own choice; nor can she
> drop the domestic charges devolving on her as an indi-
> vidual, for the exercise of the most splendid talents that
> were ever bestowed. And yet she must not shrink from the
> extra responsibility implied by the very fact of her posses-
> sing such talents.[55]

Elizabeth Gaskell was summing it up not only for her
friend but for herself. From the time of her own earliest
achievements she was subjected to counsel of the 'Be good
sweet maid and let who will be clever' type, such as that
of Carlyle, writing to congratulate her on *Mary Barton*: 'May
you live long to write good books, or do silently good actions
which in my sight is far more indispensable.' She by no
means laughed off these remarks. In her more relaxed way
she was as concerned with the problem as Charlotte Brontë.

> One thing is pretty clear, *Women* must give up living an
> artist's life, if home duties are to be paramount. It is
> different with men, whose home duties are so small a part
> of their life. However we are talking of women. I am sure
> it is healthy for them to have the refuge of the hidden
> world of Art to shelter themselves in when too much

[55] *Life of Charlotte Brontë*, ch. 16.

pressed upon by daily small Lilliputian arrows of peddling cares; it keeps them from being morbid as you say; and takes them into the land where King Arthur lies hidden, and soothes them with its peace. I have felt this in writing, I see others feel it in music, you in painting, so assuredly a blending of the two is desirable. (Home duties and the development of the individual I mean), which you will say it takes no Solomon to tell you but the difficulty is where and when to make one set of duties subserve and give place to the other. I have no doubt that the cultivation of each tends to keep the other in a healthy state, – my grammar is all at sixes and sevens I have no doubt but never mind if you can pick out my meaning.

She thought over these comments of hers and possibly decided she had made Art sound too much like a hobby that whiled away the long winter evenings and kept the little woman happy by giving her a healthy interest. In a long postscript that she wrote a few days later she put forward a much tougher view about the importance of the work itself, even if it happened to be the pursuit of some art.

If Self is to be the end of exertions, those exertions are unholy, there is no doubt of *that* – and that is part of the danger in cultivating the Individual Life; but I do believe we have all some appointed work to do, which no one else can do so well; Wh. is *our* work; what *we* have to do in advancing the Kingdom of God; and that first we must find out what we are sent into the world to do, and define it and make it clear to ourselves, (that's *the* hard part) and then forget ourselves in our work, and our work in the End we ought to strive to bring about.[56]

Though few modern readers would agree that the right aim of all exertion was the advancement of the Kingdom of God and perhaps none would so shackle the cultivation of the individual life as to make it dependent on the Divine Will, yet equivalent contemporary terms could be found to make the point of view seem sympathetic and enlightened. Certainly Elizabeth Gaskell's realisation that she had 'a great number of Mes' and her intelligent struggle to sort them all out is positively fashionable if expressed in the lan-

[56] Letter to Eliza Fox, ? Feb 1850.

guage of psychology rather than of religion. At all events we have to accept that her absolute and practical Christianity was bound to direct her approach to feminine problems. To take a small example: though a much happier person than Charlotte Brontë, she shared her belief about the uses of adversity – an essential tenet of Anglo-Saxon Christianity – as is plain in her wonderful remark about Effie Ruskin: that she would have been a ·nicer woman if she had ever had smallpox.

It may be one reason why Mrs Gaskell was reluctant to take political action to forward the emancipation of women. To resort simultaneously to the Divine Will *and* to political action has often struck sincere Christians as a belt-and-braces outlook. Whatever her reasons it was with considerable hesitation that she signed the petition got up by Barbara Leigh Smith in 1856 which urged Parliament to grant married women a legal right to their own earnings. One of her stated objections was that a law would not be proof against human behaviour: 'a husband can coax, wheedle, beat or tyrannize his wife out of something and no law whatever will help this that I see.' She realised too, characteristically, that there could be faults on both sides. She was not entirely joking when she said, 'Mr. Gaskell begs Mr. Fox to draw up a bill for the protection of *husbands* against wives who will spend all their earnings'. But in the end she agreed: 'Our sex is badly enough used and legislated *against*, there's no doubt of *that* – so though I don't see the definite end proposed by these petitions I'll sign.'[57]

Both of the motives she gave for hanging back on this particular issue were typical of her whole attitude not only to the Woman Question but to any question. Social and political problems she approached as human problems; where sympathy was required she gave it freely, where emotional involvement was required she became fully involved, and when action was called for she acted out of personal benevolence and understanding. She was almost incapable of theorising. In her letters when she came anywhere near a theory her habitual chattiness, which sometimes rose to eloquence, stuttered into what was, for her, inarticulacy.

Her general views can however be gleaned even if they

57 Ibid., 1 Jan. 1856.

are not neatly stacked up. To an extent they were reactionary; her opinion of women was not always as high as it might have been. She rightly blamed the sort of education they received, and her vigilance when it came to the upbringing of her own daughters, her anxiety to select the right school for each of them, and her admonitions that they should not express uninformed opinions all indicated her belief in the improvement of the female mind. But she seemed to think that women suffered from certain intrinsic deficiencies that were beyond the power of education to remedy.

> They've tact, and sensitiveness and genius, and hundreds of fine and lovely qualities, but are at best angelic geese as to matter requiring serious and long scientific consideration. I'm *not* a friend of Female Medical Education.[58]

(She was referring to the proposed establishment of a Training School for Nurses at St Thomas's Hospital.) Part of her complaint against women chimed with that of J. S. Mill: their failure to take advantage of the opportunities that *were* offered to them. At a meeting in support of Florence Nightingale's work, 'the ladies (stupid creatures) did not fill the space allotted to them; but the men more than did'.[59]

But some of her ideas cut right across the most sacred received thinking of her day. She lamented that girls could not take the initiative but had to wait for marriage till someone 'gave them a chance'. She saw wifely submission as a soft option, to be rejected. 'I am sometimes coward enough to wish that we were back in the darkness where obedience was the only seen duty of women.'[60] She realised to the full the need of every woman to have some work of her own, from spinsters left alone after a lifetime of looking after ageing parents to great ladies in search of novelty:

> Lady Errol, Mrs. Daubeny and Mrs. Galton the three officer's wives who are with the Camp in the Crimea, dress as Vivandieres and wash their husband's shirts, cook their dinners etc. and say 'they never were so happy in their lives.'[61]

She knew that the domestic round of the English middle-

58 Letter to unidentified correspondent, 31 Oct 1856.
59 Letter to Parthenope Nightingale, 18 Jan 1856.
60 Letter to Eliza Fox, ? April 1850.
61 Letter to Marianne Gaskell, 13 Oct 1854.

class home was not enough to satisfy women of larger gifts. She pitied Parthenope Nightingale who, to free her sister Florence,

> has annihilated herself, her own tastes, her own wishes in order to take up all the little duties of home, to parents, to poor, to society, to servants – all the small things that fritter away time and life;[62]

and approved of Charlotte Brontë's friend Miss Taylor, who

> on receiving her portion of her father's property, said she did not see why she was to be debarred from entering into trade because she was a woman, so, although she had a very fair income she emigrated to Melbourne, I think; and there set up a large shop, which is doing very well indeed.[63]

As these views were the product of feeling as well as thought it followed that she was particularly ready to like women who worked. She was untouched by the prevailing snobbery which despised governesses. Some of her best friends were governesses.

These were her private views, imparted informally. But, although she distrusted political action, she was not backward in publicly intervening in the general issues that affected womankind. Most often it was a particular case that enlisted her support; a striking example was that of a girl who had been seduced and decoyed into prostitution by the very people who were supposed to be helping her, a story which Mrs Gaskell most movingly imparted to Charles Dickens,[64] appealing for his aid on the grounds of his known benevolence to prostitutes. (He was moved and he did help.) But though her goodwill was usually inspired by individual cases it was by no means desultory or capricious. Neither was it limited to prostitutes. The condition of seamstresses was a contemporary scandal which claimed the attention of such a champion as Harriet Beecher Stowe, such a reporter as Henry Mayhew and such an imaginative sympathiser as Thomas Hood whose *The Song of the Shirt* harrowingly depicted their plight. And to the details of their situation –

---

[62] Letter to Emily Shaen, 27 Oct 1854.
[63] Letter to George Smith, ? July 1855.
[64] Letter to Charles Dickens, 8 Jan 1850.

the pitiful pay, bestially long hours, unhealthy surroundings and poor prospects – Elizabeth Gaskell was thoroughly alive. She conferred with Mrs Beecher Stowe, she quoted Thomas Hood; she did what she could.

George Eliot was even more unfortunate in father and brother than Charlotte Brontë had been for they understood none of her ambitions and gifts. She felt great natural affection for her father and, as his death approached, dreaded the loss of his 'purifying sustaining influence' in words more often used by men about women in the nineteenth century. His lordly ingratitude for all her devoted services to him seemed in the eyes of friends to evoke her grief rather than her anger. Cara Bray described Mr Evans's behaviour in his last illness:

> He takes opportunities now of saying kind things to M.A.; contrary to his wont. Poor girl, it shows how rare they are by the gratitude with which she repeats the commonest expressions of kindness.[65]

But, accurate as this comment no doubt was and though Cara Bray in such an emergency was not likely to be shown the anger, it was there. Six years earlier George Eliot had written her father a letter explaining her refusal to go to church; significantly she had found it impossible to have a meaningful discussion with him about it. Her brother Isaac's mean-minded views about her future had already alienated her: he had made it plain that the only thing to be done with her was to marry her off, and he quickly got irritated when this failed to happen. At the time of her religious dissent he apparently decided that this unfeminine freethinking would effectively frighten off any suitors and that there was therefore no point in providing her with an establishment; she ceased to exist. The letter to her father expressed the strong resentment she felt towards both of them for their attitudes.

> From what my Brother more than insinuated and from what you have yourself intimated I perceived that your establishment at Foleshill is regarded as an unnecessary expense having no other object than to give me a centre in society – that since you now consider me to have placed

[65] Letter to Sara Hennell, 11 Sep 1848.

an insurmountable barrier to my prosperity in life this one object of an expenditure held by the rest of the family to be disadvantageous to them is frustrated – I am glad at any rate this is made clear to me, for I could not be happy to remain as an incubus or an unjust absorber of your hardly earned gains which might be better applied among my Brothers and Sisters with their children.[66]

The episode with Dr Brabant did nothing to reconcile her to the masculine point of view. No doubt she displayed her partiality for him too openly, too openly that is for his weak-headed vanity, but according to his daughter Rufa Hennell he promptly, at the first sign of trouble, put all the blame on the inexperienced young woman, 'as though the fault lay with her alone'. In later life George Eliot, having clearly seen through him in the meanwhile, alluded to him when necessary with a very healthy spitefulness.

But pushed around, blamed and despised though the spinster might be, before her union with Lewes George Eliot tended to see the trials of the married woman more vividly than her joys. In this of course she was not alone. While she was staying at a pension in Geneva in 1849 the Marquise de Saint Germain, a fellow guest, condoled with her on her lack of religion, saying darkly that she might get married and *then* she would need it. 'Le mariage, chère amie, sans la foi religieuse . . .' – words failed her. Eight years before this George Eliot had found words for much the same concept in speaking of her sister Chrissey:

My dear Sister is rather an object of solicitude on many accounts – the troubles of married life seem more conspicuously the ordinance of God, in the case of one so meek and passive than in that of women who may fairly be suspected of creating half their own difficulties.[67]

Once happily settled with Lewes she gave the brighter side of the picture, and in her new security she was free to lament the treatment of herself as a representative of the female sex but without the pain of feeling there was anything personal in it. On her visit to Munich in 1858 she

[66] Letter to Robert Evans, 28 Feb 1842.
[67] Letter to Maria Lewis, 23 Oct 1841.

experienced one of the classic grievances of the nineteenth-century intellectual, or even mildly intelligent, woman.

> It is quite an exception to meet with a woman who seems to expect any sort of companionship from the men and I shudder at the sight of a woman in society, for I know I shall have to sit on the sofa with her all the evening listening to her stupidities, while the men on the other side of the table are discussing all the subjects I care to hear about.[68]

She was also free to consider the practical measures that were increasingly being taken for the amelioration of the lot of women. As her fame grew, her support became in great demand, in spite of the irregularity of her life which made her in some circles a less than ideal partisan. From the first she realised that such struggles were not for her, as far as thorough involvement was concerned; her temperament was not right. One peaceful autumn she spoke of her longing for

> a heaven made up of long autumn afternoon walks, quite delivered from any necessity of giving a judgement on the Woman Question or of reading newspapers about Indian Mutinies. I am so glad there are thousands of good people in the world who have very decided opinions and are fond of working hard to enforce them – I like to feel and think everything and do nothing, a pool of the 'deep contemplative' kind.[69]

Throughout her life she refused to commit herself to any women's cause. Where wrongs existed she was neither ignorant nor unsympathetic: the plight of seamstresses and prostitutes engaged her full compassion. And she did not withhold her support: she and Lewes were annual subscribers to the Elizabeth Garrett Anderson Hospital; she sent money to the Working Women's College; she approved of the setting up of the *Englishwoman's Journal;* from the first she gave both moral and financial support to Emily Davies in her plans for the founding of Girton College (once with the rousing words that 'a great campaign has to be

[68] Letter to Sara Hennell, 10/13 May 1858.
[69] Ibid., 21 Sep 1857.

victualled for'[70]), advised her about the curriculum, got to know some of the students, and followed the history of the College as well as that of Newnham, with keen interest; she usually agreed that women should have a vote. But she always had reservations.

They were the reservations of a mind too subtle and too reflective to take the kind of plain straightforward view on any of these issues that would lead to committed action. In one mood she described Women's Suffrage as 'an extremely doubtful good' and dissuaded Sara Hennell from canvassing on its behalf.[71] Convinced as she was of the necessity of improving women's education she was realistic to the point of despondency: 'It is not likely that any perfect plan for educating women can soon be found, for we are very far from having found a perfect plan for educating men.' Perhaps her most eloquent and explanatory statement was the following:

I feel too deeply the difficult complications that beset every measure likely to affect the position of women and also I feel too imperfect a sympathy with many women who have put themselves forward in connexion with such measures to give any practical adhesion to them. There is no subject on which I am more inclined to hold my peace and learn, than on the 'Women Question'. It seems to me to overhang abysses, of which even prostitution is not the worst. Conclusions seem easy so long as we keep large blinkers on and look in the direction of our own private path.[72]

In fact even if she had worn blinkers and concentrated on her own private path the issues would hardly have become simpler, for her own road was a very different one from that trodden by other women of her day. For one thing, she was a genuine intellectual, who wore her knowledge elegantly – Charlotte Brontë's learning sounds dreadfully ponderous by comparison – and whose thought, in maturity, seemed to have none of the half-baked quality too often characteristic of the self-taught. This is how she struck the librarian from Harvard, John Fiske, in 1873:

[70] Letter to Emily Davies, 22 Nov 1867.
[71] Letter to Sara Hennell, 12 Oct 1867.
[72] Letter to Mrs Nassau John Senior, 4 Oct 1869.

I never saw such a woman. There is nothing a bit masculine about her; she is thoroughly feminine and looks and acts as if she were made for nothing but to mother babies. But she has a power of *stating* an argument equal to any man; equal to any man do I say? I have never seen any man, except Herbert Spencer, who could state a case equal to her. I found her thoroughly acquainted with the whole literature of the Homeric question; and she seems to have read all of Homer in Greek, too, and could meet me everywhere. She didn't talk like a bluestocking – as if she were aware she had got hold of a big topic – but like a plain woman, who talked of Homer as simply as she would of flat-irons... I have often *heard* of learned women, whose learning, I have usually found, is a mighty flimsy affair. But to meet a woman who can meet you like a man, on such a question, and not *putting on any airs*, but talking sincerely of the thing as a subject which has deeply interested her – this is, indeed, quite a new experience.[73]

It must have been impossible for such a woman, however creatively imaginative, to have fully understood the limitations of minds less brilliant than hers, either in general or when it came to the Woman Question. She wrote a lot about stupidity which, interestingly, she regarded as a deficiency of the heart rather than of the head, and rightly thought of it as a bugbear, but she could only observe it.

Secondly she was not plagued by the stresses which Elizabeth Gaskell had felt, both for Charlotte Brontë and for herself, as a result of conflict between domestic duties and authorship. Deeply as George Eliot appreciated the domesticity that provided the 'solitude à deux' which meant so much to her, she loathed housekeeping, and once she had found devoted and efficient servants, she sloughed off all such cares to a surprising extent and gave herself single-mindedly to her writing. She lived with a man who regarded her work as her main duty and encouraged her to view it in that light.

She never had any wish to flout the conventions but her strong-minded and open adherence to a union which was neither legal nor socially approved set her involuntarily apart from most other women. And her ultimate triumph

[73] Letter to Mrs John Fiske, 23 Nov 1873.

in such a situation set her even farther apart. By living with Lewes she broke the most important of the Victorian commandments, but through sheer personal achievement lived to be received by crowned heads.

It was during a meeting with one of these crowned heads that the following conversation, recorded by Lewes, took place.

> The other day at dinner Madonna was talking with Bright about woman's suffrage, and the Princess Louise interposed with, 'But you don't go in for the superiority of women, Mrs. Lewes?' 'No.' 'I think,' said Huxley, 'Mrs. Lewes rather teaches *the inferiority of men*.'[74]

Without hearing the tone of voice it is not clear exactly what T. H. Huxley meant by his rejoinder; it may have been merely an automatic quip. But he did seem to realise that George Eliot could never preach a simplistic doctrine.

George Eliot was painfully conscious that there was a great deal she was ignorant of but she was incapable of wilfully ignoring anything. She dreaded convenient simplifications; to employ one would be 'like talking of "your Majesty's happy reign" to a successful monarch whose reign had been one of blood and fire to half a population, who happen to be at a distance and out of sight'.[75] So she could never entirely separate the needs of women from the needs of men. Acknowledging, even emphasising, what she considered to be the different capabilities of the two sexes, she always saw them as interdependent. Certainly the education of women should be improved, but chiefly so that there should be no inequality to upset the just balance of relationships.

> There lies just that kernel of truth in the vulgar alarm of men lest women should be 'unsexed.' We can no more afford to part with that exquisite type of gentleness, tenderness, possible maternity suffusing a woman's being with affectionateness, which makes what we mean by the feminine character, than we can afford to part with the human love, the mutual subjection of soul between a man and a woman – which is also a growth and revelation

[74] Letter to Mrs Elma Stuart, 12 Aug 1877.
[75] Letter to Mrs Charles Bray, 18 March 1865.

beginning before all history. The answer to those alarms of men about education is, to admit fully that the mutual delight of the sexes in each other must enter into the perfection of life, but to point out that complete union and sympathy can only come by women having opened to them the same store of acquired truth or beliefs as men have, so that their grounds of judgement may be as far as possible the same.[76]

Certainly it was a shame for women to be idle; the good of society required that everyone should do the work for which he or she was most fitted. Certainly women should be 'secured from suffering the exercise of any unrighteous power' but so should 'every other breathing creature'.[77]

[76] Letter to Emily Davies, 8 Aug 1868.
[77] Letter to Mrs Peter Taylor, 30 May 1867.

Chapter II

If you please, no reference to examples in books. Men
have had every advantage of us in telling their own
story. Education has been theirs in so much higher a
degree; the pen has been in their hands.[1]

Jane Austen, pen in hand, gives this speech to Anne Elliot,
the heroine of *Persuasion*, without, apparently, attaching to
the words any kind of resentment or rebellion. And as Anne
gracefully accepts this limitation of women's scope, so do
nearly all the other women characters accept all the other
limitations. Significantly, the only person who utters anything like feminist sentiments is Mrs Elton, the half-educated
vulgarian in *Emma*. She laments that wives have to leave
their own homes for those of their husbands: 'I always say
that this is quite one of the evils of matrimony'; and that
they have to consult their husbands before making decisions
even in domestic matters: 'You know, Mrs. Weston, you and
I must be cautious how we express ourselves.' But these remarks are only part of her terrible sparkling vivacity. She
is actually far more triumphant at having acquired a husband herself (she alludes to Mr E. as frequently as today's
women columnists allude to their husbands) and at having
friends who have achieved marriage ('Mrs. Jeffereys – Clara
Partridge, that was – and the two Milmans, now Mrs. Bird
and Mrs. James Cooper') than anyone else in the novels.
And in any case she is the very last person with whom a
reader would identify.

But however elegantly they conceal their triumph, marriage is the aim of all Jane Austen's heroines and we do not
see them again, except in prophetic glimpses, after the hour
of their success, and they do all succeed. Married couples
are present in the novels, of course, and sometimes play a
considerable part in the working out of events, but the hearts
that Jane Austen sets herself to explore belong to women in

[1] *Persuasion*, ch. 23.

a state of hope and expectation rather than of marital fulfilment, or disillusionment as the case may be. They likewise
belong to women in a state of competition, who exist in an
element where solidarity could be fatal.

The heroines cannot openly and straightforwardly strive
towards their goal because society forbids it. The more
spirited girls, like Elizabeth Bennet, in *Pride and Prejudice,*
act with half-conscious cunning. The supine ones, like Fanny
Price in *Mansfield Park,* employ the technique of lying down
and going limp which we have seen work so well in the sit-
down demonstrations of our own age. But though the
methods are different the objective is always individual and
exclusive.

It follows from this that there is not going to be much
examination of the more general rôle of women in society:
if they should have a vote, for example, or if their contribu-
tion should be purely domestic. In her novels, as in her life,
Jane Austen seems to accept that all these efforts to get
married should take place within existing conditions and
seems to have no wish to alter conditions so that the efforts
would be unnecessary. Again and again we hope that 'seems'
is going to be the operative word and we are always disappointed. There *are* hints, sometimes strong ones, that she
is dissatisfied with the traditional status of woman, but they
keep disappearing. They do re-emerge, however, in a different guise: as the ambiguities, discrepancies and illogic of
a creative artist, who is presenting experience, including her
own, not discussing ideas. As far as the Woman Question is
concerned Jane Austen could well be described as a latent
socialist who helps to make capitalism work and it is more
than worthwhile to follow the resulting conflict and even
to pin flags on to the map.

'Men of sense do not want silly wives.' How Mr Knightley,
the hero of *Emma,* can say this when his own, sensible,
brother has married a silly woman is as marvellous as how
Jane Austen can say it, remembering the more or less sensible male characters she has created who have done the
same: Mr Bennet, Mr Palmer, Colonel Forster, Mr Allen;
though it is true that actively wanting a silly wife and getting
one by mistake can be two different things.

Beauty, not mind or character, is what the men in Jane

Austen's novels – the men she approves of as well as the villains – actually consider first. Catherine Morland, in *Northanger Abbey*, and Fanny Price have to become swans before anyone will look at them. Captain Wentworth, in *Persuasion*, thinks seriously of Anne again only from the moment when another man, Mr Elliot, admires her looks. Many scenes exude the spirit of a Miss World contest. Sir Walter Elliot is the middle-aged man watching the event on television.

> The worst of Bath was, the number of its plain women. He did not mean to say that there were no pretty women, but the number of the plain was out of all proportion. He had frequently observed, as he walked, that one handsome face would be followed by thirty or five and thirty frights; and once, as he had stood in a shop in Bond-street he had counted eighty-seven women go by, one after another, without there being a tolerable face among them.[2]

We know that Sir Walter has not been very successful in recent years with women. (Mrs Clay's attentions are not very flattering.) After his wife's death he made 'several very unreasonable applications' which were rejected. As his rank and, at the time, wealth would have made him perfectly eligible with women of suitable age, we can only imagine that he proposed to dashing young women who were not impressed. This fact completes the picture.

But if Sir Walter is a Miss World spectator Mr Darcy in *Pride and Prejudice* is a judge, as he first of all purses his lips and then licks them in contemplation of Elizabeth's figure.

> Though he had detected with a critical eye more than one failure of perfect symmetry in her form, he was forced to acknowledge her figure to be light and pleasing.[3]

Although Jane Austen is realistic enough to show men assessing women according to their beauty she consistently makes her male characters in speech put greater value on their minds. The resulting conflict between what she wishes were true and what she knows actually happens leads to very significant confusions and ambiguities.

When Louisa Musgrove in *Persuasion* becomes engaged

[2] Ibid., ch. 15. [3] *Pride and Prejudice*, ch. 6.

to Captain Benwick, Anne says tactfully 'There are on both sides good principles and good temper', knowing that this is the utmost that can be said for Louisa, but Captain Wentworth, with whom she is having the discussion, will not be tactful.

> I confess that I do think there is a disparity, too great a disparity, and in a point no less essential than mind. I regard Louisa Musgrove as a very amiable, sweet-tempered girl, and not deficient in understanding; but Benwick is something more. He is a clever man, a reading man – and I confess that I do consider his attaching himself to her, with some surprise ... A man like him, in his situation! With a heart pierced, wounded, almost broken! Fanny Harville was a very superior creature; and his attachment to her was indeed attachment.[4]

This speech cannot be taken at its face value. When Captain Wentworth was himself courting Louisa, who was at that time prettier than Anne, he did not seem conscious of these deficiencies in her but now it is important that he should convince Anne, who has in the meanwhile regained much of her beauty, that he prefers and has always really preferred intelligent women, like her. His speech is a motivated set piece. If we took it seriously, which is probably what Jane Austen intended, his surprise at Benwick's conduct would be either naïve or insincere; he is a man of the world and must have realised what the secluded Anne has long since realised about Benwick: 'He had an affectionate heart. He must love somebody.'

Emma puts similar emphasis on the importance of intelligence in women when marriage is in question, and similar ambiguity is the result. Harriet Smith, acting under Emma's influence, has refused Robert Martin; Mr Knightley is angry and speaks plainly to Emma about Harriet's inadequacy.

> She is not a sensible girl, nor a girl of any information. She has been taught nothing useful, and is too young and too simple to have acquired anything herself. At her age she can have no experience, and with her little wit, is not likely to have any that can avail her. She is pretty, and she is good tempered, and that is all.

[4] *Persuasion*, ch. 20.

This lordly but accurate comment leads, a little further on, to the following dialogue:

> 'I am very much mistaken if your sex in general would not think such beauty, and such temper, the highest claims a woman could possess.'
> 'Upon my word, Emma, to hear you abusing the reason you have, is almost enough to make me think so too. Better be without sense than misapply it as you do.'
> 'To be sure!' cried she playfully. 'I know *that* is the feeling of you all. I know that such a girl as Harriet is exactly what every man delights in – what at once bewitches his senses and satisfies his judgement.'[5]

This passage is complicated. The opinions of Jane Austen and two of her characters swirl round in it, hers not only colliding with theirs but theirs with each other's. On any reading of the book after the first, Emma's next remark, 'Were you yourself ever to marry, she is the very woman for you', seems crudely obvious with its hint of what is to come and the laboured irony with which the clue is planted, but at a first reading, when we do not know what is to come, most readers find it reasonably inconspicuous, and we are free to concentrate on the uneasiness behind Emma's teasing, dangerous assertion. She does not really wish to think that men prefer pretty, stupid, submissive girls. Even in her small circle she must have seen that men sometimes do, apart from the example of her sister, but, with her own high opinion of herself, she cannot like the idea in general and certainly does not entertain it in particular; her feelings for Mr Knightley are already present though unacknowledged. Later, when she is led to believe that Mr Knightley *is* going to choose Harriet, her thoughts about his resulting degradation are franker than most people's would be; she has no charitable inhibitions whatever and we hear nothing of Harriet's sweetness and prettiness.

Mr Knightley's dishonesty is of a subtler kind, and seems not to have been intended by Jane Austen, who really means us to think Emma is clever; she says so in the first sentence. The modern reader may question Emma's powers; we see her doing one thing more quickly than we could ourselves,

[5] *Emma*, ch. 8.

49

that is, solving Mr Elton's riddle, but she has had years of practice. Boldly as Mr Knightley lays down the law about men of sense and silly wives, he does eventually marry rather a silly one, silly, that is, compared with the one really gifted woman in the book, Jane Fairfax. It is one of the ambiguities of this novel that Frank Churchill, the immature, brash young man, is the one who has the confidence to take on the intellectual young woman whose brains and whose talents are intimidatingly superior to those of any company we see her in. And in this connection we recall the author's comment about the marriage of Jane's friend, Miss Campbell, a very ordinary girl but the choice of Mr Dixon, who in fact, being rich and not mercenary, could equally well have chosen Jane. Jane Austen explains it as 'that luck which so often defies anticipation in matrimonial affairs, giving attraction to what is moderate rather than to what is superior'. An uncomfortable thought, if one is superior oneself.

A third example of this attempt to assure us that men like intelligent girls occurs in the relaxed conversation that Darcy has with Elizabeth soon after they have become engaged.[6] Elizabeth wants Darcy to account for his having fallen in love with her and the first quality he actually mentions is the liveliness of her mind. Presumably this is the impression we are meant to retain, but in fact she has made him say it. She steers the talk: 'Now, be sincere; did you admire me for my impertinence?' He could hardly reply 'Yes' or 'As a matter of fact it was for your figure'.

Given Jane Austen's own nervousness about intellect in women it is inevitable that she should sometimes make her heroines react in the same way, quite undermining her and their claims about the attractiveness of mind. Even the right-thinking Anne Elliot cannot translate an Italian song from a concert bill without adding: 'I do not pretend to understand the language. I am a very poor Italian scholar.' Mr Elliot seizes his opportunity and gallantly contradicts her.

Yes, yes, I see you are. I see you know nothing of the matter. You have only knowledge enough of the language to translate at sight these inverted, transposed, curtailed Italian lines, into clear, comprehensible, elegant English.

[6] *Pride and Prejudice*, ch. 60.

You need not say anything more of your ignorance. Here is complete proof.[7]

This speech leaves us with the impression that Anne really is a capable Italian scholar, but also with the feeling that only male approval can bestow the ultimate accolade, not the woman's own realisation of her capabilities.

Even the high-spirited Elizabeth Bennet is eager to run herself down. She is obviously a keen and discriminating reader. Her knowledge of eighteenth-century treatises on the picturesque, for example, has been so well assimilated that her impertinence to Mr Darcy, Miss Bingley and Mrs Hurst floats delicately on the air as she runs away from them in the garden at Netherfield.

Stay where you are. You are charmingly group'd and appear to uncommon advantage. The picturesque would be spoilt by admitting a fourth.[8]

She has grasped the theories well enough to be able to select and apply one particular point to one particular situation, rudely but so elegantly that the Bingley sisters have no idea they are being called cows, or at best, trees.

Yet when Miss Bingley, who is not a reader (she chooses a book because it is the second volume of Darcy's and cannot keep her mind on it for five minutes even so), tries to make Elizabeth seem bookish, Elizabeth denies too much.

'Miss Eliza Bennet', said Miss Bingley, 'despises cards. She is a great reader, and has no pleasure in anything else.' 'I deserve neither such praise nor such censure', cried Elizabeth. 'I am *not* a great reader, and I have pleasure in many things.'[9]

She turns off the attack very neatly, pretending that the first part of Miss Bingley's gibe is meant as a compliment but realising that in calling her a great reader, Miss Bingley is being as offensive as in saying that she has no other pleasures. Elizabeth is always quick to rebut any suggestion that she is bookish, almost too quick. Certainly it was a popular accusation at the time, often levelled at young women. Lady Middleton in *Sense and Sensibility* dislikes the Miss Dashwoods on this account, among others.

[7] *Persuasion*, ch. 20.   [8] *Pride and Prejudice*, ch. 10.   [9] Ibid., ch. 8.

Because they were fond of reading she fancied them satirical, perhaps without exactly knowing what it was to be satirical, but *that* did not signify. It was censure in common use, and easily given.[10]

It is rather sad to see the quick-witted, independent Elizabeth so eager to sound feather-brained. She is dancing with Mr Darcy.

'We have tried two or three subjects already without success and what we are to talk of next I cannot imagine.'
'What think you of books?' said he smiling.
'Books – Oh! no. I am sure we never read the same, or not with the same feelings.'
'I am sorry you think so; but if that be the case, there can at least be no want of subject. We may compare our different opinions.'
'No, I cannot talk of books in a ball-room; my head is always full of something else.'[11]

Jane Austen's attitude to reading in general is mixed. In her day to read widely was almost the only way to improve one's mind and keep in touch, especially for women. Yet she does not regard it as necessarily a sign of grace that a character should be a reader. Mary Bennet makes a fool of herself with her extracts and quotations; Mary Musgrove simply enjoys changing her library book; Marianne Dashwood's comically exaggerated plan of self-reform is to take principally the form of encyclopaedic reading and Colonel Brandon significantly is to be the provider of the books. It is true that the first thing we hear about Sir Walter Elliot in the very first sentence of *Persuasion* is that he 'was a man who, for his own amusement, never took up any book but the Baronetage' and we rightly expect the worst, but in the same novel Captain Harville, whom we are certainly supposed to admire and like, is specifically said to be 'no reader'.

So far, there is nothing very surprising about this, but Jane Austen's treatment of Anne Elliot as a reader, especially as a reader of poetry, calls for considerable comment. We accept that Jane Austen had no poetry in her but it is shocking she should be so philistine about those who have.

Anne Elliot is not ashamed to appear bookish. She is older

[10] *Sense and Sensibility*, ch. 36.   [11] *Pride and Prejudice*, ch. 18.

and more truly independent than Elizabeth Bennet, and is grateful for the support books have given her in times of suffering far worse than anything we see Elizabeth enduring. It is not only in the past they have helped her, but also in the present pain and confusion of being in Captain Wentworth's company soon after their meeting again. One would have thought this was a distressing enough situation but there is more than a hint of comedy in the way Jane Austen shows her on a country walk, with a family group that includes Captain Wentworth, desperately trying to steady herself by silently repeating

> some few of the thousand poetical descriptions extant of autumn . . . that season which has drawn from every poet, worthy of being read, some attempt at description, or some lines of feeling.

She cannot help, however, overhearing a conversation between Captain Wentworth and Louisa Musgrove which marks their increasing sympathy and intimacy with each other and

> could not immediately fall into a quotation again. The sweet scenes of autumn were for a while put by – unless some tender sonnet, fraught with the apt analogy of the declining year, with declining happiness, and the images of youth, and spring all gone together, blessed her memory.[12]

Jane Austen is not far from giving us here the stereotyped masculine sketch of the soulful literary lady, with her poetical descriptions and her tender sonnets, a P. G. Wodehouse poetess, for example.

The same tone is heard a few pages later in the scene where Anne advises Captain Benwick about his reading.

> Having talked of poetry, the richness of the present age, and gone through a brief comparison of opinion as to the first-rate poets, trying to ascertain whether *Marmion* or *The Lady of the Lake* were to be preferred, and how ranked the *Giaour* and *The Bride of Abydos*; and moreover how the *Giaour* was to be pronounced, he shewed himself so intimately acquainted with all the tenderest songs of

---

[12] *Persuasion*, ch. 10.

the one poet, and all the impassioned descriptions of hopeless agony of the other; he repeated, with such tremulous feeling, the various lines which imaged a broken heart, or a mind destroyed by wretchedness, and looked so entirely as if he meant to be understood, that she ventured to hope he did not always read only poetry; and to say, that she thought it was the misfortune of poetry, to be seldom safely enjoyed by those who enjoyed it completely; and that the strong feelings which alone could estimate it truly, were the very feelings which ought to taste it but sparingly.[13]

There is nothing intrinsically funny or wrong about one bereaved person trying to console another, so why is Jane Austen writing satirically, as the vocabulary alone shows she is doing – hopeless agony, tremulous feeling, broken hearts? Her misunderstanding of the nature and function of poetry, a misunderstanding characteristic of the half-educated in any age, is not meant to be funny, but is part of the mockery nevertheless.

The mechanism of the plot suggests one reason. It will not be long now before we see that Captain Benwick's grief if not affected is very shallow. So the tone of the passage just quoted is a fair clue, and it is capped by the irony of the paragraph which follows.

Captain Benwick listened attentively, and seemed grateful for the interest implied; and though a shake of the head, and sighs which declared his little faith in the efficacy of any books on grief like his, noted down the names of those she recommended and promised to secure and read them.

Very soon, too, Anne will be happy again; we are being given clues all the time.

But the basic reason is that Jane Austen finds people of literary sentiment funny. This is borne out by a passage which occurs when Anne is reflecting on the news of Louisa Musgrove's engagement to Captain Benwick.

She would learn to be an enthusiast for Scott and Lord Byron; nay, that was probably learnt already; of course

13 Ibid., ch. 11.

they had fallen in love over poetry. The idea of Louisa
Musgrove turned into a person of literary taste, and sentimental reflection, was amusing, but she had no doubt of
its being so. The day at Lyme, the fall from the Cobb,
might influence her health, her nerves, her courage, her
character to the end of her life.[14]

Poor Louisa Musgrove, she can never get it right. She is
first written off as being no more than a pretty, good-natured,
unaffected girl; now that she has become a 'person of literary
taste and sentimental reflection' she is laughed at. There is
no doubt that Jane Austen finds literary ladies, including
her heroine, splendid material for a laugh; and if her targets
are not literary ladies they are womanish men. Captain
Benwick is not a manly man. This is indicated throughout the
book; Admiral Croft, no close observer in general, notices it
('James Benwick is rather too piano for me') and Charles
Musgrove has to explain that he is brave really. And what
makes women and sissies sensitive to poetry is ill-health,
timidity and weak nerves. Jane Austen actually says so in
the last sentence of this extract. It shows what she thinks
about poetry. It shows what she thinks about her own
characters, even the best of them. It certainly shows what
she thinks about women.

And yet Jane Austen exempts the women she likes from
many of the weaknesses, both of character and of status, that
women exemplify in much eighteenth- and nineteenth-century literature. They are not dolls, teases or clothes horses.
They are not guardian angels or men's consciences. They do
not find themselves in nursing the sick or being good to the
poor.

Young ladies should take care of themselves. Young ladies
are delicate plants. They should take care of their health
and their complexion.[15]

These are ominous words, but Mr Woodhouse sees all his
acquaintances as dolls, frail and badly-made, and in need of
protection. No one can digest anything but gruel or with-
stand the mildest breeze. He answers enquiries as to his
household's health after the incident of the gypsies with the

[14] Ibid., ch. 18.   [15] *Emma*, ch. 34.

message that they are 'all very indifferent', and his reaction
to the idea of the ball at the Crown is eloquent:

> I could not bear it for Emma! Emma is not strong. She
> would catch a dreadful cold. So would poor little Harriet.
> So you would all. Mrs. Weston, you would be quite laid
> up.[16]

And it is not only women whose health he worries about. If
Mr Knightley, who is described as having 'a great deal of
health, activity and independence', rides in the rain or walks
on a muddy night he is the object of equally tender anxiety.

Jane Austen's own opinion is probably heard when Mrs
Croft lightly rebukes her brother Captain Wentworth when
he feels

> how impossible it is, with all one's efforts, and all one's
> sacrifices, to make the accommodation on board, such as
> women ought to have.

She calls this talk 'idle refinement' and adds:

> I hate to hear you talking so, like a fine gentleman, and as
> if all women were fine ladies, instead of rational creatures.
> We none of us expect to be in smooth water all our days.[17]

Several of Jane Austen's heroines are flirtatious – the word
'arch' is often used of Elizabeth Bennet and that is presumably what it means – but they are not designing coquettes.
They say 'no' when they mean 'no' and 'yes' when they
mean 'yes'. On the occasion when Mr Collins persists in
attributing Elizabeth's refusal to her wish of increasing his
love by suspense 'according to the usual practice of elegant
females', she replies most feelingly:

> I do assure you, sir, that I have no pretension whatever
> to that kind of elegance which consists in tormenting a
> respectable man. I would rather be paid the compliment
> of being believed sincere ... Do not consider me now as
> an elegant female intending to plague you, but as a rational
> creature speaking the truth from her heart.[18]

Dress is not a primary consideration with the girls Jane
Austen wishes us to admire. In all the novels, only four

16 Ibid., ch. 29.   17 *Persuasion*, ch. 8.
18 *Pride and Prejudice*, ch. 19.

women pay great attention to fashion: two vulgarians, one hoyden and one moron. It is not that the heroines do not care about their appearance; they do, and no doubt always look charming and appropriate, but they have 'no taste for finery or parade'. The comment of one of the vulgarians about Emma's wedding – 'very little white satin, very few lace veils; a most pitiful business!' – defines the attitude. Jane Austen would not dream of being, in a novel, so minute and specific as, for example, Richardson is about Clarissa's clothes.

Being good to the poor is not an exclusively feminine activity. Mr Darcy, according to his housekeeper, is 'affable' to them, and so, according to Harriet, is Mr Elton. According to Jane Austen, Emma's attitude to the needy is both feeling and sensible; we believe this to be true, and none the less when Emma, being Emma, cannot help exploiting her own genuine benevolence as a sexual gambit on Harriet's behalf. Mr Elton, doing the same on his own behalf, dashes out of the Vicarage as he sees the girls passing by on their way to the humble cottage. Emma reflects:

> To fall in with each other on such an errand as this; to meet in a charitable scheme; this will bring a great increase of love on each side. I should not wonder if it were to bring on the declaration.[19]

Jane Austen does not consider that nursing the sick is a necessarily feminine skill either. Charles Musgrove, when his son is injured, thinks: 'This was quite a female case, and it would be highly absurd in him, who could be of no use at home, to shut himself up', and soon afterwards Anne voices his thoughts: 'Nursing does not belong to a man; it is not his province.' This is obviously the accepted notion, and one is sorry to see Anne subscribing to it, but the novels as a whole give us a much more balanced, realistic picture. Women are not instinctively good at nursing. Mary Musgrove is hopeless. So is Mrs Norris; so is Lady Bertram. (One looks ahead to the wonderful description of Mrs Nickleby 'coming into the room with an elaborate caution, calculated to discompose the nerves of an invalid rather more than the entry of a horse-soldier at full gallop'.) When Tom Bertram is ill it is his

[19] *Emma*, ch. 10.

brother Edmund who shines in the sickroom, and the absent Fanny loves him all the better for it.

Yet when women are good nurses – Elinor Dashwood, Mrs Harville – it becomes them. The readers like them for it, and in the assessing eye of the male it is as good as an accomplishment. When Elizabeth says to Mr Darcy, more truly perhaps than she realises: 'To be sure you know no actual good of me – but nobody thinks of *that* when they fall in love', Darcy replies: 'Was there no good in your affectionate behaviour to Jane, while she was ill at Netherfield?'[20]

Though Mr Darcy attributes his reformation, as far as the breaking down of his pride is concerned, to Elizabeth, there is no idea that she is to be his habitual guardian angel. Jane Austen does not claim this rôle for her heroines, partly because she feels ambivalently on the subject of their goodness, frequently showing it to be a mixture of ignorance and naïveté rather than a steady moral attitude. Jane Bennet is an excellent example. Her forgiving spirit is, in fact, a neurotic inability to blame anyone, and her recourse to theories of conspiracy, when trying to find excuses for Miss Bingley's part in separating her from Mr Bingley, is not so much good as simple-minded. Elizabeth tartly points out that if she cannot provide some excuse for the conduct of the 'interested parties' who have worked on Miss Bingley, she will have to think badly of somebody. But Elizabeth herself is not spared. When she is expounding to Mr Darcy her philosophy of not dwelling on unpleasant memories he does not scruple to say that it is based on ignorance.

Henry Crawford tries the purifying-influence approach with Fanny (he has already said 'You have some touches of the angel in you') and she corrects him quite vigorously, for her.

'Shall I go? Do you advise it?'
'I advise! – you know very well what is right!'
'Yes. When you give me your opinion, I always know what is right.'
'Oh, no! – do not say so. We all have a better guide in ourselves, if we would attend to it, than any other person can be.'[21]

[20] *Pride and Prejudice*, ch. 60.
[21] *Mansfield Park*, ch. 42.

Fanny, of course, would have declined to do or be anything suggested by Mr Crawford and at other points Jane Austen does seem to be indicating that men *can* be redeemed by women. But she does so in comments about hypothetical situations, unions which in fact never took place. Two of the worst men in the novels, Willoughby and Mr Elliot, seem to be on the point of marrying good women, Marianne Dashwood and Anne Elliot. When it becomes known that they are not going to after all, and friends such as Colonel Brandon and Mrs Smith feel free to tell all they know about their villainy, the friends naturally have to explain their apparent irresponsibility in not having told all before and this is the best line they could take.

> To suffer you all to be so deceived; to see your sister – but what could I do? I had no hope of interfering with success; and sometimes I thought your sister's influence might yet reclaim him.[22]

> My heart bled for you, as I talked of happiness. And yet, he is sensible, he is agreeable, and with such a woman as you, it was not absolutely hopeless.[23]

The suggestion of a true good angel situation, the Frank Churchill/Jane Fairfax marriage, is in fact equally deceptive. Observers of the couple and the bridegroom himself dwell on the bride's uplifting influence; Mr Knightley gloomily:

> He may yet turn out well. With such a woman he has a chance;[24]

Emma spitefully:

> It is fit that the fortune should be on his side, for I think the merit will be all on hers;[25]

and Frank himself idiotically:

> She is a complete angel. Look at her. Is she not an angel in every gesture?[26]

But he is insincere and the onlookers are mistaken. None of them has noticed that his association with her up to that

[22] *Sense and Sensibility*, ch. 31.
[23] *Persuasion*, ch. 21.   [24] *Emma*, ch. 49.
[25] Ibid., ch. 48.   [26] Ibid., ch. 54.

time has done him no good at all and that her presence, as at the Box Hill party, actually makes him worse. Jane Austen, incidentally, told her friends that Mrs Frank Churchill died young.

'My aunt Philips wants you so to get husbands, you can't think.' So does Jane Austen; there is no pretence at all that getting husbands is not the point of each novel. Interest and surprise lie only in the sort of husband and the circumstances in which he is got. So much is known in general and shown by Jane Austen in particular about the social and economic advantages of marriage for women in those days, that the necessity can be passed over without further remark. What does call for comment is the way in which her heroines, while recognising the need for marriage, do not allow themselves to be utterly trapped by it. They do not panic.

Jane and Elizabeth Bennet are good examples of this. Their future is extremely precarious. They have little fortune; the famous entail could turn them out of their home at any time; they meet so few eligible men that even Jane with all her beauty and sweetness is nearly twenty-three before she attracts someone as suitable as Mr Bingley, and apparently she has had no serious proposals before. Elizabeth's case is perhaps worse, in that she is not so pretty and docile as Jane. Yet when Bingley more or less jilts Jane, it is for him she grieves not for the status he could offer her. And when Elizabeth has reason to believe that Darcy will never renew his proposals, not knowing or not caring that her feelings have changed, she can say with conviction: 'If he is satisfied with only regretting me, when he might have obtained my affections and hand, I shall soon cease to regret him at all.'[27] These are brave and dignified words, with spinsterhood looming. In *The Watsons* Jane Austen gives us the beginnings of a terrifying sketch of a desperate woman, but her heroines never despair, not even Elizabeth when Mr Collins says: 'In spite of your manifold attractions, it is by no means certain that another offer of marriage may ever be made to you.'[28]

Emma goes further than Elizabeth, supported possibly by her thirty thousand pounds. Mary Crawford, who has a similar dowry, is resigned to *waiting* after the disaster at

[27] *Pride and Prejudice*, ch. 57.   [28] Ibid., ch. 19.

Mansfield Park, but Emma actually declares marriage to be unnecessary to a woman who has a comfortable home, power, occupation and someone to love.[29] This is quite revolutionary and, though she goes back on her words eventually, they should be taken seriously. It is interesting that she should see that to have a loving relationship is the important thing, without the other party's necessarily being a husband.

> And as for objects for the affections, which is, in truth, the great point of inferiority, the want of which is really the great evil to be avoided in *not* marrying, I shall be very well off, with all the children of a sister I love so much, to care about.

In her analysis of a satisfying life Emma leaves out two things which only marriage could at that time bring: the impossibility of being called an old maid, and sex. Harriet points out the first difficulty. 'But still, you will be an old maid! and that's so dreadful!' but Emma retorts that she will be a rich old maid which makes all the difference. Sex, is of course, not mentioned. But Jane Austen does sometimes take it into account in speaking of marriage.

> That Lady Russell, of steady age and character, and extremely well provided for, should have no thought of a second marriage, needs no apology to the public.[30]

Lady Russell's steadiness can only mean lack of interest in sex, for the other benefits of marriage she could still have enjoyed. There is a similar hint in *Emma*:

> It was now some time since Miss Taylor had begun to influence his schemes; but as it was not the tyrannic influence of youth on youth, it had not shaken his determination of never settling till he could purchase Randalls.[31]

Even the highly debatable comment that middle-aged people do not want sex is more realistic than no comment at all.

Marriage, then, is the goal for everyone except the sated and the strong-minded, and even these can be tempted. A woman cannot ask, of course. That is hardly surprising considering how widely the convention still applies, but the

[29] *Emma*, ch. 10.   [30] *Persuasion*, ch. 1.   [31] *Emma*, ch. 2.

degree of passivity enforced upon girls then sounds almost lunatic: Anne Elliot can see no straightforward way of replying to Captain Wentworth's letter of proposal but has to depend, in a state of wearing suspense, on meeting him accidentally in the street and giving him what she hopes is a significant look; Elizabeth Bennet cannot even acknowledge Mr Darcy's letter though he has taken several thousand words to explain some extremely personal matters to her, a case where one would have thought the commonest courtesy would have overridden sexual taboos.

Jane Austen may or may not have thought such conventions absurd, but she makes even her most high-spirited heroines unquestioningly subscribe to the letter of the law. (We have to wait some time for the splendid scene in *Daniel Deronda* where a girl, Catherine Arrowpoint, honestly and quietly declares her love to a man.) The spirit of the law is another matter; Jane Austen's girls manage to get round it with considerable success. All girls were allowed to practise what was delicately called encouragement, but they go further. Catherine Morland's open display of her feelings for Henry Tilney, which is the only reason for his 'giving her a serious thought', is too much part of the burlesque of *Northanger Abbey* as a whole to be evidence, but three of the other heroines actively precipitate the hero's proposal. Emma shows emotion on the subject of the Churchill/Fairfax engagement in a way which she must have known, especially after her recent scene with Mrs Weston, would be misinterpreted by Mr Knightley and such a misunderstanding was bound to lead to something more tender and intimate. Elizabeth sets the scene in much the same way with an emotional outburst of gratitude to Darcy which would have moved the stoniest heart to some warm response; and she has already sent an intelligible message by Lady Catherine, for that is what that scene boils down to. The most telling example is the final version of the proposal scene in *Persuasion*. The cancelled chapter shows Anne contributing in a small way to her own destiny. When she finds she is to be alone with Captain Wentworth she politely says she will call on Mrs Croft another time.

But the Admiral would not hear of it; and if she did not return to the charge with unconquerable perseverance, or did not with a more passive determination walk quietly out of the room (as she certainly might have done), may she not be pardoned?[32]

In the chapters which took the place of this one, however, she does everything. Her moving words to Captain Harville on the subject of woman's fidelity, spoken aloud in a room where Captain Wentworth is writing and not even talking to anyone else, are as near to a declaration as a conventional novelist could with propriety let her heroine go, perhaps much nearer.

But a decent pretence that women do not propose is consistently kept up; it is often thrust at us. Mary Crawford is as liberated a person as the Jane Austen world could contain, and at first she speaks quite airily about her part in *Lover's Vows.*

Who is to be Anhalt? What gentleman among you am I to have the pleasure of making love to?

adding that she is not surprised

at this want of an Anhalt. Amelia deserves no better. Such a forward young lady may well frighten the men.[33]

But later even she has serious qualms, first when Anhalt is to be played by Charles Maddox and then when Edmund agrees to take the part. The subject of the main scene between them is

love – a marriage of love was to be described by the gentleman and very little short of a declaration of love be made by the lady.[34]

The worldly Miss Crawford gets almost incoherent with agitation when she has to do this. She asks Fanny to rehearse with her so that she can harden herself a little, 'for really there *is* a speech or two –'.

Have you ever happened to look at the part I mean? Here it is. I did not think much of it at first – but upon my word –. There, look at *that* speech, and *that*, and *that*. How am I ever to look him in the face and say such things?'

[32] *Persuasion*, cancelled chapter.
[33] *Mansfield Park*, ch. 15.   [34] Ibid., ch. 18.

If such a sophisticate is reduced to dithering indecision by merely acting an almost-proposal, how wild must be the notion of a woman in real life declaring her feelings to a man.

Fortunately, there are more devious ways. 'Some of those little attentions and encouragements which ladies can so easily give, will fix him, in spite of himself',[35] says John Dashwood, advising Elinor how to get Colonel Brandon. The little attentions include accomplishments, which are all aimed at catching men; the idea that a woman might cultivate her talents and personality for their, or her, own sake has no place in Jane Austen's scheme of things.

Music, with its obvious entertainment value, is a good example. Mr Knightley shows how men expect women to minister to them in this way.

> A very pleasant evening, particularly pleasant. You and Miss Fairfax gave us some very good music. I do not know a more luxurious state, sir, than sitting at one's ease to be entertained a whole evening by two such young women.[36]

'And the silken girls bringing sherbet.'

Emma Woodhouse and Elizabeth Bennet are both very indifferent performers, but the standard of the performance has nothing to do with what is essentially a sexual gesture. Those who love them do not mind: Harriet assures Emma that she will always think that she plays as well as Jane Fairfax or that if there is any difference nobody would ever find it out, and Darcy tells Elizabeth that no one admitted to the privilege of hearing her could think anything wanting. They realise their own inadequacies but do nothing to modify them, nor do they ever hold back from performing. They are not really humble about their singing and playing; they think of themselves as clever people who have not taken their gifts seriously enough; amateurs, in fact. Mary Crawford hits them off beautifully in speaking of the Miss Owens who 'would sing if they were taught or sing all the better for not being taught'. What does it matter? It is all a means to an end. The description of Mary's own music is perfectly honest.

> A young woman, pretty, lively, with a harp as elegant as herself; and both placed near a window, cut down to the

---

[35] *Sense and Sensibility*, ch. 33.   [36] *Emma*, ch. 21.

ground and opening on a little lawn, surrounded by shrubs in the rich foliage of summer, was enough to catch any man's heart.[37]

And Mrs Jennings is quite right in deducing from Colonel Brandon's interest in Marianne's singing a love not of music but of her.

Music as an accomplishment has a barefaced relationship to sexual status. Mrs Weston, who is married and pregnant, and Anne Elliot, who is on the shelf, do not give solo performances; the former has no need to, for the latter it is useless. They accompany the dancing. Brides often celebrate their marriages by giving up music altogether: Lady Middleton and Mrs Elton do. They are worthless women, it is true, but we cannot help thinking of the much nobler Natasha in *War and Peace* who does exactly the same thing.

Conversation is the other commodity that Mr Knightley in his Grand Turk mood requires from young women. The eighteenth century put little value on women's conversation. Lord Chesterfield said they were 'to be talked to as below men and above children' and it was from this unhappy level that presumably they were supposed to respond. The conduct books of the period certainly suggest that their rôle was to minister to men's conversations – those that were sufficiently trivial to be carried on in the drawing room in the first place – having mastered just enough of the subject to put in an intelligent comment, or, better, question, here and there. Some of Jane Austen's conversations do indeed sound rather like that. Emma is listening to the Knightley brothers who are talking animatedly about 'their own concerns and pursuits', principally connected with the Donwell property. When she does join in, it is as a feed.

I did not thoroughly understand what you were telling your brother about your friend Mr. Graham's intending to have a bailiff from Scotland, to look after his new estate. But will it answer? Will not the old prejudice be too strong?[38]

Sometimes we are irritated by remarks like Mr Knightley's: 'What does Weston think of the weather; shall we have rain?' Why on earth could an intelligent, observant woman, who

37 *Mansfield Park*, ch. 7.   38 *Emma*, ch. 12.

65

had lived in the country all her life, not prophesy the weather as well as her husband? But on the whole there is considerable equality between the sexes in conversation. Only pseudo-feminists like Mrs Elton really put into practice the idea that it is for gentlemen to speak about serious subjects like politics.

> If you mean a fling at the slave-trade, I assure you that Mr. Suckling was always rather a friend to the abolition.[39]

She cannot say that she herself is a friend to the abolition, though she is quoting Maple Grove with approval as usual. (Henry Tilney's silencing of his sister and Catherine Morland, on their walk to Beechen Hill, by bringing round the conversation to politics is too much part of the general joke to be evidence on this point, especially as Catherine is made to break the silence by one of the most idiotic remarks of her life.)[40]

Women were allowed, even encouraged, to show in their conversation that they had read. The various lists of books recommended for them in Jane Austen's day, stereotyped, limited and dreary, were published alongside other details of required behaviour. Literary allusions, as long as they were not too far-ranging or assertive, were held to be perfectly feminine, and indeed to be a desirable indication of the improved mind – an accomplishment within an accomplishment, in fact. Most of these literary tropes must have sounded terribly contrived and ill-digested; even Jane Austen's heroines cannot always carry them off. Listen to Emma.

> She has the advantage, you know, of practising on me, like La Baronne d'Almane on La Comptesse d'Ostalis, in Madame de Genlis' *Adelaide and Theodore*, and we shall now see her own little Adelaide educated on a more perfect plan.[41]

And Fanny's derivative remarks creak even more; her little speech about memory comes, as several critics have pointed out, almost straight from Dr Johnson, and we feel like Mary Crawford who 'untouched and inattentive, had nothing to say'.[42]

[39] Ibid., ch. 35.
[40] *Northanger Abbey*, ch. 14.
[41] *Emma*, ch. 53.
[42] *Mansfield Park*, ch. 22.

Miss Bingley includes a thorough knowledge of modern languages in her list of necessary accomplishments. In *Persuasion* we have an excellent example of the way in which this accomplishment, too, can be used for sexual manoeuvre. In the incident at the concert in Bath, already described, Anne Elliot's mastery of Italian is cleverly exploited by Mr Elliot as though it were a weapon of his own, to increase intimacy, to exercise proprietorial airs and to distract attention from a rival at a critical moment.[43] After her translation of the song, compliment follows fulsome compliment until the interval during which Anne manages to get a seat at the end of a bench, away from Mr Elliot and accessible to Captain Wentworth whom she has just seen. It works: Captain Wentworth comes up and talks to her, with increasing warmth and sympathy.

> He even looked down towards the bench, as if he saw a place on it well worth occupying; when, at that moment, a touch on her shoulder obliged Anne to turn round. It came from Mr Elliot. He begged her pardon, but she must be applied to, to explain Italian again. Miss Carteret was very anxious to have a general idea of what was next to be sung.

Captain Wentworth retreats.

The fact that dancing and elegant walking are considered to be essential female allurements is hardly surprising but sometimes the frankness of reference to the latter is rather startling. When Miss Bingley, who has an elegant figure and walks well, is trying to attract Mr Darcy she gets up and parades around the room in front of him like a street walker. He goes on reading. She invites Elizabeth to join her. He looks up. But when she then asks him to join them he declines, saying that one of the reasons they are walking is 'because you are conscious that your figures appear to the greatest advantage in walking' in which case 'I can admire you much better as I sit by the fire'. 'Oh! shocking!' cries the delighted Miss Bingley. It is rather. Mr Darcy really is a Miss World judge.[44]

The plot of each of Jane Austen's books depends a great deal on dancing and the women characters display their full

43 *Persuasion*, ch. 20.
44 *Pride and Prejudice*, ch. 11.

characters by means of it, Fanny 'gliding about with quiet, light elegance and in admirable time', Harriet bounding about 'in a continual course of smiles', Emma leading off 'with genuine spirit', Anne relegating herself to the piano. Henry Tilney's famous, and significant, comparison of dancing with marriage[45] is illustrated at every turn, for example, when Emma has to stand second to Mrs Elton. 'It was almost enough to make her think of marrying.' And so she does, and becomes 'a Mrs Knightley for them all to give way to'.

Jane Austen invests dancing heavily with symbolism. The ball at the Crown just alluded to is an extreme example, with its two fraught situations: Mr Knightley inviting Harriet to dance when she is scorned by Mr Elton, in circumstances of such drama that it is no wonder she mis-interprets her rescuer's motives: Emma, in a glow of gratitude suggesting to Mr Knightley that they should dance together, apparently for the first time.

> 'Whom are you going to dance with?' asked Mr. Knightley.
> She hesitated a moment, and then replied, 'With you, if you will ask me.'
> 'Will you?' said he, offering his hand.
> 'Indeed I will. You have shown that you can dance, and you know we are not really so much brother and sister as to make it at all improper.'
> 'Brother and sister! no, indeed!'[46]

It is like a first kiss.

What of the men whom all these sustained and systematic efforts are to secure? Jane Austen presents them as on the verge of being something rather unpleasant though they never go quite over the edge. They have traces of arrogance, conceit and sadism, but these traces are well-concealed. They teach, humiliate, punish, frustrate and tantalise the women they love, but only to a degree which Jane Austen manages to disguise as acceptable behaviour. And we have only to think of scenes from other novels to realise how tentative she is.

Man as teacher, for example: Jane Austen gives us nothing

45 *Northanger Abbey*, ch. 10.
46 *Emma*, ch. 38.

as unpleasant and painful as the scene in *Sons and Lovers* where Paul teaches Miriam algebra. Certainly she shows her heroes instructing ignorant girls in subjects that have so far passed them by. Henry Tilney's lecture to Catherine on the picturesque is the most obvious example.[47] But the multiple and shifting satire prevents us from knowing quite how to take it; if we had to respond seriously to a sentence like this:

> His instructions were so clear that she soon began to see beauty in everything admired by him, and her attention was so earnest that he became perfectly satisfied of her having a great deal of natural taste . . .

we might feel that Paul's rage at Miriam's stupidity is more wholesome. There do seem to be indications, however, in the technique of this passage as a whole that Jane Austen has more animus against Henry Tilney in his character of pedagogue than the pervasive irony lets us easily see. Henry makes very heavy weather of his lecture; it sounds dreadfully pompous and we cannot help recalling Elizabeth Bennet's brief, witty and telling application of the same material. It is interesting, too, that some of his instructions are summarised in the style of Jingle:

> He talked of foregrounds, distances and second distances – side-screens and perspectives – lights and shades. . . . He suffered the subject to decline and by an easy transition from a piece of rocky fragment and the withered oak which he had placed near its summit, to oaks in general, to forests, the enclosure of them, waste lands, and government, he shortly found himself arrived at politics;

a style very similar to that used to convey Mrs Elton's monologue at the strawberry-picking party at Donwell.[48]

Edmund Bertram's tutorial relation to Fanny Price is altogether more natural as it starts earlier, when she is nine, and is at a more basic level.

> Edmund prepared her paper, and ruled her lines with all the good will that her brother could himself have felt, and probably with somewhat more exactness. He continued with her the whole time of her writing, to assist

[47] *Northanger Abbey*, ch. 14.   [48] *Emma*, ch. 42.

her with his penknife or his orthography, as either were
wanted.[49]

As Fanny grows up the instruction becomes more sophisticated:

He recommended the books which charmed her leisure
hours, he encouraged her taste, and corrected her judgement;

but it is still justifiable because he is older and really does
know more than she does.

But the superiority based on the man's being older is seen
also in cases where the woman has had time to catch up.
Jane Austen's heroes are always older than the women they
marry; this is axiomatic (not only for her, of course, but for
most nineteenth-century novelists) and anything else is unthinkable and improper. (In *Lady Susan* the objections of
the de Courcy family to Reginald's marrying her are based
less on her being a scheming bitch than on her being twelve
years older than himself. It is relevant to remember that
one of Jane Austen's brothers married a woman twelve years
older than himself.) The heroes often pull rank and they
often pull age. In the scene from *Northanger Abbey* recently
cited Henry says:

Consider how many years I have had the start of you. I
had entered on my studies at Oxford, while you were
a good little girl working your sampler at home.

Catherine accepts this, with further depreciation of herself:
'Not very good, I am afraid.' Emma is the one who challenges
the attitude.

'To be sure; our discordancies must always arise from my
being in the wrong.'
'Yes', said he smiling, 'and reason good. I was sixteen
years old when you were born.'
'A material difference, then', she replied, 'and no doubt
you were much my superior in judgement at that period of
our lives; but does not the lapse of one-and-twenty years
bring our understanding a good deal nearer?'
'Yes, a good deal *nearer.*'

[49] *Mansfield Park*, ch. 2.

'But still, not near enough to give me a chance of being right if we think differently.'

'I have still the advantage of you by sixteen years' experience, and by not being a pretty young woman and a spoiled child.'[50]

To man as seducer Jane Austen does not pay anything like enough attention, either because he, like man as teacher, figured prominently in the eighteenth-century novel – and indeed Lovelace could never be surpassed – or simply because it is a subject she prefers not to dwell on, or because she is forced into a sort of unworldly sophistication by the popular trials of the romantic heroine, as lampooned by Sir Walter Scott in his review of *Emma*.

She was regularly exposed to being forcibly carried off like a Sabine virgin by some frantic admirer. And even if she escaped the terrors of masked ruffians, an insidious ravisher, a cloak wrapped forcibly around her head, and a coach with the blinds up driving she could not conjecture whither, she still had her share of wandering, of poverty, of obloquy, of seclusion, and of imprisonment.[51]

Northanger Abbey as part of the general burlesque adopts a facetious attitude to seducers.

When the hour of departure drew near, the maternal anxiety of Mrs. Morland will be naturally supposed to be most severe ... Cautions against the violence of such noblemen and baronets as delight in forcing young ladies away to some remote farmhouse, must, at such a moment relieve the fullness of her heart. Who would not think so? But Mrs. Morland knew so little of lords and baronets, that she entertained no notion of their general mischievousness, and was wholly unsuspicious of danger to her daughter from their machinations.[52]

This note is struck later in the introductory description of Captain Tilney.

He cannot be the instigator of the three villains in horsemen's greatcoats, by whom she will hereafter be forced

[50] *Emma*, ch. 12. [51] *Quarterly Review*, March 1816.
[52] *Northanger Abbey*, ch. 2.

into a travelling-chaise and four, which will drive off with incredible speed.[53]

Of the four novelists with which this book deals only Jane Austen would present rape as funny. And, apart from that, she and Mrs Morland are being naïve. Seduction and rape were real hazards not only during the period she was describing but long before and ever since. With a goose like Catherine it was especially likely. There is greater realism in some of her other novels. Lydia Bennet and Maria Rushworth do not count; Wickham and Crawford are as much seduced as seducing. But *Sense and Sensibility* really does deal with the subject, though it is much softened by being presented in the form of two coherent, well-composed stories told in a low voice by one of the most shadowy men in fiction.[54] We never see Mrs Brandon or Miss Williams; their histories do not harrow us. Towards the end of the book Marianne is haunted by fears that Willoughby might have intended to seduce her, a quite plausible fear, especially in view of the unchaperoned expedition to Allenham. Marianne's dread of something that did not happen brings the subject much nearer, as do some of the casual comments in *Emma* about the unpleasantness of 'solitary female walking', the dangers Jane Fairfax was facing in her walk back to Highbury from Donwell alone and what might have happened to Harriet when the gypsies attacked her.

The heroes, of course, cannot be seducers, not even reformed ones, but they can be pretty nasty. 'Teazing, teazing man!' exclaims Elizabeth about Mr Darcy, and indeed the heroes do lead the heroines a dance. What causes Elizabeth's annoyance is his unloving behaviour at the Longbourn dinner and then his going away from Netherfield altogether at a time when she has just decided that she does love him after all and when she suspects that in spite of everything he still loves her. A little later, when they are safely engaged, she taxes him with his behaviour and he attributes it to his embarrassment and uncertainty about her feelings; she finds this reasonable but the readers may not.

However Darcy does not make Elizabeth suffer long or deeply. Far worse is Captain Wentworth's treatment of Anne

[53] Ibid., ch. 16.
[54] *Sense and Sensibility*, ch. 31.

Elliot, whom he subjects to six years of active and wearing grief.

> 'Tell me if, when I returned to England in the year eight, with a few thousand pounds, and was posted into the Laconia, if I had then written to you, would you have answered my letter? would you in short have renewed the engagement then?'
> 'Would I!' was all her answer; but the accent was decisive enough.
> 'Good God!' he cried, 'you would! It is not that I did not think of it, or desire it, as what could alone crown all my other success. But I was proud, too proud to ask again. I did not understand you. I shut my eyes, and would not understand you, or do you justice.'[55]

We would expect Frank Churchill to be vindictive and he is. Throughout the book he seems to be punishing Jane Fairfax for having stooped to a secret engagement with him though he coerced her into it with threats of going mad. His account of their final quarrel acknowledges with almost indecent honesty his wish to hurt her.

> In short, my dear madam, it was a quarrel blameless on her side, abominable on mine; and I returned the same evening to Richmond, though I might have staid with you till the next morning, merely because I would be as angry with her as possible. Even then, I was not such a fool as not to mean to be reconciled in time; but I was the injured person, injured by her coldness, and I went away determined that she should make the first advances.[56]

From Mr Knightley, the paragon, we would expect greater generosity but we do not get it.

> I should like to see Emma in love, and in some doubt of a return; it would do her good.[57]

It is an unpleasant wish to make for anyone, however bumptious.

The real demon of cruelty is kind Edmund Bertram. We must, I suppose, overlook his obtuseness at not seeing that Fanny is in love with him; presumably he cannot help being obtuse. But there is something horribly systematic about

[55] *Persuasion*, ch. 23.   [56] *Emma*, ch. 50.   [57] Ibid., ch. 5.

the way in which he hurts Fanny and some of the moments he chooses to turn the knife in the wound are most ingeniously selected. To take only a few examples: at a time when his infatuation for Mary Crawford is reaching a critical stage, he practically tells Fanny he has never thought *her* pretty; it is Sir Thomas who has made the discovery.[58] When Henry Crawford proposes to Fanny, unsuccessfully, and she is in a state of great agitation about it, Edmund makes it quite clear he wants her to marry Crawford, and partly because of his love for Crawford's sister: 'You are aware of my having no common interest in Crawford.' This is bad enough in general, but some of his particular comments on the situation are diabolical.

> I wish he had known you as well as I do, Fanny. Between us, I think we should have won you. My theoretical and his practical knowledge together, could not have failed. He should have worked upon my plans.[59]

Perhaps worst of all is when he presses, by strong approval and encouragement, the woman who loves him into the service of the woman he loves. The circumstances are trivial – Fanny is to hear Mary read her part in the play – but the feelings are not.[60] It is as though Anne Elliot really had had to nurse her rival Louisa back to health; Wentworth wants her to but Jane Austen will not permit it. (She is wise, but it is tantalising to think what George Eliot might have made of it: such fantasies of smothering with pillows, mixing the medicine wrong, opening the window too wide.)

The least unkind of the heroes is Henry Tilney. In character he is a confirmed tease, of his sister as well as of Catherine, whose naïve, ill-expressed notions he is for ever mocking to her face, in casual remarks as well as in the sustained parody of her romantic fears with which he enlivens the journey to Northanger Abbey. Yet when serious feelings are at stake, he is completely serious and responsible. He leaves Northanger immediately after the quarrel with his father and sets out for Fullerton; aware of Catherine's love he does not keep her in suspense a moment longer than is necessary.

When Kate Millett describes in *Sexual Politics*[61] the doctrine of 'shoot and screw' to be found in the plays of

[58] *Mansfield Park*, ch. 21.   [59] Ibid., ch. 35.
[60] Ibid., ch. 18.   [61] *Sexual Politics*, ch. 1.

Jean Genet, we do not, probably, instantly think of Jane Austen. But we might if the vocabulary did not head us off, for shooting, as a male activity, is used in her novels with inescapable symbolism. On the occasion of Mr Bingley's return to Netherfield Mrs Bennet, even more anxious than before to have him marry Jane, speaks as follows:

> When you have killed all your own birds, Mr. Bingley, I beg you will come here, and shoot as many as you please, on Mr. Bennet's manor. I am sure he will be vastly happy to oblige you, and will save all the best of the covies for you.[62]

A few days later, when Mr Bingley and Mr Darcy come to dinner at Longbourn, it is in this guise that they are referred to: 'The two, who were most anxiously expected, to the credit of their punctuality as sportsmen, were in very good time.'[63] It is the one pursuit that Lydia, in a state of honeymoon rapture, seizes on to convey Wickham's attractions.

> Lydia was exceedingly fond of him. He was her dear Wickham on every occasion; no one was to be put in competition with him. He did everything best in the world; and she was sure he would kill more birds on the first of September, than anybody else in the country.[64]

There are lesser examples in the other novels: Willoughby and Charles Musgrove make up for lack of satisfaction in their marriages by 'sporting of every kind', while Admiral Croft, who is extremely happily married, 'sometimes took out a gun but never killed'.

Driving in those days – a gig, a curricle, a barouche – was a masculine accomplishment entirely comparable with driving a motor car today. Men exploited both the possession of the vehicle and their skill in handling it to impress women; they fancied themselves, rightly or wrongly, as drivers; and they could be sorted out and assessed according to this criterion by girls, even by girls as inexperienced as Catherine.

> But the merit of the curricle did not all belong to the horses; Henry drove so well, so quietly, without making any disturbance, without parading to her, or swearing at

---

[62] *Pride and Prejudice*, ch. 53.
[63] Ibid., ch. 54.   [64] Ibid., ch. 51.

them; so different from the only gentleman-coachman whom it was in her power to compare him with! And then his hat sat so well, and the innumerable capes of his great-coat looked so becomingly important! To be driven by him, next to being dancing with him, was certainly the greatest happiness in the world.[65]

On the fateful expedition to Sotherton from Mansfield Park everyone realises the significance of Mrs Grant's suggestion that Julia should sit beside Henry on the barouche box, and of her wording of the suggestion ('As you were saying recently that you wished you could drive, Julia, I think this will be a good opportunity for you to take a lesson'). Mrs Grant wants her brother to marry Julia and she is as good as saying so. Maria's jealous bad temper at the seating arrangements is not the exaggeration it would be if these were the only factor in question, and neither is Julia's triumphant pleasure, nor Henry's attempts to explain the matter away to Maria later. For Jane Austen, sitting beside the driver is a symbol of sexual achievement. It is one of the two aspects of Anne's marriage that Mary Musgrove is jealous about; she does not like seeing her 'the mistress of a very pretty landaulette'.

In face of all this male dominance which caused women such suffering ('that silent torture of an unloved woman, condemned to suffer thus because she is a woman and must not speak', as Julia Kavanagh said later in the century),[66] what solidarity do Jane Austen's heroines display? The answer, unfortunately, is almost none. Some pairs of sisters give each other invaluable support – Jane and Elizabeth Bennet, Elinor and Marianne Dashwood – but Maria and Julia Bertram give way to the most unpleasant and spiteful rivalry, closing ranks again only when both have been deserted by Henry Crawford. Women friends and acquaintances consistently throw each other to the wolves. After Willoughby's jilting of Marianne, Lady Middleton, whose husband incidentally is more loyal, 'determined that as Mrs. Willoughby would at once be a woman of elegance and fortune, to leave her card with her as soon as she

[65] *Northanger Abbey*, ch. 20.
[66] *English Women of Letters* (1862) ch. 18.

married'.[67] Mary Crawford, after the most perfunctory of expostulations with her brother when he has declared his aim of making Fanny Price fall in love with him at a time when he himself has no serious idea of her at all, leaves her calmly to her fate,[68] for which we might have been prepared by Mary's way of talking about the Bertram sisters earlier on; little as they deserve she is heartless in the extreme.[69]

The only two women who make a great show of standing by their female friends are Mrs Elton and Isabella Thorpe. Mrs Elton's vulgar insensitive espousal of the cause, as she considers it, of Jane Fairfax, is one of the main themes of *Emma*. Less developed but telling is Isabella's patronage of Miss Andrews.

> I think her as beautiful as an angel, and I am so vexed with the men for not admiring her! I scold them all amazingly about it ... The men think us incapable of real friendship you know, and I am determined to show them the difference.[70]

Emma is more honest, which perhaps explains her creator's lenient treatment of her unpardonable scandal-mongering about Jane Fairfax. She is bound to take the line that Emma's betrayal of Jane Fairfax – in imparting to Frank Churchill her suspicions about Jane's attachment to Mr Dixon – is wrong, but she is not really very severe, not half severe enough, many readers might think.

It is only fair to add that in her novels Jane Austen does not show us much male solidarity either. With the exception of the Darcy/Bingley friendship, there is no example of the traditional couple of males hunting together and even this is rather a dubious example as Darcy dominates Bingley in much the same way that Emma dominates Harriet and there is not much solidarity *there*.

What is the fate, the future of Jane Austen's heroines, after the excitement of the courtship and the triumph of the wedding, a time when women are more important than ever again in their lives? (Consult Mrs Elton on the status of a bride.) 'Nothing very bad. The fate of thousands': Mr

---

[67] *Sense and Sensibility*, ch. 32. [68] *Mansfield Park*, ch. 24.
[69] Ibid., ch. 17. [70] *Northanger Abbey*, ch. 6.

Knightley is speaking of the grown-up life of spoiled children, but the remark would apply equally to the married lives of the dancing, singing, talking young women of whom we lose sight soon after the ceremony. Jane Austen is careful that the wedding bells should ⁄ actually sound out, metaphorically and literally ('Henry and Catherine were married, the bells rang and everybody smiled'); she never stops at the engagement, perhaps because in her day so many engagements were never fulfilled because one of the couple died. We see this in the novels with the sad story of Fanny Harville.

The heroines are going to be happy. They have taken a whole book each to make their choice and to ensure that they are chosen, so this is likely. We hear of 'the perfect happiness of the union' (*Emma*), and of 'the comfort and elegance of their family party at Pemberley' (*Pride and Prejudice*); we are told that 'Anne was tenderness itself, and she had the full worth of it in Captain Wentworth's affection' (*Persuasion*) and that 'the happiness of the married cousins must appear as secure as earthly happiness can be' (*Mansfield Park*).

What wives contribute to society can be seen in Jane Austen's portraits of those who are already married or who even have died before the story begins.

> Lady Elliot had been an excellent woman, sensible and amiable; whose judgment and conduct, if they might be pardoned the youthful infatuation which made her Lady Elliot, had never required indulgence afterwards. – She had humoured, or softened, or concealed his failings, and promoted his real respectability for seventeen years; and though not the very happiest being in the world herself, had found enough in her duties, her friends and her children, to attach her to life, and make it no matter of indifference to her when she was called on to quit them.[71]

> While Lady Elliot lived, there had been method, moderation and economy, which had just kept him within his income; but with her had died all such right-mindedness, and from that period he had been constantly exceeding it.[72]

---

[71] *Persuasion*, ch. 1.   [72] Ibid.

These pasages are bleakly realistic. To modern readers the idea of a spirited woman's devoting seventeen years, or even one, to promoting a man's respectability and covering up for him generally is uncongenial. The portrait of bustling Charlotte Collins, née Lucas, with 'her home and her house-keeping, her parish and her poultry' is much less depressing.

Lady Elliot is later seen, however, through the eyes of those she loved and who loved her, her friend Lady Russell and her daughter Anne; the picture improves and we can see the charms of such a situation. The archetypal good wife and mother of Jane Austen's day and of many other days both earlier and later, with duties, ties, loyalties and allegiances, living through others, with no impulses of her own, is here surrounded unexpectedly with a sort of glow.

> 'I own that to be able to regard you as the future mistress of Kellynch, the future Lady Elliot – to look forward and see you occupying your dear mother's place, succeeding to all her rights, and all her popularity, as well as to all her virtues, would be the highest possible gratification to me. You are your mother's self in countenance and disposition; and if I might be allowed to fancy you such as she was, in situation, and name, and home, presiding and blessing in the same spot, and only superior to her in being more highly valued! My dearest Anne, it would give me more delight than is often felt at my time of life!'
>
> Anne was obliged to turn away, to rise, to walk to a distant table, and, leaning there in pretended employment, try to subdue the feelings this picture excited. For a few moments her imagination and her heart were bewitched. The idea of becoming what her mother had been; of having the precious name of 'Lady Elliot' first revived in herself; of being restored to Kellynch, calling it her home for ever, was a charm which she could not immediately resist.[73]

But the glow fades, for Anne and for us, and when at the end of the book she says 'If I mistake not, a strong sense of duty is no bad part of a woman's portion', we may well feel like snapping, 'of everybody's portion'.

The most significant description of the happy, occupied

[73] Ibid., ch. 17.

wife and mother is that of Isabella Knightley. Mr Woodhouse is lamenting

> over the destiny of poor Isabella; which poor Isabella, passing her life with those she doated on, full of their merits, blind to their faults, and always innocently busy, might have been a model of right feminine happiness.[74]

This is intriguing. What does Jane Austen really think? We know she considers Isabella a fool. Can she be seriously recommending this undiscriminating, imperceptive, trivial woman as an exemplar of 'right feminine happiness'? Does she in her heart think so poorly of women, or does she think so poorly of marriage, as to consider a degree of dimness a positive advantage to anyone embarking on it? It would be easy to say simply that the remark is meant ironically, but it does not sound ironical either by itself or in context. It is certainly comic but it is Mr Woodhouse Jane Austen is laughing at. She has been careful to establish, however, that Mr Woodhouse, though practically half-witted, can be right where nearly everyone else is wrong; he sees at once that Frank Churchill is 'not the thing'. Mr Woodhouse, alone of all the characters in the book, thinks Isabella has a terrible time. Does the author think so too?

When a really unhappy marriage occurs in the novels, such as that of the Bennets or the Willoughbys, it is treated either humorously or summarily; we are not encouraged to dwell on the tragedy of it. On the other hand, a happy marriage such as that of the Crofts is bathed in a lingering rosy light.

In the novels all Jane Austen's fears about childbirth are suppressed. Nobody dies in childbed and many of the characters do not conceive at all: Maria Bertram, for example, experiences marriage and a passionate love affair without becoming pregnant. Isabella Knightley, who is having a child every year, is, overtly, the object of congratulation not of sympathy. Mrs Jennings gloomily forecasts that Edward Ferrars and Lucy will have a child every year but it is only because they will be poor that she is gloomy about it. The Morlands have ten children yet Mrs Morland is far from being a 'poor animal'. Mrs Price would have been indolent and inefficient with no children at all.

[74] *Emma*, ch. 17.

Mrs Weston's pregnancy, which gives rise to considerable anxiety in *Emma*, would have been fairly worrying even today in view of her age.

Yet though everything that Jane Austen thought she knew about women's lot in marriage is smoothed and softened to fit the masculine viewpoint of the novels, occasionally she gives herself away. Most revealing is Mrs Weston's comment when Mr Knightley says what a good wife she is: 'Thank you. There will be very little merit in making a good wife to such a man as Mr. Weston.'[75] Marriage is a state where women struggle and endure. There can be no virtue in effortless contentment.

Throughout the nineteenth-century novel the rôle of woman was depicted increasingly as less passive and more independent than it had been. Even Fanny Price has more spine than Fanny Burney's Evelina. When Mr Knightley teasingly asks Emma, 'What do you deserve?' and in the cheerful confidence of her recent engagement she replies, 'Oh! I always deserve the best treatment because I never put up with any other',[76] she is exaggerating but not inventing. However, there was a long way to go. The presentation of three women characters – Lady Susan, Mrs Croft and Mary Crawford – shows how long.

Lady Susan is a woman who has to do the best for herself in a society where she is very much at a disadvantage. Instead of a gentle supine selfishness, which might pass as virtue, she displays active and conscious cunning. A dominating, clever woman surrounded by remarkably flabby men, she moulds her own destiny and that of others. But, artistically, she is the least powerful and convincing of all the heroines, and – which is important – one whom Jane Austen decided not to present to the world. She is allowed to triumph, but is unequivocally condemned for her unblushing career of self-help.

Mrs Croft, the nearest Jane Austen could get to a professional woman, is, with all her voyages and experiences and knowledge of the navy, still only a sailor's wife, and in any case she could not have accomplished what she did if she had had children. Her status is made quite plain in Jane Austen's comment: 'Mrs. Croft (was) looking as intelligent

[75] Ibid., ch. 5.   [76] Ibid., ch. 54.

81

and keen as any of the officers around her.'[77] How pleasant and how unthinkable if she had said that the officers looked as intelligent and keen as Mrs Croft. It would have been as though Emma and not Mr Knightley had said that they had 'every right that equal worth can give, to be happy together',[78] or as though Tennyson's Princess, having expounded the equality of the sexes, had told the Prince to put his sweet hand in hers and trust in her.

Mary Crawford is as nearly a 'modern woman' as Mrs Croft is a career woman; she is realistic, outspoken and fair-minded, but Jane Austen does not allow her to be appreciated. What finally condemns her in Edmund's eyes is the fact that she can openly and honestly discuss the elopement of her brother and Maria Rushworth, and show no signs of 'modest loathings' while doing so.[79] She is the only person in the book, with the exception of the monstrous Mrs Norris, to show any sort of humanity towards Maria's final plight. Henry Crawford will certainly be accepted by society again before long – as Jane Austen herself points out, with some resentment but not enough – even if a few mothers lock up their daughters; Maria never will be, and when Mary urges on the Bertram family a marriage between Henry and Maria it is only of the welfare of Maria, whom she has never liked, that she can be thinking. But even as we warm to Mary's liberality, Jane Austen as novelist cons us into feeling that Mary is being coarse and improper, and when Mary comments that, if only Fanny had accepted Henry, his affair with Maria 'would have all ended in a regular standing flirtation, in yearly meetings at Sotherton and Everingham' – a perfectly sensible, even a wise remark – we are pressured into thinking that it is not sensible but crude. Yet only a few pages later Jane Austen in her own person says something very similar, to the effect that if Mr Rushworth marries again it is to be hoped that next time he will be betrayed with good humour and good luck. Apparently what Maria did wrong was to sin bad-temperedly and to get found out.

To talk of conflict between Jane Austen's ideals for women and her basic acceptance of a male-dominated society is perhaps to use too dramatic a word; but some sort of stress and

[77] *Persuasion*, ch. 18.   [78] *Emma*, ch. 53.
[79] *Mansfield Park*, ch. 47.

ambivalence we do find – and must enjoy without asking for more. When Miss Bingley wishes that conversation and not dancing were the chief occupation at a ball, her brother replies that while no doubt it would be more rational it would not be near so much like a ball. We might wish that the stress and ambivalence had been much greater and more exciting, but the resulting work would not have been near so much like Jane Austen.

Chapter III

Between the publication of Jane Austen's *Persuasion* and
Charlotte Brontë's *Jane Eyre* great social changes occurred.
They had begun in Jane Austen's time, of course, and she
had apparently not taken much notice of them, but by 1847,
the date of the publication of *Jane Eyre*, they could no longer
be ignored and in any case Charlotte Brontë had no wish to
ignore them. Mr Suckling's fling at the slave trade turned,
with her, into serious author's comment.

In her novels she not only shows the changes brought
about by the growth and spread of the industrial revolution
but tends to approve of them, as in this passage from the
end of *Shirley*, where Robert Moore, the mill-owner, re-
prieved from the threat of bankruptcy by the repeal of the
Orders in Council, prophesies a bright future.

> I can line yonder barren Hollow with lines of cottages,
> and rows of cottage-gardens ... The copse shall be fire-
> wood ere five years elapse: the beautiful wild ravine shall
> be a smooth descent; the green natural terrace shall be a
> paved street: there shall be cottages in the dark ravine,
> and cottages on the lonely slopes: the rough pebbled track
> shall be an even, firm, broad, black, sooty road, bedded
> with the cinders from my mill: and my mill shall fill its
> present yard ... I will get an act for enclosing Nunnely
> Common, and parcelling it out into farms ... The house-
> less, the starving, the unemployed, shall come to Hollow's
> Mill from far and near.

The tone is apocalyptic. Caroline, Moore's future wife, does
protest a little, but she knows quite well that progress must
come before prettiness. And at the end the narrator con-
firms it all.

> The other day I passed up the Hollow, which tradition
> says was once green, and lone, and wild; and there I saw
> the manufacturer's day-dreams embodied in substantial

stone and brick and ashes – the cinder-black highway, the cottages, and the cottage gardens; there I saw a mighty mill, and a chimney, ambitious as the tower of Babel.[1]

However unattractive some of these details may be, the tone is the quietly elegiac voice of acceptance and its rhythm hauntingly recalls the conclusion of *Wuthering Heights*.

We think of those two romantic preservationists, Fanny Price and Marianne Dashwood: Fanny with her general suspicion of Mr Repton's improvements and Marianne with her distress at the idea of the dead leaves of Norland being swept up and her preference for a picturesquely ragged village community to a tidy prosperous one. Though Jane Austen is laughing at Marianne's exaggeration and a little at Fanny's sentiment, both girls are her heroines and she does not really dissociate herself from them. She, too, liked things as they were.

The difference between the attitudes of the two authors, on this and on other issues, particularly the Woman Question, sprang partly from a difference of class. Jane Austen and Charlotte Brontë were both daughters of clergymen, but there, socially, the resemblance ended. Patrick Brontë had social pretensions – he changed his name from Brunty – but he was a self-made man of humble origins, whom Haworth provided with none of the polished society which might have made his manners more relaxed and easy. And Branwell Brontë established a positively downward trend with the unambitious work he undertook (imagine any of Jane Austen's brothers as a booking clerk on the railway) and the low company he preferred to keep. The family was poor and the girls, though their school friendships brought and kept them in touch with people of wealth and property, had to go out to work.

It was a similarly insecure background that Charlotte Brontë gave her heroines. They come from much the same social class as Jane Austen's heroines, at least from its lower echelons. Caroline Helstone, for example, the portionless niece of a country vicar, is on much the same footing as Emma Watson. Two of them, Jane Eyre and Lucy Snowe, have fallen from relatively high estate. They are all ladies of course. Jane, in spite of her lowly status and unimpressive

[1] *Shirley*, ch. 37.

looks, is still recognised by the servants as a social superior; as Bessie says, 'You are genteel enough, you look like a lady'[2] and even Hannah, when every circumstance works to mislead her, concludes, 'You look a raight down dacent little crater',[3] her egalitarian North Country way of saying much the same thing. Lucy Snowe can, if she chooses, mix with the de Bassompierres on terms of equality. Shirley Keeldar, when Sir Philip Nunnely seems about to propose, meets with no more opposition from his mother than Elizabeth Bennet does from Lady Catherine de Bourgh.

But there is the question of work. Jane Austen's women for the most part live unthinkingly on the labour of others. The dark world of paid employment – and it is consistently presented as gloomy – casts its shadow over only a few of them. But Charlotte Brontë's most important women characters have to work. And this necessity looms so large as to affect her presentation of women as a whole. Work gives Jane Eyre, Lucy Snowe and Frances Henri greater freedom of a sort, and however unwelcome, than their more sheltered sisters in the drawing rooms of Mansfield Park and Pemberley. It gives them wider experience, however unpleasant, and more urgent and realistic needs. It certainly brings them face to face with the Woman Question.

Charlotte Brontë's own passionate nature with all its aspirations and consequent frustrations would no doubt have burst through Godmersham Park as it did through Haworth, and it is impossible to do more than suggest where her views came from. But it is possible to define them and particularly, of course, her views on the status of women, without having to decide on their exact source. A comparison of certain passages from her novels with essentially similar ones from the work of Jane Austen will begin to demonstrate Charlotte Brontë's strikingly different attitude.

Firstly: two scenes where a gentleman reads Shakespeare aloud to the ladies. In *Mansfield Park* Henry Crawford, chiefly to further his pursuit of Fanny, declaims with excellent effect some passages from *Henry VIII*. Fanny has been reading it to her aunt before his arrival but there is no question of her continuing now. The ladies listen and their only response to the performance can be praise. Henry dominates the scene completely and would do so even if Lady Bertram

2 *Jane Eyre*, ch. 10.   3 Ibid., ch. 29.

were more talkative and Fanny less determined to give him no encouragement.

In *Shirley* Caroline Helstone, spending an evening at Hollow's Cottage, formally though they are her distant cousins, with Robert and Hortense Moore, takes the initiative in suggesting reading aloud, chooses the play, *Coriolanus*, and, brushing aside Hortense's hint that 'when the gentleman of a family reads, the ladies should always sew', joins Robert in the reading, catechises him about it afterwards and draws rather outspoken morals from it with a view to improving his character.[4] Yet Caroline is no Elizabeth Bennet; she is more like Fanny Price.

Secondly: two sustained passages of which amateur acting is the subject. We know from *Mansfield Park* what Jane Austen thought of it and particularly her horror at the indelicacy of women taking parts which called on them to display themselves in front of young men to whom they were not married and to utter sentiments of love, even if it was only maternal love, in public. A great deal of the early part of *Mansfield Park* depends on this theme, and the evils resulting from the performance of *Lover's Vows* are the worst the author can devise.

In *Villette* there are absolutely none of these 'modest loathings'. Even the conventional Mme Beck, even the hidebound M. Paul, see nothing wrong in women appearing on the stage in front of a considerable audience including a number of strange men. Some of the girls take men's parts and are expected to wear trousers. The play they are presenting is all about love and flirtation. In taking part Lucy has nothing worse than shyness to overcome, not principle – though she refuses to wear trousers – and when it comes to the point she throws herself into the rôle and thoroughly enjoys herself.[5]

And thirdly: two quite different views of feminine accomplishments. As we have seen, Jane Austen presents them as lures to catch men. The scene in *Emma* where the heroine plans to paint Harriet's portrait as a means of securing Mr Elton for her is a good example. Emma draws and paints purely for social and sexual reasons; when there is no such motive she puts the apparatus away. There is no question of her doing it to please or express herself.

[4] *Shirley*, ch. 6.   [5] *Villette*, ch. 14.

In *Jane Eyre* the subject is seen in quite a new light. Jane's standard of performance is no better than Emma's but her motivation is superior. In the course of her first conversation with Mr Rochester she shows her pictures to him and they are described to the reader.[6] They sound rather dreadful but they are genuine expressions of a personal vision pursued for its own sake, with diligence and as much technique as the artist can command, by a girl who, though lonely and deprived, respects and cherishes her own individuality. Her later attempts to subdue her feelings for Mr Rochester, when it really does seem that he is going to marry Blanche Ingram, are touching and brave. She draws a portrait of the sumptuous Blanche and another of her thin plain self;[7] not a way to produce great art, probably, but a higher impetus than the wish to catch a man.

Here, we might be tempted to think, is a leader, a leader in the cause of feminism, and after reading *Shirley* with its clarion calls about the fatuousness of what women are expected to do and be and its glimpses of their possible scope, we might be completely convinced. But we should be finally disappointed. Charlotte Brontë writes of individuals, each with her own frustrations and her own solution to them. She does not think in terms of a cause and can see no body of women to lead. It is the same as with her social attitudes in general; she can see no more organised way of helping the poor than the easy Cheeryble Brothers-type of hand-out that *Shirley* administers or Robert Moore's preference for hiring rather than firing as he works his way up to being a rich mill-owner.

Worse than this, Charlotte Brontë is a lost leader. In the spirit and independence of its heroine the whole of *Shirley* demonstrates the potential of woman, but at the end the heroine dwindles into a tiresome neurotic who keeps putting off her wedding day for no good reason and who, when asked to shoulder any responsibility, simply says, 'Go to Mr. Moore; ask Mr. Moore'.

The limitations and hardships of the only work available to middle-class women, that is, governessing or school teaching, are presented explicitly by Charlotte Brontë. Teaching in a school is made to seem not too bad. Lucy Snowe,

[6] *Jane Eyre*, ch. 13.   [7] Ibid., ch. 16.

Frances Henri and Jane Eyre – in her last years at Lowood and after she had escaped from Thornfield and is put in charge of a village school by St John Rivers – all have a certain independence and scope, and are supported by the hope, realised in the case of Frances and Lucy, of owning schools of their own and becoming powerful and prosperous like Mlle Reuter and Mme Beck. But governessing can be truly terrible. The novels contain eloquent emotional passages on the subject; situation is not enough, there is direct and forcible comment.

Jane Austen has already shown us something of governessing, representing it as a sort of leprosy or cancer; rather strangely in view of the fact that one governess, Miss Taylor, has an extremely happy home with the Woodhouses, on terms of family intimacy, her health the first object with Mr Woodhouse and her subservient status no bar to her making an eligible marriage. Jane Fairfax's reprieve from going as a governess is made to seem like a reprieve from hanging. Charlotte Lucas marries a lout to escape this even worse fate. Emma Watson, repudiating with all the courage of a pretty young girl the idea of marrying for money, says she would rather go as a governess and she can imagine nothing worse.

Charlotte Brontë goes further. The words of Mrs Pryor in *Shirley* are quite blood-curdling; she quotes extensively the very phrases that most wounded her in the circumstances she is describing.

I was early given to understand that 'as I was not their equal', so I could not expect 'to have their sympathy'. It was in no sort concealed from me that I was held a 'burden and restraint in society'. The gentlemen, I found, regarded me as a 'tabooed woman', to whom 'they were interdicted from granting the usual privileges of the sex', and yet who 'annoyed them by frequently crossing their path'. The ladies too made it plain that they thought me a 'bore'. The servants, it was signified, 'detested me'; *why*, I could never clearly comprehend. My pupils, I was told, 'however much they might love me, and however deep soever the interest I might take in them, could not be my friends'. It was intimated that I must 'live alone, and never transgress the invisible but rigid line which established the difference between me and my employers'. My life in this house was sedentary, solitary, constrained, joyless, toilsome.[8]

This is fine, paranoid stuff and though it is part of the characterisation – Mrs Pryor has marked paranoid tendencies – it is meant to sound like serious reportage as well. Mrs Pryor forgets that her life as Shirley Keeldar's governess has been remarkably pleasant, but so does Charlotte Brontë seem to forget, when recounting the spiteful remarks of the Thornfield house party about governesses, that Jane is having a peaceful, reasonably happy time teaching Adèle.

The attitude of the men is significant. When Mr Rochester and Jane become engaged he exclaims imperiously: 'You will give up your governessing slavery at once.'[9] What was quite suitable for an unknown young woman is not good enough for his future wife, however bigamous he may be. One is reminded of Mr Willcox in *Howard's End* who was calmly ready to sell a house for a boys' preparatory school which he considered too damp for himself and his family. It is an essential part of Paul Emanuel's wooing of Lucy that he should set her up as the proprietress of a school rather than leave her as an employed teacher.

But with all this dire talk we are shown that there are worse things than governessing. One is boredom and the feeling that life is slipping away with nothing worthwhile done. Caroline is so driven by the frustrations of her life ('It is scarcely *living* to measure time as I do at the Rectory. The hours pass, and I get them over somehow, but I do not *live*',)[10] that she asks her uncle for permission to go as a governess. Mr Helstone, his mind working on the same lines as Mr Rochester's and Paul Emanuel's, gives her the strongest reason he can for not complying: 'I will not have it said that my niece is a governess.' The conversation ends as follows:

'Put all crotchets out of your head, and run away and amuse yourself.'
'What with? My doll?' asked Caroline to herself as she quitted the room.[11]

As distressing as the ennui and the sense of futility of an unmarried girl is the torment of the unhappily married

[8] *Shirley*, ch. 21.   [9] *Jane Eyre*, ch. 24.
[10] *Shirley*, ch. 21.   [11] Ibid, ch. 11.

woman; in this case, too, teaching is a soft option as even Mrs Pryor acknowledges.

My new name sheltered me: I resumed under its screen my old occupation of teaching. At first, it scarcely procured me the means of sustaining life; but how savoury was hunger when I fasted in peace! How safe seemed the darkness and chill of an unkindled hearth, when no lurid reflection from terror crimsoned its desolation! How serene was solitude, when I feared not the irruption of violence and vice.[12]

And a third worse evil for a woman than having to teach is a loss of self respect in an illicit union. Jane Eyre is eloquent on this point.

Whether is it better, I ask, to be a slave in a fool's paradise at Marseilles – fevered with delusive bliss one hour – suffocating with the bitterest tears of remorse and shame the next – or to be a village-schoolmistress, free and honest, in a breezy mountain nook in the healthy heart of England?[13]

At times, in *Shirley*, we seem to be on the brink of some eulogy of work as a positive pleasure and an opportunity for women, some noble forward-looking idea of occupation more elevated and more honourable than governessing. But it all boils down to the same dreary concept of work being marginally better than aimlessness. Caroline talking to Shirley uses very strong language indeed about both alternatives, and gives the conversation an unpleasant twist by refuting the conventional cant about the evils of women working with an argument even more reactionary.

'Caroline', demanded Miss Keeldar abruptly, 'don't you wish you had a profession – a trade?'
'I wish it fifty times a day. As it is, I often wonder what I came into the world for. I long to have something absorbing and compulsory to fill my head and hands, and to occupy my thoughts.'
'Can labour alone make a human being happy?'
'No; but it can give varieties of pain, and prevent us from breaking our hearts with a single tyrant master-torture.

[12] Ibid., ch. 24.   [13] *Jane Eyre*, ch. 31.

91

Besides successful labour has its recompense; a vacant, weary, lonely, hopeless life has none.'
'But hard labour and learned professions, they say, make women masculine, coarse, unwomanly.'
'And what does it signify, whether unmarried and never-to-be-married women are unattractive and inelegant, or not? – provided only they are decent, decorous, and neat, it is enough. The utmost which ought to be required of old maids, in the way of appearance, is that they should not absolutely offend men's eyes as they pass them in the street; for the rest, they should be allowed without too much scorn, to be as absorbed, grave, plain-looking, and plain-dressed as they please.'[14]

Marriage, as Jane Austen pointed out, is a woman's pleasantest preservative from want, and many of her women characters are gratefully conscious of this aspect of their unions. Charlotte Brontë's heroines are not compelled to fall back on marriage for financial independence; she takes care to provide for them first. Jane Eyre is left a fortune. (One is reminded of Margaret Dashwood's ridiculous wish that someone would leave all three of them a large fortune apiece.) It must give Jane great satisfaction to tell Mr Rochester that she is

> quite rich, sir. If you won't let me live with you, I can build a house of my own close up to your door, and you may come and sit in my parlour when you want company of an evening.[15]

Lucy Snowe who, we understand, never marries is put firmly on the path to prosperity and it is the man who wishes to marry her who makes her financially independent of him. Caroline Helstone's future is made secure by Mrs Pryor's offer to provide for her, some time before Robert Moore at last proposes. Shirley Keeldar is, of course, rich from start to finish.

The fact that the heroines do have a viable alternative to marriage makes their decision and their eagerness to marry more significant. Kate Millett's interesting but contrived account of *Villette*[16] seems to overlook this fact. Lucy is *not*

[14] *Shirley*, ch. 12. [15] *Jane Eyre*, ch. 37.
[16] *Sexual Politics*, ch. 3.

free at the end of the book; she does not rise above the lures of marriage and wisely choose to refrain from it. Her future husband is drowned, by Charlotte Brontë, and she is an unhappy and deprived woman for the rest of her life.

The heroines need to have somebody of their own. Lucy Snowe, indulging her modest dreams of setting up a school and becoming independent, continues:

> But afterwards, is there nothing more for me in life – no true home – nothing to be dearer to me than myself, and by its paramount preciousness to draw from me better things than I care to culture for myself only? Nothing at whose feet I can willingly lay down the whole burden of human egotism, and gloriously take up the nobler charge of labouring and living for others?[17]

Later in the book when Paulina, inspired by happiness into more insufferable condescension than usual, says patronisingly to Lucy:

> But ours, Lucy, is a beautiful life, or it will be; and you shall share it;

Lucy very properly and roundly replies:

> I shall share no man's or woman's life in this world, as you understand sharing. I think I have one friend of my own, but am not sure, and till I *am* sure, I live solitary.[18]

The important difference is that when the heroines do decide on the man they want to marry they are absolutely whole-hearted, with no reservations whatever about suitability. The readers may feel that Robert Moore, for example, will be a rather unsatisfactory husband, but Caroline has no doubts at all in spite of the shifty and even cruel behaviour she has witnessed. Jane, Caroline and Shirley never change ground; Mr Rochester, Robert Moore and Louis Moore are their first and only choices, so their steadiness is less surprising. But Lucy does a complete volte-face. Dr John is her first love and it is only on his defection that she turns to Paul Emanuel. But when she does she is thorough.

> Once – unknown and unloved, I held him harsh and strange; the low stature, the wiry make, the angles, the

[17] *Villette*, ch. 31.   [18] Ibid., ch. 37.

darkness, the manner displeased me. Now, penetrated with his influence, and living by his affection, having his worth by intellect, and his goodness by heart – I preferred him before all humanity.[19]

Those who put great emphasis on the fact, the almost certain fact, that Dr John 'was' George Smith and Paul Emanuel 'was' M. Heger have here a corrective to any excessive reliance on autobiographical material. In life M. Heger was succeeded by George Smith (succeeded only in a chronological sense as his influence was nothing like as strong); in the book the true love came second so that there could be no doubt, no hesitation, no compromise. A false start only enhanced the triumphant arrival. In life many women settle down quite happily with non-intellectual bigoted Puseyites and it looks as though Charlotte Brontë would have done the same but she was too splendidly romantic to allow any of her heroines to do so.

The force and frankness of their passion was astonishing for those times. Obviously women did sometimes, perhaps very often, declare their love to men and make straightforward sexual advances; the affair of Mary Wollstonecraft and Gilbert Imlay was not entirely unique. But that they should have been approvingly allowed to do so in a novel was unusual. For a while, it is true, they are cagey enough, concealing their feelings and being perversely guarded in the approved manner, but at a certain point they burst out with an explosiveness which must be at the bottom of the common contemporary accusation that Charlotte Brontë was coarse. Jane Eyre's outburst is famous.

I tell you I must go! Do you think I can stay to become nothing to you? Do you think I am an automaton? – a machine without feelings? and can bear to have my morsel of bread snatched from my lips, and my drop of living water dashed from my cup? Do you think, because I am poor, obscure, plain and little, I am soulless and heartless? You think wrong! – I have as much soul as you, – and full as much heart! And if God had gifted me with some beauty, and much wealth, I should have made it as hard for you to leave me, as it is now for me to leave you. I am not talking to you now through the medium of custom,

[19] Ibid., ch. 41.

94

conventionalities, or even of mortal flesh: – it is my spirit that addresses your spirit; just as if both had passed through the grave, and we stood at God's feet, equal, – as we are![20]

Lucy Snowe's words are not given us. Charlotte Brontë suddenly becomes as reticent as Jane Austen.

I spoke. All escaped from my lips. I lacked not words now; fast I narrated; fluent I told my tale; it streamed on my tongue.[21]

This, and the whole of the passage, is artistically right. Lucy has been in a terrible world of shadow and hallucination and evil, and it is better that we should not hear her describe it explicitly. But she was obviously very explicit indeed in telling Paul Emanuel of her feelings for him. It is a far cry from:

She spoke then, on being so entreated. What did she say? Just what she ought, of course. A lady always does.[22]

In their grief at loss and bereavement Charlotte Brontë's heroines are equally outspoken and passionate. Again, it is a far cry, a very far cry indeed, from Elizabeth Bennet's controlled comment:

If he is satisfied with only regretting me, when he might have obtained my affections and my hand, I shall soon cease to regret him at all;[23]

to Jane's despair, in circumstances that only seem dissimilar:

In full, heavy swing the torrent poured over me. The whole consciousness of my life lorn, my love lost, my hope quenched, my faith deathstruck, swayed full and mighty above me in one sullen mass. That bitter hour cannot be described: in truth, 'the waters came into my soul; I sank in deep mire: I felt no standing; I came into deep waters; the floods over flowed me'.[24]

Gentle reader, may you never feel what I then felt! May your eyes never shed such stormy, scalding, heart-wrung tears as poured from mine. May you never appeal to

[20] *Jane Eyre*, ch. 23.   [21] *Villette*, ch. 41.
[22] *Emma*, ch. 49.   [23] *Pride and Prejudice*, ch. 42.
[24] *Jane Eyre*, ch. 26.

Heaven in prayers so hopeless and so agonised as in that hour left my lips.[25]

Less straightforward is the chapter in *Shirley* where Caroline is rebuffed by Robert Moore. The circumstances do not sound especially searing. One evening Robert has behaved so affectionately to Caroline that at night she indulges in girlish dreams of love and marriage. When they meet next morning his manner is cool. That is all. But Charlotte Brontë continues:

> A lover masculine so disappointed can speak and urge explanation; a lover feminine can say nothing; if she did, the result would be shame and anguish, inward remorse for self-treachery. Nature would brand such demonstration as a rebellion against her instincts, and would vindictively repay it afterwards by the thunderbolt of self-contempt smiting suddenly in secret. Take the matter as you find it; ask no questions; utter no remonstrances: it is your best wisdom. You expected bread, and you have got a stone; break your teeth on it, and don't shriek because the nerves are martyrised: do not doubt that your mental stomach – if you have such a thing – is strong as an ostrich's: the stone will digest. You held out your hand for an egg, and fate put into it a scorpion. Show no consternation: close your fingers firmly upon the gift; let it sting through your palm. Never mind: in time, after your hand and arm have swelled and quivered long with torture the squeezed scorpion will die, and you will have learned the great lesson how to endure without a sob.

This should seem more highly-coloured than the circumstances warrant; it does not, in fact, for Charlotte Brontë rarely sounds too highly-coloured for any situation; the passion is too genuine for questions of appropriateness to occur. In any case, the passage could be justified as heralding the long agony which Caroline is indeed going to suffer. But Charlotte Brontë goes on to claim irrelevance for the purple passage, ironically, as she was too scrupulous an artist to be carelessly irrelevant.

But what has been said in the last page or two is not germane to Caroline Helstone's feelings, or to the state of

[25] Ibid., ch. 27.

things between her and Robert Moore. Robert had done her no wrong; he had told her no lie; it was she that was to blame, if any one was: what bitterness her mind distilled should and would be poured on her own head. She had loved without being asked to love, – a natural, sometimes an inevitable chance, but big with misery.[26]

Caroline's appropriation of blame to herself is not supported by Charlotte Brontë. To love without being asked to love is in her eyes no crime.

Fully to understand the men whom Charlotte Brontë sets up as the objects of her heroines' devotion, worship almost ('I could not, in those days, see God for his creature: of whom I had made an idol'),[27] we must look back at Haworth Parsonage, and at Patrick and Branwell Brontë.

The male-dominated family with its attendant women occurs in the novels, but ambiguously. The most notorious ministering angel is Paulina Home de Bassompierre. At Bretton as a little girl she points out that boys are more important than girls and waits hand and foot – most tiresomely Lucy Snowe thinks – on both her father and Graham.[28] As a young woman in Villette she actually postpones saying her prayers in order not to keep her father waiting for his breakfast.[29] Charlotte Brontë's attitude to Paulina is in general so ambivalent that one hardly knows how to take these references. Her attitude to Mrs Bretton is complex, too, but surely there is resentment, justifiably, in Lucy's comment about this incident at the concert.

> 'This room is stiflingly hot,' said Dr. Bretton, rising with sudden impatience. 'Lucy – mother – will you come a moment to the fresh air?'
> 'Go with him, Lucy', said Mrs. Bretton. 'I would rather keep my seat.'
> Willingly would I have kept mine also, but Graham's desire must take precedence of my own; I accompanied him.[30]

Mr Rochester, Paul Emanuel, Robert Moore and Louis Moore are all, in varying ways and degrees, bossy men;

[26] *Shirley*, ch. 7.   [27] *Jane Eyre*, ch. 24.   [28] *Villette*, chs. 2 and 3.
[29] Ibid., ch. 32.   [30] Ibid., ch. 20.

97

nineteenth-century fathers or brothers. The first two are old enough to be the fathers of the girls they marry, as, in Jane's case, Mrs Fairfax tactlessly points out. Their ascendancy and authority are carefully plotted.

In Mr Rochester's case it is the ascendancy not only of age but of rank, and of great wealth and possessions. The first descriptions of battlemented Thornfield establish this even before its owner appears. He is also Jane's employer and she is only the governess. His authority is complete; he is in every sense the master, as he makes clear during the first evening Jane spends in his presence.

'Here is Miss Eyre, sir', said Mrs. Fairfax, in her quiet way. He bowed, still not taking his eyes from the group of the dog and child.
'Let Miss Eyre be seated', said he: and there was something in the forced stiff bow, in the impatient yet formal tone, which seemed further to express, 'What the deuce is it to me whether Miss Eyre be there or not? At this moment I am not disposed to accost her.'

Go into the library – I mean, if you please – (Excuse my tone of command; I am used to say 'Do this,' and it is done: I cannot alter my customary habits for one new inmate.) – Go then, into the library; take a candle with you; leave the door open; sit down to the piano, and play a tune.[31]

Paul Emanuel is the arbiter of Lucy's fate from the first. Her reception at Mme Beck's pensionnat depends on him. Providentially he comes on the scene at the critical moment. He is Mme Beck's cousin and she consults him. Without a word to Lucy, or even a nod or a smile, he gazes intently at her and then pronounces, an oracular utterance which settles her future. Had he not accepted her she would immediately have been turned out into 'the lonesome, dreary, hostile street' and might not have survived.[32] Then he is not only emperor at Mme Beck's, making the girls smile or weep and changing the atmosphere of the whole establishment according to his moods; he has influence in the town as well. He makes speeches unembarrassedly in the presence of royalty and holds up his head in the most distinguished company.

31 *Jane Eyre*, ch. 13.   32 *Villette*, ch. 7.

The supremacy of Louis Moore is harder for Charlotte Brontë to establish. He is a tutor, the male equivalent of a governess, almost a menial and moreover employed by the heroine's uncle. Neither is he very much older than Shirley; he is thirty. This counts as a grave deficiency in a book which maintains that husbands ought to be considerably older than their wives. Shirley gives as one of her reasons for not marrying Sir Philip the fact that he is the same age as herself. But Shirley says she has never thought of Louis as young and indeed he is exceptionally staid and self-contained. His ascendancy is entirely that of character and he wields it even in trivial domestic circumstances. When Shirley is toasting bread,

> 'You are overheated now,' he said, when she had retained the fork for some time: 'let me relieve you.'
> And he took it from her with a sort of quiet authority, to which she submitted passively – neither resisting him nor thanking him.[33]

If he shows signs of slipping into subservience, she pushes him back into a position of authority. When the plot is moving towards its dénouement there occurs a scene which is otherwise irrelevant: she forces him to control her very life. She has been bitten by a dog that is said to be rabid and she fears the onset of hydrophobia. She makes Louis promise to preside over her sickbed, to turn her relatives and the surgeons out,

> and, lastly, if I give trouble, with your own hand administer to me a strong narcotic: such a sure dose of laudanum as shall leave no mistake.[34]

But Louis, of course, in being a teacher has the greatest advantage that any Brontë hero could have. Shirley is no longer his pupil but the teacher/pupil relationship that existed between them formerly is revived at various stages in the book, deliberately to mark the advance of their sexual relationship, Shirley pushing her hair back behind her ears when he tells her to and reciting French poetry with a schoolgirlish eagerness to copy the master's accent.[35] Throughout the book Shirley insists that for women improvement is an essential part of marriage and that she will only

[33] *Shirley*, ch. 26.　　　[34] Ibid., ch. 28.　　　[35] Ibid., ch. 27.

99

marry someone who can undertake to educate her. When Louis quite reasonably suggests that if she married Sir Philip Nunnely she 'might have the satisfaction of leading him to a higher standard – of improving his tastes', she bursts out:

Leading and improving! teaching and tutoring! bearing and forbearing! Pah! My husband is not to be my baby. I am not to set him his daily lesson and see that he learns it, and give him a sugar-plum if he is good, and a patient, pensive, pathetic lecture if he is bad. But it is like a tutor to talk of the 'satisfaction of teaching'. – I suppose *you* think it the finest employment in the world. I don't – I reject it. Improving a husband! No. I shall insist upon my husband improving me, or else we part.[36]

This is sad, reactionary, mixed-up stuff. Even Jane Austen saw marriage as a state of *mutual* improvement.

Man as teacher is not always surrounded by thunderclouds of passion, however. Robert Moore teaching and helping Caroline is a quiet echo of Edmund Bertram counselling Fanny Price.

'If you please, Robert, will you mend me a pen or two before you go?'
'First, let me rule your book, for you always contrive to draw the lines aslant.'[37]

Sometimes she lost herself in the maze, and when so lost, she would, now and then ... carry her book to Robert in the counting-house, and get the rough place made smooth by his aid. Mr. Moore possessed a clear, tranquil brain of his own; almost as soon as he looked at Caroline's little difficulties they seemed to dissolve beneath his eye; in two minutes he would explain all – in two words give the key to the puzzle.[38]

Mr Rochester teaches Jane nothing at all, except the inadvisability of accepting a proposal from a man who immediately adds, 'God pardon me'. She is his superior in morals, honesty, self-respect and even in worldly wisdom. But as Winifred Gérin has aptly pointed out, the really strange thing about Mr Rochester is that he is *not* M. Heger.

[36] Ibid., ch. 36.   [37] Ibid., ch. 5.   [38] Ibid., ch. 6.

St John Rivers does teach Jane. It is the first gambit of his plan to marry her, and the fact that she has no wish whatever to learn Hindostanee is symbolic of the fact that she has no wish whatever to marry him.

Though Mr Rochester was the first of Charlotte Brontë's heroes that the public met, *The Professor* of course was her first novel. It is a complete example of the artistic identification of sex and tuition; the erotic relationship and the tutorial relationship are equated and the plot so shaped as to formulate their integral connection. We know from Charlotte Brontë's poems that she regarded the association of male teacher and female pupil – and it was axiomatic that the teacher should be a man and the pupil a woman – with a sensuous fervour that it does not normally inspire beyond the pupil's adolescence, if it ever inspires it at all. The terrible doggerel verses included in *The Professor* set the tone.

> Low at my master's knee I bent,
> The offered crown to meet;
> Its green leaves through my temples sent
> A thrill as wild and sweet.

Success in school is not the only event they describe. The wild sweet thrill of graduation and prize-winning has been preceded by the wilder sweeter thrill of a sickroom visit from the master. (Charlotte Brontë, being denied by convention the ordinary bedroom scene, makes resourceful use of sickbeds.)

> One day when summoned to the bed,
> Where pain and I did strive,
> I heard him, as he bent his head,
> Say, 'God, she *must* revive!'
>
> I felt his hand with gentle stress,
> A moment laid on mine,
> And wished to mark my consciousness
> By some responsive sign.[39]

The teller of the story, the professor William Crimsworth, is eloquent though disingenuous about the relationship of the master and the pupil in general. He does not meet her in

[39] *The Professor*, ch. 23.

101

the guise of 'a partner at a ball or a gallant on the pro-
menade'. She is not dressed 'in satin and muslin, with hair
perfumed and curled, neck scarcely shaded by aerial lace,
round white arms circled with bracelets, feet dressed for the
gliding dance'. He finds her in the schoolroom, plainly
dressed, possibly resentful, with no desire to flirt, her real
self. 'In short, to the tutor, female youth, female charms are
like tapestry hangings, of which the wrong side is continually turned towards him.'[40] In this situation can emerge
real sympathy, real compatability; it is how the true choices
of life are made.

Crimsworth notices Frances Henri from the start but it is
the purity of her English accent which first intrigues him,
the first aptitude of hers by which he is really struck, that
is, something which brings her up nearer to his own level.[41]
His interest and good opinion are confirmed when she sub-
mits a *devoir* on the subject of Alfred and the cakes in which
he discerns 'some proofs of taste and fancy'. It acts on him
like a love letter or a declaration of some sort; he values it
sentimentally as Louis does Shirley's composition – in
French, so as to approach *his* standard – on *La Première
Femme Savante*. It gives him the strength and the spirit to
tantalise her cruelly, giving back all the other work with no
comment on hers. His eventual approval as a teacher gives
her exactly the same improvement in looks[42] as Mr Rochester's proposal of marriage does to Jane.

Crimsworth is always 'the Master', a title which we
know Charlotte Brontë used ambiguously, as when she was
writing to Heger and called him touchingly 'the only master
I ever had'. After Frances has left the school and he finds her
by chance in the Protestant Cemetery, she greets him with the
passionate cry, 'Mon maître! mon maître!' When soon after
this he plans to make her his wife he assesses her feeling
for him by weighing up her behaviour as a pupil, docile,
smiling and attentive.[43] During the period of courtship it is
not so much that the new relationship is thought of in terms
of the old but that they are in fact the same. Wondering
whether to visit her, Crimsworth says: 'I thought she might
possibly be wishing for her master. I knew I wished for my
pupil.'[44] Still tantalising, he does not commit himself: 'We

[40] Ibid., ch. 14.   [41] Ibid., ch. 15.   [42] Ibid., ch. 18.
[43] Ibid., ch 19.   [44] Ibid., ch. 22.

met as we had always met, as master and pupil – nothing more.' But at least 'the frost of the Master's manner might melt' and the teacher and the future husband become one after a proposal conducted entirely in teacher/pupil terms.[45] He remains 'Monsieur', however, to the last pages of the book and she remains docile, smiling and attentive as she devotes her life to making him 'the master in all things'.

If not artistically, emotionally *The Professor* is a run-through for *Villette*. Many of the situations are the same, with interesting additions, all representing recognisable stages of a love affair, for example, the occasion where M. Paul tries to show Lucy off to his men friends and she resentfully lets him down.[46] Another situation is his ridiculous suspicion that she had more experience than she admits to. In both cases it is her scholarship that is ostensibly the quality in question.

M. Paul's kindness as a teacher ebbs and flows. When Lucy is diffident and unresponsive he is encouraging, but when she has surmounted the preliminary difficulties of the subject and is enthusiastically responsive he is scared and sarcastic.[47] One is reminded of Branwell Brontë who, having admired Mary Taylor when she was indifferent to him, 'instantly conceived a sort of contempt for her' when she responded.[48]

Altogether the presentation of the teacher/pupil relationship in *Villette* is much more passionate and much more harrowing than that of *The Professor*. Every aspect is heightened: the love of the protagonists (the schoolroom fairly crackles), the torture the master inflicts by withdrawing his presence and apparently his affection, the agony of the pupil at his withdrawal, and the attractions of the teacher. Here the fact that the teacher speaks in *The Professor* and the pupil in *Villette* is obviously most relevant. Crimsworth, describing himself, is lenient to his own shortcomings, both those which are important, like sadism and conceit, and those which are trivial, like being short-sighted and having to wear glasses, hinting at them but glossing them over. Lucy, speaking of Paul, positively dwells on his demerits, and these three in particular, but because she loves him and

45 Ibid., ch. 23.   46 *Villette*, ch. 35.   47 Ibid., ch. 30.
48 Letters to Ellen Nussey, 20 Nov. 1840.

is describing her feelings M. Paul, paradoxically, seems far more attractive than his predecessor.

The imperfect hero is in any case someone Charlotte Brontë can willingly accept, for herself and her women characters. Jane Austen's heroines expect, and get, perfection. 'How unlike what a man should be', exclaims Emma of Frank Churchill as she turns to the morally superior Mr Knightley. Charlotte Brontë's heroes are very much unlike what men should be, Rochester particularly, but it is probably not so much adult tolerance that makes her endure and love her creatures as an extension of her adolescent weakness for cads, like Zamorna. (This sympathy broke down in real life when it came to Branwell's final degradation.) Her early devotion to the Byronic, even the Satanic, hero is well described by Winifred Gérin in her chapter expressively called 'Zamorna against all Comers'.[49]

Paul Emanuel is of course less wicked than Rochester, but he is foul-tempered, sadistic and arrogant. So is Rochester but he is more; he is a seducer. Charlotte Brontë was not one to think that seduction, even in the grand manner, was good for a laugh, as Jane Austen seems often to have done. She knew too much about its sad realities. Yet she was remarkably lenient towards Rochester's attempted seduction of Jane, for to trick someone with her moral principles into a bigamous marriage, the truth of which was bound to come out some day – after all Mr Mason kept turning up – was comparable to Lovelace's drugging and raping Clarissa. Jane's innocence, when all was disclosed, would not have kept her from shame and misery any more than Clarissa's did her. It is interesting that Charlotte Brontë allows Jane to forgive Rochester and to marry him after all. Both Clarissa before her and Ruth after her refuse to marry the seducer on the simple but passionate grounds that they do not *like* men who have behaved so towards them.

Mr Rochester does not regard himself as a seducer. His motives, as well as his powers of self-deception, are superior to Zamorna's. He feels he is atoning for his past profligacy by his great goodness in bigamously marrying Jane. At the moment of betrothal he actually says, 'It will atone . . . It will expiate at God's tribunal'. He has bought women all his life and now considers he is acting differently, though in the

[49] *Charlotte Brontë*, ch. 8.

famous clothes-buying scene Jane tells him roundly that he is treating her as his English Céline Varens.[50] His attitude is, in fact, his undoing, for Jane's annoyance at being kept by him, as she herself expresses it, causes her to write to her uncle in Madeira with news of the proposed marriage.

Man as spy has an important place in the novels. Charlotte Brontë's attitude to spying in general is entirely ad hoc. Mme Beck systematically going through suitcases and bundles of letters, though approved of for her efficiency at it, is morally condemned.[51] There is no suggestion that William Crimsworth, eavesdropping on an intimate conversation between M. Pelet and Mlle Reuter, is equally guilty or indeed guilty at all.[52] Paul Emanuel is the master spy, but then of course he is a devout Roman Catholic; Charlotte Brontë seriously considers that this would account for it. Lucy is deeply shocked when he points to a window overlooking the pensionnat and shamelessly describes his proceedings:

> That is a room I have hired, nominally for a study – virtually for a post of observation. There I sit and read for hours together: it is my way – my taste. My book is this garden; its contents are human nature – female human nature. I know you all by heart.

By these methods he has been saved from marrying Zélie St Pierre and has got to know the real nature of the pupils. When Lucy objects that from that distance he could not see what happened in the garden at night he goes, in her opinion and perhaps in ours, from bad to worse:

> By moonlight I possibly might with a glass – I use a glass – but the garden itself is open to me. In the shed, at the bottom, there is a door leading into a court, which communicates with the college; of that door I possess the key and thus come and go at pleasure.[53]

Mr Rochester is not above using such methods to discover the true character of the girl in whom he is already beginning to feel interested.

> The next day I observed you – myself unseen – for half an hour while you played with Adèle in the gallery. It was a

[50] *Jane Eyre*, ch. 24.   [51] *Villette*, ch. 8.
[52] *The Professor*, ch. 12.   [53] *Villette*, ch. 31.

snowy day, I recollect, and you could not go out of doors. I was in my room; the door was ajar: I could both listen and watch. Adèle claimed your outward attention for a while; yet I fancied your thoughts were elsewhere: but you were very patient with her, my little Jane; you talked to her and amused her a long time. When at last she left you, you lapsed at once into a deep reverie: you betook yourself slowly to pace the gallery. Now and then, in passing a casement, you glanced out at the thick-falling snow; you listened to the sobbing wind, and again you paced gently on and dreamed.[54]

Neither is Louis Moore above it. When Shirley and her relatives are out he wanders through the parlours.

He makes discoveries. A bag, a small satin bag, hangs on the chair-back. The desk is open, the keys are in the lock; a pretty seal, a silver pen, a crimson berry or two of ripe fruit on a green leaf, a small, clean, delicate glove – these trifles at once decorate and disarrange the stand they strew.

He goes through everything thoroughly and notes down his conclusions.

I have seen and handled many of her possessions, because they are frequently astray. I never saw anything that did not proclaim the lady: nothing sordid, nothing soiled; in one sense she is as scrupulous as, in another, she is unthinking: as a peasant girl, she would go ever trim and cleanly. Look at the pure kid of this little glove, – at the fresh unsullied satin of the bag.[55]

This is nanny's talk, and it is really rather ludicrous that the suitor should be summing up the loved one's character by rummaging through her personal possessions, but Louis clearly feels, like Mr Rochester and Paul Emanuel, that snooping is a perfectly fair way for a man to assess a woman's character.

Finally, man the tamer. Of the heroines, Jane Eyre and Lucy Snowe have the most of Charlotte Brontë herself in them. (Shirley we know to have been based on Emily Brontë, and however little like Emily she may seem – no one, I imagine would ever have guessed, except possibly for the

[54] *Jane Eyre*, ch. 27.   [55] *Shirley*, ch. 29.

dog-bite incident, unless Charlotte had said so – her creator's intentions have to be borne in mind.) And Charlotte Brontë had no wish to be tamed by a man. She wished to devote herself, not to be dominated.

Lucy and Jane react in a similar way. Jane's dedication in marriage is rhapsodically described:

> I have now been married ten years. I know what it is to live entirely for and with what I love best on earth. I hold myself supremely blest – blest beyond what language can express; because I am my husband's life as fully as he is mine. No woman was ever nearer to her mate than I am: ever more absolutely bone of his bone, and flesh of his flesh. I know no weariness of my Edward's society: he knows none of mine, any more than we do of the pulsation of the heart that beats in our separate bosoms; consequently, we are ever together. To be together is for us to be at once as free as in solitude, as gay as in company. We talk, I believe, all day long: to talk to each other is but a more animated and an audible thinking. All my confidence is bestowed on him, all his confidence is devoted to me; we are precisely suited in character – perfect concord is the result.[56]

But the passage makes it clear that it is not only a question of ecstasy but also of equality (though the reference to Adam and Eve is disquieting). At the time when they were first engaged Jane was in an inferior position which she resented and which Mr Rochester did nothing to smoothe over with his lavish offers of silks, jewels and foreign travel. Now she is rich; she has proved she can live alone and keep sane and useful, which is more than he was able to do; and events have justified her earlier decision. And above all she is sighted. Rochester is not allowed to see until her equality has been established and then it is only a partial restoration.

Lucy Snowe would have been as devoted a wife as Jane. Merely her correspondence with Paul Emanuel during his three years absence is, touchingly, made to sound like a blissfully happy marriage. Yet there is equality here, too. She is now a prosperous headmistress; she counts in Villette. And, more important, her religion has been formally recognised. Paul writes that he wishes her to remain a Protestant

[56] *Jane Eyre*, ch. 38.

as it is right for her. He speaks civilly of Protestantism, too, in a way he has never done before.

But when Charlotte is creating a character in terms of Emily rather than herself the situation changes completely. No doubt Charlotte wished Emily to be tamed. The aggressiveness in Emily's character that showed forth so repellently in such incidents as the punching of Keeper, her general awkwardness which hampered Charlotte's social life while they were both in Brussels, and the terrifying intractability she displayed in her last illness, and many other unrecorded events must, in spite of Charlotte's great love for her sister, have left deep resentment and a wish that she had been less indomitable. So Shirley must be tamed, but by her own request; no violence is to be done. It is not to be a case of Katherina and Petruchio; Shirley must ask for such treatment.

> Did I not say I prefer a *master*? One in whose presence I shall feel obliged and disposed to be good. One whose control my impatient temper must acknowledge. A man whose approbation can reward – whose displeasure punish me. A man I shall feel it impossible not to love, and very possible to fear.[57]

This sounds like a good working relationship between a man and a dog or a man and a horse. The idea of man and animal thus implied, there follows a series of references to Shirley in terms of wild animals. 'Lioness! she has found her captor', says Caroline.[58] A few pages later Louis, too, calls her a lioness and himself her keeper. Later still she is a leopardess and a pantheress. And her future husband sums it all up:

> Pantheress! – beautiful forest-born! – wily, tameless, peerless nature! She gnaws her chain: I see the white teeth working at the steel! She has dreams of her wild woods, and pinings after virgin freedom.[59]

Winifred Gérin makes the point that an advantage of the male pseudonym was that it allowed an outspokenness which a female could not be supposed to adopt.[60] This is potentially

[57] *Shirley*, ch. 31.
[58] Ibid., ch. 35.
[59] Ibid., ch. 36.
[60] *Charlotte Brontë*, ch. 6.

true, but as Charlotte Brontë had no great experience of any kind of male talk, licentious or otherwise, the liberty made calls on her fantasy rather than her observation with often unfortunate results. G. H. Lewes has not been the only one to object to the scene where Shirley brawls with Mr Sympson.[61] He makes a now outmoded distinction between the boldness which a man and woman respectively might employ, but says that even for a man 'such vulgarities would be inexcusable'. It is a complicated situation. Here is Charlotte Brontë as Currer Bell, abandoning the unmistakable, feminine tone of *Jane Eyre* and using the less revealing third-person technique, depicting a girl with decidedly masculine characteristics engaged in a slanging match with an effeminate middle-aged man, her uncle and guardian, to whom the conventions of the time dictated that she should show respect, in a way which shocks a liberal-minded and sophisticated critic on grounds of both artistic taste and verisimilitude.

It has often been pointed out as an example of Jane Austen's limitations that she never shows men talking to each other when no women are present. (This, incidentally, is not quite true: Mr Knightley's hints to Emma that Mr Elton is not likely to marry the penniless Harriet, based as they are on what he has heard Mr Elton say in exclusively male company, give a most vivid and convincing, though fleeting, impression of men's conversation.) The same could never be said of Charlotte Brontë who bravely and frequently tackles the problem of men talking and writing letters to each other and, of course, in *The Professor* goes to the, then, unusual lengths of writing an entire book not only from a man's point of view but as a man. The fact that *The Professor* is not a very satisfying novel and has never been popular is due to various causes, but failure to carry out this masculine impersonation is not, I think, one of them.

Charlotte Brontë is well aware of the conditioning to which the women of her day were subjected. She shows the independent Lucy Snowe, terrified out of her wits by having seen the ghost in the attic, falling straight into her traditional rôle.

The sight of the gentlemen did me good and gave me

61 *Shirley*, ch. 31.

courage: it seemed as if there were some help and hope, with men at hand.[62]

But she also observes in men and women the perpetual shifting of their conventional attributes and responses: the masculine in Mme Beck:

At that instant she did not wear a woman's aspect but rather a man's;[63]

the feminine in M. Paul, seeing

in his vexed, fiery and searching eye, a sort of appeal behind all its menace.[64]

The response of her heroine to these approaches is shifting, too. To Mme Beck's challenging suggestion that without a moment's warning she teach an unruly class, Lucy reacts like an untried soldier being shamed by his superior into bravery.

Power of a particular kind strongly limned itself in all her traits, and that power was not *my* kind of power; neither sympathy, nor congeniality, nor submission, were the emotions it awakened. I stood – not soothed, nor won, nor overwhelmed. It seemed as if a challenge of strength between opposing gifts was given, and I suddenly felt all the dishonour of my diffidence, all the pusillanimity of my slackness to aspire.

To M. Paul's appeal she replies generously as a superior, though it is a similar ordeal that he wants her to undergo, and 'for a moment his rigid countenance relaxed with a quiver of content'.

Ambiguous also is Charlotte Brontë's attitude to effeminate-looking men. She had liked Willie Weightman (Celia-Amelia). But in her novels the character who is constantly spoken of in feminine analogies is Alfred de Hamal in *Villette*, a man whom we are meant to despise, a heartless, unprincipled fop. Here is Lucy's first view of him, at a ball:

I believe I could have picked out the conquering de Hamal even undirected. He was a straight-nosed, very correct-featured little dandy. I say *little* dandy, though he was not beneath the middle standard in stature; but his

[62] *Villette*, ch. 22.   [63] Ibid., ch. 8.   [64] Ibid., ch. 14.

110

lineaments were small, and so were his hands and feet; and he was pretty and smooth, and as trim as a doll: so nicely dressed, so nicely curled, so booted and gloved and cravated – he was charming indeed . . . I observed with deep rapture of approbation, that the Colonel's hands were scarce larger than Miss Fanshawe's own, and suggested that this circumstance might be convenient, as he could wear her gloves at a pinch.

As a suitor of Ginevra Fanshawe he is a rival of Dr John, who soon afterwards appears. Lucy compares them.

He carried his hat in his hand; his uncovered head, his face and fine brow were most handsome and manly. *His* features were not delicate, not slight like those of a woman, nor were they cold, frivolous and feeble; though well cut, they were not so chiselled, so frittered away, as to lose in power and significance what they gained in unmeaning symmetry.[65]

Later she sees de Hamal again, in a picture gallery.

I had caught a glimpse of a head too pretty to belong to any other than the redoubted Colonel de Hamal. What a very finished, highly polished little pate it was! What a figure, so trim and natty! What womanish feet and hands! How daintily he held a glass to one of his optics![66]

But though Lucy's contempt for de Hamal remains constant to the last pages, her admiration of the manly man, Dr John, dwindles considerably.

There is a surprising amount of transvestism in the novels: surprising, not in the statistical sense in which George Eliot was once criticised, for presenting too many deaths per community for the national average; but in the sense of being in excess of the real demands of the plot. One important example is Alfred de Hamal's impersonation of the nun, which spreads frighteningly and symbolically over the entire book until the moment when the discarded clothes are left on Lucy's bed. Another is Mr Rochester's dressing up as a gypsy woman in order to have private conversations with certain ladies at the Thornfield house party under the pretence of telling their fortunes.[67] It is all quite unnecessary;

[65] Ibid., ch. 14.   [66] Ibid., ch. 19.   [67] *Jane Eyre*, chs. 18 and 19.

even in the Victorian age, even in girls' boarding schools, it *was* possible for men to approach women privately without these dramatic and rather childish expedients. There is something important to Charlotte Brontë's plans in the dressing-up itself. Then, too, there is the incident, already alluded to, of the school play where Lucy has to take a man's part and there occurs a strange, significant little scene between her and Zélie St Pierre, already rivals for the favour of M. Paul, as to the extent to which she will wear men's clothing. Zélie spitefully insists that she make a complete change; Lucy resists obstinately, saying that she will wear some of the clothes, enough to suggest a man, but no more. M. Paul, called on to arbitrate, decides in favour of Lucy, and the tension slackens.

> Once alone, I grew calm, and collectedly went to work. Retaining my woman's garb without the slightest retrenchment, I merely assumed, in addition, a little vest, a collar, and cravat and a paletot of small dimensions.[68]

Kate Millett attempts to show that Lucy is in love with Ginevra. Though this conclusion is simplistic there are many passages that seem to lead to it. Lucy intensely admires Ginevra's beauty.

> How pretty she was! How charming she looked, when she came down on a sunny Sunday morning, well-dressed and well-humoured, robed in pale lilac silk, and with her fair long curls reposing on her white shoulders.

> Beautiful she looked: so young, so fresh, and with a delicacy of skin and flexibility of shape altogether English, and not found in the list of continental female charms.[69]

She notices and records the details of Ginevra's dress and at one point says something which certainly sounds lover-like:

> In *my* eyes, you will never look so pretty as you did in the gingham gown and plain straw bonnet you wore when I first saw you.[70]

This really is a man-to-woman remark; it is very like, for example, John Rokesmith's speech to his wife Bella in *Our Mutual Friend*:

[68] *Villette*, ch. 14.   [69] *Ibid.*, ch. 9.   [70] Ibid.

In such a dress as you are wearing now, you first charmed me, and in no dress could you ever look, to my thinking, more graceful or more beautiful.[71]

The scene in which Lucy drinks out of Ginevra's coffee cup at breakfast and gives her her rolls is invested with the same kind of feeling as that in which later she shares food with M. Paul. She throws herself wholeheartedly into her part in the school play which requires that she shall court a girl, played by Ginevra, and win her from a rival. The rival resembles Dr John, a fact which could give point to all Lucy's anxiety at Dr John's infatuation with Ginevra, an anxiety which she attributes to concern for his welfare but which could obviously have another interpretation. But beyond a certain point, the critical point, she does not go and it then seems as though Ginevra is the keener of the two. In fact, if one were looking for a theory to propound, it would probably be easier to prove that Ginevra rather than Lucy had lesbian tendencies.

When she took my arm, she always leaned upon me her whole weight; and as I was not a gentleman, or her lover, I did not like it.[72]

Everything can more easily be explained by this faculty of Charlotte Brontë's, already alluded to, to see and represent the bi-sexuality present in every human being. She herself can quite naturally address the same loving words to both men and women. In a letter to Ellen Nussey, lamenting the fact that Ellen contemplates leaving the neighbourhood she says:

Why are we to be divided? Surely it must be because we are in danger of loving each other too well – of losing sight of the *Creator* in idolatry of the *creature*.[73]

This exact language is used by Jane Eyre about Mr Rochester in a speech already quoted, and the same consequences are to follow the excessive love: they *are* divided.

Certain men and women are seen to be each other's physical counterparts. We know how Charlotte Brontë saw a startlingly close resemblance to Emily in G. H. Lewes. We

[71] *Our Mutual Friend.* bk. 4, ch. 5.   [72] *Villette,* ch. 27.
[73] Letter to Ellen Nussey, 20 Feb 1837.

read in *Villette* M. Paul's insistence that the growing rapport between Lucy and himself is a physical as well as a spiritual identity.

> Do you see it, mademoiselle, when you look in the glass? Do you observe that your forehead is shaped like mine – that your eyes are cut like mine? Do you hear that you have some of my tones of voice? Do you know that you have many of my looks?[74]

And above all Charlotte Brontë's creative powers extend to imagining the reaction of a woman imagining she is a man, as when Lucy says of Mme Beck as she rootles through Lucy's personal possessions:

> Had I been a gentleman I believe Madame would have found favour in my eyes, she was so handy, neat, thorough in all she did.[75]

Here, because Lucy is the narrator, this can be said. In *Shirley* it has to be deduced. That Shirley was Emily as she would have been if prosperous and in good health we know from Charlotte herself. That Emily 'should have been a man' we know from M. Heger, that highly-experienced observer of young women. Shirley is a faithful portrait, we can be sure, and so is much more than an early example of the boyish heroine or the heroine who by force of circumstances has to act like a man in a man's world, for example, Bathsheba in *Far From the Madding Crowd*.

Mrs Gaskell quotes M. Heger as saying that Emily should have been 'a great navigator. Her powerful reason would have deduced new spheres of discovery from the knowledge of the old; and her strong imperious will would never have been daunted by opposition or difficulty; never have given way but with life.' From what we know of Emily this is a sound comment (the first part of the sentence certainly indicates the method of *Wuthering Heights*), and it is in this guise that posterity has continued to see her; John Osborne makes Jimmy Porter describe a certain young man as 'a female Emily Brontë'. But in Shirley Charlotte Brontë has turned all this masculinity into make-believe, into a sort of joke. It is as though she could not bear to present a woman who was *really* masculine.

[74] *Villette*, ch. 31.   [75] Ibid., ch. 13.

Shirley has a man's name – it is a handicap to the novel that in the twentieth century the name has acquired such strong associations of cute, pre-pubertal femininity – and, as a landowner, a man's status and from these facts alone would have sprung considerable jocularity in those days. Shirley herself, rather defensively, leads the way:

> I am an esquire! Shirley Keeldar, Esquire, ought to be my style and title. They gave me a man's name; I hold a man's position: it is enough to inspire me with a touch of manhood, and when I see such people as that stately Anglo-Belgian – that Gerard Moore before me, gravely talking to me of business, really I feel quite gentleman-like.

She is talking to Mr Helstone, the very person to pick up such a remark and pursue it.

> Mrs. Pryor, take care of this future magistrate, this church-warden in perspective, this captain of yeomanry, this young squire of Briarfield, in a word: don't let him exert himself too much: don't let him break his neck in hunting: especially, let him mind how he rides down that dangerous hill near the Hollow.[76]

He calls Shirley Captain Keeldar; the name sticks and is used by Robert Moore as well.

Shirley, like Lucy Snowe, thinks of women as if she were a man and they were possible mates.

> If she had had the bliss to be really Shirley Keeldar, Esq., Lord of the Manor of Briarfield, there was not a single fair one in this and the two neighbouring parishes, whom she should have felt disposed to request to become Mrs. Keeldar, lady of the manor. This declaration she made to Mrs. Pryor, who received it very quietly, as she did most of her pupil's off-hand speeches, responding – 'My dear, do not allow that habit of alluding to yourself as a gentleman to be confirmed: it is a strange one. Those who do not know you, hearing you speak thus, would think you affected masculine manners.[77]

Charlotte Brontë seems basically to agree with Mrs Pryor. None of Shirley's 'masculine manners' *is* confirmed. Her

[76] *Shirley*, ch. 11.   [77] Ibid., ch. 12.

whistling turns out to be an affectionate imitation of Louis. Her pistol-packing is straight out of *Annie Get Your Gun*. Her leading of the defiant march against the Dissenters is Sunday School heroics. More important, her mind lacks the qualities which M. Heger saw in Emily's.

Emily had a head for logic, and a capability of argument, unusual in a man, and rare indeed in a woman, according to M. Heger. Shirley seems completely deficient in an ability to put two and two together, even on the most everyday level. Knowing pretty well that Caroline loves Robert Moore, she is outraged at a suggestion that she has been encouraging him herself and indeed she does not do so, but it seems never to have occurred to her that Caroline could misinterpret the situation and needs a hint to put her mind at rest. Similarly she does not see that Robert Moore could misinterpret her extremely oncoming attitude to him; her anger when he does propose seems most unjust, as not only he but all their circle of friends have been persuaded with every show of reason that she would accept.[78] She makes eloquent and explicit claims to be treated as an honest woman but in fact she is not very honest.

But if she falls short of Emily in reasoning power, she does conform to the rest of M. Heger's comment, in

> her stubborn tenacity of will, which rendered her obtuse to all reasoning where her own wishes, or her own sense of right, was concerned.[79]

This is Shirley to the life; it is interesting that Charlotte Brontë should have made one half of the portrait – the capriciousness which is supposed to be typically feminine – so much more graphic than the other, to the detriment of her declared intention, and it is strange that Shirley, the manly woman, turns out to be more of a silly little thing than Jane Eyre or Lucy Snowe.

Though for herself Charlotte Brontë seemed largely resigned to living in a man's world, for her heroines she was not; there was at least a show of resentment, as we have seen in the passages already quoted about boys getting better treatment than girls, which was the first and the basic dis-

[78] Ibid., ch. 20.
[79] *Life of Charlotte Bontë*, ch. 11.

advantage of the situation of women as Charlotte Brontë knew it and as she presented it in her novels.

The home life of some of her heroines shows all the possible frustrations experienced by women in that age. The virtual necessity of staying in the same place, for example: Jane Austen's heroines did not find this much of a burden; after all the emotional complications in which Emma, Harriet and Mr Elton were communally involved, they all found it perfectly possible to go on living in the same small village and meeting every day without intolerable embarrassment or pain, even to the extent, ultimately, of Mr Elton's conducting the marriage service of both girls. Caroline Helstone, on the other hand, who has only to contend with the collapse of her secret hopes of marriage with Robert Moore, which apparently nobody has suspected or commented on, feels she cannot stay any longer in Briarfield. But escape is impossible, because she is a woman. When the love schemes of Arthur Bell Nicholls went wrong he could and did leave Haworth.

The inevitable consignment of women to the home while the men go out is poignantly presented. Even when there are storms outside, the women are in a weak rather than a sheltered position, as they wait in anxiety and ignorance.

All the afternoon the two ladies sat and sewed, till the eyes and fingers, and even the spirits of one of them were weary. The sky since dinner had darkened; it had begun to rain again, to pour fast; secret fears began to steal on Caroline that Robert would be persuaded by Mr. Sykes or Mr. Yorke to remain at Whinbury till it cleared, and of that there appeared no present chance. Five o'clock struck, and time stole on; still the clouds streamed; a sighing wind whispered in the roof-trees of the cottage; day seemed already closing; the parlour-fire shed on the clear hearth a glow ruddy as at twilight.[80]

This is eloquent enough, but in *Villette* she is completely explicit:

How often, while women and girls sit warm at snug firesides, their hearts and imaginations are doomed to divorce from the comfort surrounding their persons, forced out by

[80] *Shirley*, ch. 6.

117

night to wander through dark ways, to dare stress of weather, to contend with the snow-blast, to wait at lonely gates and stiles in wildest storms, watching and listening to see and hear the father, the son, the husband coming home.[81]

And as they wait and worry they sew. It is not always use-less work; it is sometimes making shirts for the men of the family, it is sometimes darning stockings. But it is made to sound dreadfully boring; for the middle-class women in the stories, that is to say. When Caroline, at Hollow's Cottage, is nearly paralysed with the tedium of darning all the after-noon, she finds Sarah, Hortense Moore's servant, by herself in the kitchen, also sewing but cheerful and full of advice for her less fortunate superior. Her own servant Fanny has no problems of ennui either and is ready with sympathy and suggestions for her mistress who has.

We find little solidarity among middle-class women in the novels; Shirley and Caroline come closest to it, but there are strange betrayals in their friendship. No ingenuity of ex-planation on the author's part can quite conceal Shirley's negligent behaviour towards Caroline in her serious illness, nor can the emotional requirements of the plot prevent it from seeming rather odd that Shirley did not confide in Caroline her fears about the dog bite. For most of the book they have all the appearance of being rivals for the love of Robert Moore; Caroline is convinced they are and that she is the loser; we guess they are not only because we know about nineteenth-century plots. There are pairs of rivals in all the novels, Mlle Reuter and Frances Henri, Jane Eyre and Blanche Ingram, Lucy Snowe with, first, Zélie St Pierre and then Justine Marie Sauveur, Ginevra Fanshawe with Paulina de Bassompierre, and Lucy Snowe with both of them. Mary Wollstonecraft thought it was not necessary for women to be rivals, but Charlotte Brontë and most nine-teenth-century novelists found it inevitable.

This is straightforward sexual rivalry, but older women can be rivals, too; sometimes their rôle is to interfere with the sexual schemes of the younger women on behalf of their own candidates, as do Mme Walravens and Lady Ingram; sometimes they are activated by simple irritation at the

81 *Villette*, ch. 25.

younger women's existence and distinctive personality, like Mrs Reed. But they are gorgons, bizarre and menacing in appearance, figures of nightmare. Poor mad Mrs Rochester fits into the second category rather than the first. Her madness has destroyed her sexual claims in nearly all eyes but her own; she still feels herself to be Rochester's wife as her tearing up of Jane's wedding veil shows, but to her husband, and to her brother and his lawyer, she is just a legal fact. Jane, to her credit, sees her still as a human being with emotional and spiritual claims and here for a moment she rather parts company with her author.

Jane Eyre gets on as pleasantly with the Rivers girls as Charlotte Brontë must have done with her sisters, being able both to work and relax in their company. Lucy Snowe, however, gives a very jaundiced picture of the society of women.

> If the other teachers went into town or took a walk on the boulevards or only attended mass they were very certain (according to the accounts brought back) to meet with some individual of the 'opposite sex', whose rapt, earnest gaze assured them of their power to attract.[82]

Her contempt for their conversation is matched by her conviction that they cannot be silent.

> I was not accustomed to find in women or girls any power of self-control, or strength of self-denial. As far as I knew them, the chance of a gossip about their usually trivial secrets, their often very washy and paltry feelings, was a treat not to be readily foregone.[83]

If women cannot keep faith with, or even like each other, it is a hard world for them indeed, for Charlotte Brontë presents men as being really rather dreadful. We have already seen how mean and cruel even the heroes can be. Charlotte Brontë can condone *their* faults, but where her sympathies are not engaged she can be quite ferocious. Her picture of the curates in *Shirley* is savage. It is caricature, of course, but her full-length portrait of Mr Helstone is not; it is photographic in its realism and worth studying in some detail as an example of what women were up against.

---

[82] Ibid., ch. 12.   [83] Ibid., ch. 25.

He made no pretence of comprehending women, or comparing them with men; they were a different, probably a
very inferior order of existence; a wife could not be her
husband's companion, much less his confidante, much less
his stay.[84]

Women were not only inferior in ability but also in morals.

Some suspicion of clandestine meetings haunted him;
having but an indifferent opinion of women, he always
suspected them: he thought they needed constant watching.[85]

Acting on these convictions he made his wife miserable – she
has died before the story begins – and is seen to be making
his niece Caroline equally wretched. He cannot in the least
understand her longings to do something worthwhile. A few
domestic accomplishments should be enough for women:

Stick to the needle – learn shirt-making and gown-making,
and pie-crust-making, and you'll be a clever woman some
day;[86]

and three square meals a day and a roof over their heads
ought to be all they need:

She has her meals, her liberty, a good house to live in, and
good clothes to wear, as usual: a while since that sufficed
to keep her handsome and cheery, and there she sits now,
a poor little, pale, puling chit enough. Provoking![87]

Mr Helstone's sexual tastes are consistent with these views.
Socially he is very popular with girls as he assumes an easy
gallantry which springs from contempt. Here is his estima-
tion of the relative charms of the Misses Sykes:

As Mary was the most sensible, the least coquettish of the
three, to her the elderly widower was the least attentive.
At heart he could not abide sense in women: he liked to
see them as silly, as light-headed, as vain, as open to ridi-
cule as possible ... Hannah was his favourite. Harriet,
though beautiful, egotistical, and self-satisfied, was not

[84] *Shirley*, ch. 4.   [85] *Ibid.*, ch. 10.   [86] Ibid., ch. 7.   [87] Ibid., ch. 11.

quite weak enough for him: she had some genuine self-respect amidst much false pride ... Hannah, on the contrary, demanded no respect; only flattery: if her admirers only *told* her that she was an angel, she would let them *treat* her like an idiot. So very credulous and frivolous was she; so very silly did she become when besieged with attention, flattered and admired to the proper degree, that there were moments when Helstone actually felt tempted to commit matrimony a second time.[88]

In spite of his deplorable attitudes, however, he enlists a small amount of our sympathy when Caroline is so ill, by his complete ignorance that he has contributed to her state and by his rudimentary attempts to help her. Coming from him, the finding of the silver fork, that she had used as a child on her arrival at the Rectory, is indeed 'a happy thought, a delicate attention'. And almost pathetic is his admission that he simply cannot give women what they want unless it is something tangible and material.

When they pine for they know not what – sympathy – sentiment – some of these indefinite abstractions – I can't do it: I don't know it; I haven't got it.[89]

Joe Scott, with his anti-women remarks and attitudes is a working-class echo of the Rector, but as he is only a common fellow he is not taken too seriously; he is made a figure of fun whereas Mr Helstone is dangerous.[90]

Paternal tyranny, though a feature of life at Haworth from Charlotte's infancy, plays no part in her work. The notion that a daughter must marry according to her father's wish had been fluctuating in the novel since the eighteenth century. Jane Austen positively sends the idea up, in two comic scenes in *Pride and Prejudice*: when Elizabeth has just had a proposal from Mr Collins and later when she thinks Mr Darcy has written to her father, rather than to herself, renewing his offer. She also makes it clear in *Mansfield Park* that Sir Thomas, however forceful his advice, cannot compel Fanny to marry Crawford. Dickens, on the other hand, in some extremely unpleasant passages of *Nicholas Nickleby*, shows the authority of Mr Bray to be absolute in disposing of Madeline in marriage.

[88] Ibid., ch. 7.   [89] Ibid., ch. 24.   [90] Ibid., ch. 18.

It is not that Charlotte Brontë depicts triumphant rebellion but that she removes the source of oppression. Jane Eyre, Lucy Snowe, Frances Henri and Shirley Keeldar are all orphans and Caroline is fatherless. To an extent Mr Sympson in *Shirley* represents paternal authority, but is ludicrous and easily routed. Jane Eyre has an uncle who is vital to the plot, as indeed Mr Sympson, as the employer of Louis Moore, is to that of *Shirley*; it is essential to the story that Jane should let Mr Eyre know she is going to marry Mr Rochester, but her psychological reasons for doing so are perfectly plausible: they are not only a natural wish for some dowry to make her a little independent of the Grand Turk, but an equally natural wish for quasi-fatherly approval.

In Charlotte Brontë's world women expect and find objectionable attitudes in men. It is gracious of a man to listen to a woman's point of view.

> He listened so kindly, so teachably; unformalized by scruples lest so to bend his bright handsome head, to gather a woman's rather obscure and stammering explanation, should imperil the dignity of his manhood.[91]

A man's superior judgement allows him to censor the pictures a woman looks at[92] and what she reads,[93] even to cutting pages out of books. A man can expect a woman to perform the most distasteful tasks of sick-nursing.

> Women who are worthy of the name ought infinitely to surpass our coarse, fallible self-indulgent sex, in the power to perform such duties.[94]

If he gives her presents he has a right to expect some return and to be able to calculate exactly where he stands from her reception of them.[95] Man runs mad at any idea of rival intellect in women.[96] He sneers at women who have not managed to get married.[97]

To an extent women can retaliate. A woman can pretend to regard a man as just a grown-up child: Charlotte Brontë, on the threshold of marriage, generalises from her fiancé's behaviour:

> Man is indeed an amazing piece of mechanism when you see, so to speak, the full weakness of what he calls his

[91] *Villette*, ch. 19.   [92] Ibid.   [93] Ibid., ch. 29.   [94] Ibid., ch. 19.
[95] Ibid., ch. 9.   [96] Ibid., ch. 30.   [97] *Shirley*, ch. 10.

122

strength. There is not a female child above the age of eight but might rebuke him for spoilt petulance of his wilful nonsense.[98]

As a novelist she can show man satirically – a bull in a field of cows, for example:

> Surrounded only by women and children, there was nothing to cross and thwart him; he had his own way and a pleasant way it was.[99]

She can not only cut him down to size, she can cut him up: maim him (Robert Moore), drown him (Paul Emanuel), blind him (Mr Rochester). But it is all done from a position of weakness; it is a cornered animal spitting and snarling.

The potential awfulness of being a woman is presented most vividly in *Shirley*, but we are to suppose that the young women who marry, Shirley and Caroline, are going to be happy, although in the course of the book we are shown, in both Mrs Helstones, two of the most unhappily married women in fiction. But truly in Charlotte Brontë's world if matrimony has some pain, celibacy has no pleasure. The state of old maids, suggested by Jane Austen in the character of Miss Bates, is now worked up into an explicit major theme.

The chapter in *Shirley*, 'Old Maids', starting, significantly, with a glance at the condition of the poor and deprived, develops from Caroline's depression at the thought that Robert Moore does not love her after all, to a full-scale exposition of the subject of unmarried women. Two prototypes are presented to us, Miss Mann and Miss Ainley. Caroline, seeing spinsterhood threatening herself, goes to visit them, and their spotless little cottages, their good works, their loneliness, their ugly faces and their primness strike terror into our hearts as well as into hers. There is a dead weight of misery and desolation over the whole scene, for though the two women are good and Miss Ainley is positively contented, these virtues have been achieved through frightening renunciation and the lifelong strangling of hope.

A later chapter which shows Caroline, having found good works and strenuous exercise an insufficient cure for her malaise, steadily sinking under the disappointment of her expectations and the monotony of her life, takes the form

---

[98] Letter to Ellen Nussey, 27 May 1854.   [99] *Villette*, ch. 33.

of a soliloquy which, in turn, becomes a rousing exhortation in Dickensian style comparable with the rhetorical adjuration which follows the death of Jo the crossing sweeper in *Bleak House*.[100] The whole passage must be read to get the full emotional force of Charlotte Brontë's views, but the gist is that hope lies not in resignation and thoughts of heaven, but in what society could and ought to do for single women.

> I believe single women should have more to do – better chances of interesting and profitable occupation than they possess now.

Once more, this time sarcastically, Caroline equates spinsters with the poor.

> Old maids, like the houseless and unemployed poor, should should not ask for a place and an occupation in the world: the demand disturbs the happy and rich: it disturbs parents.

She gives a withering picture of the wiles employed by girls to get a husband in an 'overstocked matrimonial market'. And she concludes, no longer in her own language but expressing her real feelings:

> Men of England! look at your poor girls, many of them fading round you, dropping off in consumption or decline; or, what is worse, degenerating to sour old maids, – envious, backbiting, wretched, because life is a desert to them: or, what is worst of all, reduced to strive, by scarce modest coquetry and debasing artifice, to gain that position and consideration by marriage which to celibacy is denied. Fathers! cannot you alter these things? Perhaps not all at once; but consider the matter well when it is brought before you, receive it as a theme worthy of thought: do not dismiss it with an idle jest or an unmanly insult . . . Keep your girls' minds narrow and fettered – they will still be a plague and a care, sometimes a disgrace to you; cultivate them – give them scope and work – they will be your gayest companions in health; your tenderest nurses in sickness; your most faithful prop in age.

It is not surprising to find that the idea of escape is central to the novels of Charlotte Brontë. Jane Eyre's childish cry, 'I

100 *Shirley*, ch. 22.

can never get away from Gateshead till I am a woman' and her brave shout of defiance, 'Good-bye to Gateshead' as she crosses the hall when leaving it against her expectation, while still a little girl, lead on to her feelings after eight years at Lowood. For most of these years she has been happy enough but suddenly she feels trapped.

> I went to my window, opened it, and looked out. There were the two wings of the building; there was the garden; there were the skirts of Lowood; there was the hilly horizon. My eye passed all other objects to rest on those most remote, the blue peaks; it was those I longed to surmount; all within their boundary of rock and heath seemed prisonground, exile limits. I traced the white road winding round the base of one mountain, and vanishing in a gorge between two: how I longed to follow it further! ... I tired of the routine of eight years in one afternoon. I desired liberty; for liberty I gasped; for liberty I uttered a prayer; it seemed scattered on the wind then faintly blowing.[101]

So she goes to Thornfield and, again, is happy enough, but still feels a need for wider horizons.

> When I took a walk by myself in the grounds; when I went down to the gates and looked through them along the road; or when ... I climbed the three staircases, raised the trap-door of the attic, and having reached the leads, looked out afar over sequestered field and hill, and along dim sky-line – then I longed for a power of vision which might overpass that limit; which might reach the busy world, towns, regions full of life I had heard of but never seen; then I desired more of practical experience than I possessed; more of intercourse with my kind, of acquaintance with variety of character, than was here within my reach.[102]

But Mr Rochester arrives and Thornfield becomes quite enough for her (it is sad to think that the wide world she rightly hankered after she probably never did see, after her eventual marriage) till the day when the bigamous marriage ceremony is broken off and she has to escape once more, this time from mortal sin, as she considers it, and this time tearing herself away in agony of mind and body. It is a beautiful

[101] *Jane Eyre*, ch. 10.   [102] Ibid., ch. 12.

summer morning as she leaves Thornfield, with dew and bird-song, and in spite of all the dangers she encounters in the next few days and the grief which never leaves her even after she has been rescued by the Rivers family, the fresh air and the open countryside remain for her symbols of personal freedom and independence, directly in contrast with the stale air and suffocation which the thought of being Mr Rochester's 'slave' – she uses the word – evokes.

Foreign countries, of course, are a cliché of escape. Frances Henri, in a state of subservience in Belgium, keeps England before her eyes as a way out. Lucy Snowe, hemmed in and dispossessed in England, looks to Belgium for her escape. Her action is a fit beginning to the long arduous road to freedom which we watch her painfully treading throughout *Villette*. When goaded by M. Paul, at the height of their running sexual battle,

> I broke out afresh with a cry that I wanted to be liberated – to get out into the air – I was almost in a fever.

The language sounds strangely modern; she does want to be liberated. But there is decided ambiguity. In the magnificent chapter at the end of the book where Lucy, drugged by her enemies, shakes off the sedative and breaks out of the pensionnat to wander through the streets and parks of Villette alone in a festive mob, she seems a heroine, the glorious prototype of all struggling imprisoned women, until we reflect that she is looking for the reactionary Paul Emanuel; she is looking for a man.

Chapter IV

Jane Austen, Charlotte Brontë and Elizabeth Gaskell all had at least one clergyman in their lives. All three were sincerely religious and presented their heroines as believers who conducted themselves according to Christian principles. But there the resemblance ends.

At first sight Jane Austen's heroines seem hardly to be religious at all, and indeed at second and at third sight it is difficult to imagine the high-spirited, self-reliant Elizabeth Bennet on her knees, though presumably she did take to God in prayer the whole story of Lydia's elopement, if not of Darcy's proposal. Emma Woodhouse, a regular church-goer, seems completely to ignore the practical influence which Christianity might be expected to have on her own behaviour. Even after her folly and unkindness to Harriet have been made apparent by Mr Elton's proposal to herself, a moment when it would be most natural for a religious woman to examine her conscience in the presence of God, she seizes on the bad weather as a good excuse for not going to church as it would be so awkward to meet Mr Elton. When at last she humbly acknowledges her own defects, her reflections are secular and sensible rather than religious, and she takes far more notice of Mr Knightley than she does of God.

But at least twice in the novels Jane Austen shows us the mighty power of religion, that is, we can easily deduce it from her low-voiced hints. It is not the general piety of Fanny Price that offers us this vision but Jane Austen's statement that, if Mary Crawford had married Edmund Bertram, Fanny's conscience would have subdued her own love for Edmund even to the point where she would feel able to marry someone else. We have seen Fanny's desperate love for Edmund, based on so much more than inclination: on childhood loneliness, suffering and insecurity. We have seen how it poisons her reactions to Mary Crawford, preventing her from appreciating Mary's few but genuine good qualities.

Yet religion for her is an equally strong force, or rather a marginally stronger one. Perhaps the example of Marianne Dashwood is even more convincing. Her love for Willoughby, no deeper perhaps than Fanny's for Edmund, but wilder and more frantic in its expression, is eventually conquered, as she says herself, not only by reason but by religion.

Reason could never be enough by itself. That other case of intemperate passion, Maria Bertram's love for Henry Crawford – unsanctioned from the first as she is already engaged to Mr Rushworth – can in its early stages be controlled by pride and resolution. Indeed Maria behaves very strong-mindedly when Henry's faithlessness is first revealed, on her father's return from Antigua. But pride and resolution are in the end inadequate. Reason would certainly have advised her not to elope with Henry Crawford and so forfeit for ever her lofty and enviable social position as Mrs Rushworth, but unsupported reason cannot restrain her. She has never been a religious girl and nothing else is strong enough to save her.

Charlotte Brontë's women characters differ greatly from each other where religion is concerned. Caroline Helstone, rector's niece and Sunday School teacher, is without question a devout girl. But the misery she undergoes through her disappointment in love and the loneliness and frustration of her life is a trial quite unassuaged by the consolations of religion. And the two old maids, Miss Ainley and Miss Mann, whom in desperation she tries to emulate, are not very inspiring in this respect. Miss Ainley's self-abnegation seems negative and depressing, and the good works of both have no more than overtones of religion and those chiefly because the good works are necessarily done within the framework of the church.

Lucy Snowe is a Protestant before she is a Christian. Her acid bigotry is sectarian rather than spiritual and the neurotic tantrums into which the least whiff of Roman Catholicism sends her are unedifying and even comic. Paul Emanuel is a better representative of his creed. Roman Catholic he may be and bigoted he certainly is, but he has deeds of truly Christian kindness to his credit. In the end each respectfully allows the other freedom of worship, but what would have happened in the course of normal family life, especially with regard to the upbringing of children, is another matter; it may be one more reason why Paul Emanuel has to be drowned. The Protestant/Catholic conflict is such a strong theme in the book that, had there not been several much stronger ones as well, the novel might have come into the increasingly popular category of tales based on sectarian controversy. As it is, it is curious that Charlotte Brontë does not make the status of the Virgin Mary in Catholicism more of a debating point; here was an excellent opportunity for sarcasm and diatribe, which she could exercise not only as a Protestant but as a woman.

The religious content of *Jane Eyre* is misleading. At three important points in the plot Jane apparently turns to God for support: at Lowood, under the influence and admonitions of Helen Burns; at Thornfield when Rochester tries to persuade her to live with him; and at Marsh End, when St John Rivers urges her to marry him and go with him to the mission field. But in all three cases commonsense is as much at stake as morality, and indeed, as has often been pointed out in connection with Jane's flight from Rochester, sheer prudence is her guide as much as anything; or perhaps it is something nobler: an intelligent interpretation of what she has actually observed – that is, Rochester's contempt for his mistresses – and heroically applied to her own situation with no weak reservations about its being different in her case. At Lowood, too, the Christian virtue of meek endurance fits in with what commonsense tells Jane even as a child, that to stay at school is the only way to escape Gateshead and to get an education which will eventually lead to independence. The St John Rivers episode is particularly ambiguous. What St John is urging Jane to do is eminently moral: marriage and missionary work are both ordained by God. Jane's scruples are not religious as they were in her opposition to Rochester's proposals; they belong to the realm of romantic delicacy: she does not love St John. So when she appeals for supernatural aid in her tussle with him she is invoking religion against religion.

When we turn to Elizabeth Gaskell we find a very different portrait of the religious woman. With her, reason and religion do not always arrive at much the same answer, with reason as the public face and religion the private energy. In some of her heroines she shows us women who interpret everything openly in terms of their religion, who feel and act voluntarily, almost spontaneously, in terms of their rela-

129

tionship with God. Here, for example, is Miss Jessie Brown, in a scene from *Cranford*. Recently bereft of her father, she is kneeling at the deathbed of the cantankerous sister whom she has devotedly nursed and for whom she has sacrificed her hopes of marriage. She has just had to tell Miss Brown of the death of their father.

> A strange look, which was not distress, came over Miss Brown's face. She did not speak for some time, but then we saw her lips form the words, rather than heard the sound – 'Father, mother, Harry, Archy;' – then, as if it were a new idea throwing a filmy shadow over her darkened mind – 'But you will be alone, Jessie!' Miss Jessie had been feeling this all during the silence, I think; for the tears ran down her cheeks like rain, at these words, and she could not answer at first. Then she put her hands together tightly and lifted them up, and said – but not to us – 'Though He slay me, yet will I trust in Him.'[1]

This unashamedly emotional expression of religious belief agrees with Mrs Gaskell's methods in general. Formulae and abstractions were unsympathetic to her. She could not write a 'social problem novel' though she wrote about social problems, and neither could she write about anything less than the human realities of religion though in fact her experience, as born Dissenter and Dissenter's wife, had given her plenty of material for something more theoretical. But this she consistently denies the readers even when they would welcome it: in *North and South* where Mr Hale's dissent precipitates the entire plot it is positively tantalising that we are told nothing about the nature of his doubts.

In *Ruth* Mr Benson, the minister who comes to the fallen heroine's rescue, is a Dissenter, but his non-conformism contributes little more to the story than a few comic speeches given to Sally the maidservant, unless of course Mrs Gaskell thought, as she well might given the tolerance of Unitarian attitudes, that it was a mercy Ruth had not fallen among Anglicans. *Ruth* is the least cerebral of novels. It is a story of repentance and redemption straight out of the Gospels; the behaviour is that of Mary Magdalene weeping and drying Christ's feet with her hair: uninhibited, passionate and demonstrative, essentially 'womanly' behaviour. The scene

[1] *Cranford*, ch. 2.

at the christening of Leonard, Ruth's illegitimate baby, strikes a note of something like ecstacy.

> Ruth came to the presence of God, as one who had gone astray, and doubted her own unworthiness to be called His child; she came as a mother who had incurred a heavy responsibility, and who entreated His almighty aid to enable her to discharge it; full of passionate yearning love which craved for more faith in God, to still her distrust and fear of the future that might hang over her darling ... There she stood, her fair pale cheek resting on her baby's head, as he slumbered on her bosom; her eyes went slanting down under their half-closed white lids.[2]

Years later another crucial scene takes place in church, when Ruth has just met her child's father again; it has an almost apocalyptic quality.

> In this extreme tension of mind to hold in her bewildered agony, it so happened that one of her senses was preternaturally acute. While all the church and the people swam in misty haze, one point in a dark corner grew clearer and clearer till she saw (what at another time she could not have discerned at all) a face – a gargoyle I think they call it – at the end of the arch next to the narrowing of the nave into the chancel, and in the shadow of that contraction. The face was beautiful in feature (the next to it was a grinning monkey), but it was not the features that were the most striking part. There was a half-open mouth, not in any way distorted out of its exquisite beauty by the intense expression of suffering it conveyed ... Though the parted lips seemed ready to quiver with agony, yet the expression of the whole face, owing to those strange, stony and yet spiritual eyes was high and consoling. If mortal gaze had never sought its meaning before, in the deep shadow where it had been placed long centuries ago, yet Ruth's did now ... She grew still enough to hear words which have come to many in their time of need, and awed them in the presence of the extremest suffering that the hushed world had ever heard of.[3]

And everything culminates in the scene of Ruth's funeral. Mr Benson, conducting the ceremony, has lovingly prepared a

[2] *Ruth*, ch. 17. [3] Ibid., ch. 23.

sermon, 'his great, last effort in her honour', but confronted with the emotions of his weeping audience and with his memories of Ruth in the early days when she was brought so low, he puts aside his script and reads from the Apocalypse itself.

> And he said to me, These are they which came out of great tribulation, and have washed their robes, and made them white in the blood of the Lamb.
>
> Therefore are they before the throne of God, and serve him day and night in his temple and he that sitteth upon the throne shall dwell among them.
>
> They shall hunger no more, neither thirst any more; neither shall the sun light on them nor any heat.
>
> For the Lamb which is in the midst of the throne shall feed them and shall lead them into living fountains of waters, and God shall wipe away all tears from their eyes.[4]

Though Elizabeth Gaskell would never have stooped to the popular creed of her day that religion was good for women as it reconciled them to their domesticity, she did seem to feel there was a special affinity between women and religion. That women tended to be more amenable to pastoral advice she records as a social fact, in the words of Minister Holman in *Cousin Phillis*:

> I don't see the men; they are all at their business, their shops, or their warehouses; they ought to be there. I have no fault to find with them; only if a pastor's teaching or words of admonition are good for anything, they are needed by the men as much as by the women.[5]

But there is more to it than that, some special possibility of grace. In all the novels men, like women, may or may not conduct their lives according to Christian principles: in *Mary Barton* Job Legh does and John Barton does not. But there is not nearly so much joy in Heaven over the sinner that repenteth if he happens to be a man.

Today we are bound to see the religious reformation of Ruth in quite a different light, as a process of social conditioning. It is only the opinion of the world that makes her begin to repent. The God-given conscience, the instinctive response to right and wrong, which Mrs Gaskell must have

[4] Ibid., ch. 36.   [5] *Cousin Phillis*, pt. 2.

believed in, gives Ruth no indication beyond a vague unease that her early association with Mr Bellingham can be amiss, and the fact that she has been religiously brought up till the age of sixteen and is still a regular churchgoer seems not to weigh at all. Neither does the warning of old Thomas, though this is hardly surprising as his talk of the devil, going about as a raging lion seeking whom he may devour, is not sufficiently tailored to the occasion, as Mrs Gaskell herself admits with a gleam of humour. Ruth is not awakened to the realities of her situation even by Mrs Mason's terrifying denunciation:

> Don't attempt to show your face at my house again after this conduct. I saw you and your spark too. I'll have no slurs on the character of my apprentices.[6]

She reacts to it rather like an animal; she recognises wrath and attempts to modify her conduct so as to avert it without in the least seeing the reason for it. It is in Wales after she has been living with Mr Bellingham for some months that she first realises what the world thinks of her. A censorious child called Harry who is staying at the same inn has heard the grown-ups discussing Ruth and later meets her out of doors.

> Harry lifted up his sturdy little right arm and hit Ruth a great blow on the face.
> 'Oh, for shame, sir!' said the nurse, snatching back his hand; 'how dare you do that to the lady who is so kind as to speak to Sissy!'
> 'She's not a lady!' said he indignantly. 'She's a bad, naughty girl – mamma said so, she did; and she shan't kiss our baby.'
> The nurse reddened in her turn. She knew what he must have heard; but it was awkward to bring it out, standing face to face with the elegant young lady.
> 'Children pick up such notions, ma'am', said she at last, apologetically to Ruth, who stood, white and still, with a new idea running through her mind.
> 'It's no notion; it's true, nurse; and I heard you say it yourself. Go away, naughty woman!' said the boy, in infantile vehemence of passion to Ruth.[7]

It is significant that Harry's first accusation should be that

6 *Ruth*, ch. 4.　　　　　7 Ibid., ch. 6.

Ruth was no lady. The whole of her redemption can be read as an attempt to win the respect of the world rather than the forgiveness of God. By means of a lie, she secures the post of governess in a most respectable middle-class family. When Mr Bellingham meets her again, in this setting, he comments to himself how well she must have played her cards; the remark is meant to be coarse and insensitive but, in fact, the substance of it is no more than Mrs Gaskell has said herself. Later when the lie is exposed and Ruth has to do even more to fight her way back, it is the acclaim of the world, that is of the citizens of Eccleston, that marks her triumph.

Two of Mrs Gaskell's claims to fame are connected with the subject of prostitution. The first is that, unlike many Victorians, she distinguishes carefully between different types of fallen women, between those who have been seduced and those who have turned to prostitution as a way of life. She takes motives and circumstances into account and does not lump together all those who have intercourse with men to whom they are not married under the general title of fornicators. The characters in her books, reflecting the contemporary outlook, often do. The insults that are hurled at Ruth by everyone from the infant Harry, already quoted, and the chambermaid at the Welsh inn, to Mr Bradshaw, years later in Eccleston, could hardly have been more vituperative had she been the most active prostitute in Britain.

The second is that she tackles the subject of prostitution so boldly. Writing *Mary Barton* in the 1840s, she was much franker than the novelists who came just before her. To begin with, she used the word 'prostitute', which Dickens had not dared to do, except in a preface, when describing the career of Nancy in *Oliver Twist*, ten years earlier. She also used such unequivocal words as 'street-walker'. Neither did she attempt to glamourise the profession as Charlotte Brontë did.

Mr Rochester's glaring revelations of sin in *Jane Eyre* shocked the reading public of 1847, both in themselves and because they were made to an innocent young girl. But Céline Varens was a high-class courtesan not a common street-walker, which distinguished her in the eyes of Charlotte Brontë if not in the eyes of God. It probably helped the reading public swallow the pill, too; at all events they did swallow it, with happy protests. All the trappings of well-to-do immorality, the silks, scent, laughter, bright lights and expensive boudoirs, which for Charlotte Brontë went so well with fornication, sound quite convincing in a Dame aux Camélias way and were no doubt reasonably true to life. We certainly see Céline with customers, if Mr Rochester could ever be referred to as a customer. But Charlotte Brontë could not, or at any rate did not, depict the chilling realities of prostitution in the way that Elizabeth Gaskell did when speaking of Esther.

Nothing could have been more gloomily realistic than the descriptions of Esther's habitat and activities: crumpled stained finery, gin palaces, hacking coughs, dark wet street corners, everything. We see her too, by clever implication, with her customers. When she hangs about the factory gate waiting for a word with Jem Wilson, and when she accosts first John Barton and later Jem, though *we* know her motives to be pure and altruistic on these occasions, the men take her to be going through the motions of her profession – with expertise if not much finesse – and react accordingly.

Esther is both prologue and epilogue to *Mary Barton* and her story one of the book's most important themes. The first chapter concerns her mysterious disappearance and the grief it is causing her sister, the older Mary Barton, John's wife. The circumstances of her departure, 'dressed in her Sunday gown, and with a new ribbon in her bonnet, and gloves on her hands, like the lady she was so fond of thinking herself' and the much-stressed fact of her great beauty hint loudly at the truth, as does John Barton's recital of his earlier words to her:

> Esther, I see what you'll end at with your artificials, and your fly-away veils, and stopping out when honest women are in their beds; you'll be a street-walker, Esther, and then, don't you go to think I'll have you darken my door, though my wife is your sister.

The thought of 'absent Esther' spoils the comfortable tea-party of chapter 2, and in chapter 3, when Mrs Barton dies in childbed, the doctor attributes her death to anxiety about her sister. This rather wild diagnosis hardens John Barton's heart towards Esther, as the needs of the plot demand that it should be hardened.

Esther now fades into the background while the young people grow up. But thoughts of her continue to influence the motherless Mary, in a way that makes her later flirtation with Harry Carson, son and heir of a rich mill-owner, more credible than it would otherwise be.

> The sayings of her absent, the mysterious aunt Esther, had an unacknowledged influence over Mary. She knew she was very pretty; the factory people as they poured from the mills, and in their freedom told the truth (whatever it might be) to every passer-by, had early let Mary into the secret of her beauty ... So with this consciousness she had early determined that her beauty should make her a lady; ... the rank to which she firmly believed her lost aunt Esther had arrived.[8]

At the time when young Mr Carson's pursuit of Mary is at its most intense, there is a significant description of the Barton house.

> Only one (nail) had been displaced. It was Esther's bonnet nail which in his deep revengeful anger against her, after his wife's death, he had torn out of the wall, and cast into the street.[9]

John Barton's heavily symbolic hurling of the nail into the street where no doubt his earlier brutal words helped to precipitate Esther herself, leads the way to her melodramatic reappearance.

Esther has decided to intervene in a situation where history seems to be repeating itself. The only irony is that, by the time she speaks, the worst of the danger is over; otherwise she is perfectly right. Mary has genuinely believed that Harry Carson means to marry her, which is odd in an intelligent town-bred girl who has been living an unsheltered, independent life since her mother's death. Nobody else has believed it, neither Sally Leadbitter the go-between, nor Esther, nor, most importantly, Harry Carson himself. Mary, with her very natural aspirations to a life of ease and luxury, not only for herself but for her father (Mrs Gaskell is con-

[8] *Mary Barton*, ch. 3.   [9] Ibid., ch. 10.

cerned to give all her characters who have actually or nearly fallen an unselfish interest as well), has been in real peril.

Instead of speaking to Mary herself Esther approaches Mary's father, not so much, Elizabeth Gaskell explains later, because she trusts man's authority and responsibility in such a case but because she dreads showing Mary what she has become. The scene of the meeting is set in all its dreariness.

> Unceasing, soaking rain was falling; the very lamps seemed obscured by the damp upon the glass, and their light reached but to a little distance from the posts. The streets were cleared of passers-by; not a creature seemed stirring, except here and there a drenched policeman in his oil-skin cape.

The details of Esther's own appearance are itemised with equally dreary effect:

> ... her faded finery, all unfit to meet the pelting of that pitiless storm; the gauze bonnet, once pink, now dirty white; the muslin gown, all draggled, and soaking wet up to the very knees; the gay-coloured barege shawl, closely wrapped around the form which yet shivered and shook ... Much was like the gay creature of former years; but the glaring paint, the sharp features, the changed expression of the whole![10]

John Barton behaves with the self-righteous cruelty which his former actions and words would lead us to expect. In all his dealings with Esther he is far more unsympathetic than when he commits murder. He curses and rebuffs her simply because she is a prostitute, even before he recognises her. When he does, he abuses her brutally and calls her the murderer of her sister. He flings her against a lamp-post as she sinks down fainting, and strides away. She is discovered in a state which one of the policemen, put into the scene earlier, mistakes for drunkenness and is condemned to hard labour for a month.

This month is one of acute suspense for Esther, who dares not even pray for Mary in case a prayer coming from her could do positive harm. The minds of the readers, however, are put at rest during this time by a confrontation between

[10] Ibid.

Mary and Mr Carson in which he reveals that his intentions have been dishonourable and Mary spurns him.

Barton's rebuff of Esther is, of course, necessary to the plot and, when he repents of his severity, so is his failure to find her again. At this point, though Esther has had no chance to mention her fears and though he has taken her naming of Mary to apply to his dead wife rather than his daughter, he begins to identify young Mary with Esther, quite unreasonably but, at the time, with perfect accuracy.

> He often looked at Mary, and wished she were not so like her aunt, for the very bodily likeness seemed to suggest the possibility of a similar likeness in their fate and then this idea enraged his irritable mind, and he became suspicious and anxious about Mary's conduct.[11]

Esther, while intending the exact opposite, is in fact making history repeat itself.

Esther now comes out of prison and with even firmer purpose speaks to Jem Wilson, without knowing that he is in love with Mary. He too shakes off her detaining hand but with no harsher language than 'Go away, missis', and when she tells him who she is he reacts with kindness and sympathy. At this central point, half-way through the book, we hear Esther's story. Mrs Gaskell adroitly packs into it as many extenuating circumstances as she can: all the obvious ones such as the fact that her seducer promised marriage and that she was driven to prostitution by a need to provide for her sick child, and some less obvious ones such as her loyal refusal to hear a word against her lover and her unprecedented honesty in acknowledging that she was extremely happy in her three years of living in sin. Seduced girls were supposed to have hated every minute of it. Jane Fairfax who had fallen no lower than a clandestine engagement, said afterwards that she had never known the blessing of a tranquil hour. Esther's intelligence is endearing, too. She sees, as the moralists of her time did not when they tried to redeem prostitutes by means of drudgery, that drudgery can in fact lead to prostitution.

> I found out Mary went to learn dressmaking, and I began to be frightened for her; for it's a bad life for a girl to be

[11] Ibid., ch 11.

out late at night in the streets, and after many an hour of weary work, they're ready to follow after any novelty that makes a little change.[12]

Esther has now set the plot thoroughly in motion. Jem is to meet Carson and to be discovered fighting with him so as to be the clear suspect when Carson is murdered. She could be allowed to withdraw except for the tidying up process demanded by the craft of the novel. But she is constantly placed in the foreground. Several times, and particularly at the trial, Mary brings her to mind by wondering who could have told Jem about herself and Carson. She also plays a much more active part. It is she who finds and brings to Mary the incriminating piece of paper which has been used as wadding in the murderer's gun, thus burdening Mary with the knowledge that her father is the murderer. This is far from Esther's intentions – which have been to shield Jem – as the results of all her other efforts to do good have been. It is almost as though her own sad superstition that a prostitute cannot do good has some foundation.

> With her violent and unregulated nature, rendered morbid by the course of life she led, and her consciousness of her degradation, she cursed herself for the interference which she believed had led to this; for the information and the warning she had given to Jem, which had roused him to this murderous action. How could she, the abandoned and polluted outcast, ever have dared to hope for a blessing, even on her efforts to do good. The black curse of Heaven rested on all her doings, were they for good or for evil.[13]

The scene in which she appears to Mary – Biblical language seems appropriate – has a visionary, hallucinatory quality. Mary, desperately brooding over her dilemma and already unhinged by anxiety, has fallen asleep on the floor of her home, longing for her mother to be alive again and persuaded in her dreams that it is so. After midnight Esther knocks at the door.

> The moon shone clearly in at the unshuttered window, making the room almost as light as day, in its cold ghastly

[12] Ibid., ch. 14.   [13] Ibid., ch. 21.

radiance ... A strange feeling crept over Mary's heart, as if something spiritual were near; as if the dead, so lately present in her dreams, were yet gliding and hovering round her, with their dim, dread forms.[14]

This is very much the atmosphere of *The Eve of St. Agnes* and when Mary opens the door Esther melts into her dream in rather the same spirit that Porphyro melted into Madeline's.

'O mother! mother! you are come at last?' She threw herself or rather fell into the trembling arms of her long-lost, unrecognized aunt, Esther.

Elizabeth Gaskell was consciously employing the apparatus of romanticism. On approaching the house, Esther

had felt as if some holy spell would prevent her (even as the unholy Lady Geraldine was prevented, in the abode of Christabel) from crossing the threshold of that home of her early innocence.

Though the spell does not stop her entering the house it soon operates. She overacts the part of the respectable, comfortably-off mechanic's wife for which she has dressed herself to such an extent as to repel Mary and they come to no understanding. The scene ends with a highly theatrical and wholly conventional flourish. Esther turns to go and Mary, reproaching herself for her coldness, advances to kiss her.

But, to her surprise, her aunt pushed her off with a frantic kind of gesture, and saying the words – 'Not me. You must never kiss me. You!' She rushed into the outer darkness of the street, and there wept long and bitterly.[15]

Equally conventional and theatrical have been Esther's feelings on seeing herself in a glass after dressing up in her drab and worthy disguise, which 'has a sort of sanctity to the eyes of the street-walker'.

She ... thought how easy were the duties of that Eden of innocence from which she was shut out; how she would work, and toil, and starve, and die, if necessary, for a husband, a home – for children.

[14] Ibid., ch. 20.   [15] Ibid., ch. 21.

This is not only theatrical but ironical (consciously ironical: the point is repeated in *Cranford*) in view of some of the terrible situations we have seen respectable married women, such as Mrs Davenport, involved in.

Throughout the book there have been hints as to the possibility of Esther's reclamation. Even John Barton wondered if religion might help her; he was sure no earthly power could. At the end, when everything is nearly wound up, Jem tells Mary the truth about her aunt's situation. Mary's immediate reaction is to find and help her. When Jem doubtfully explains that she has already refused his help, Mary cries out in the spirit of the best nineteenth-century social reformers:

> You will never persuade her if you fear and doubt. Hope yourself, and trust in the good that must be in her. Speak to that, – she has it in her yet; – oh, bring her home, and we will love her so, we'll make her good.[16]

Jem is inspired and rushes out with redeeming zeal but after a day and a night of searching has not found her. But that evening she comes dying to the Bartons' house where she lived as a girl.

> She had come (as a wounded deer drags its heavy limbs once more to the green coolness of the lair in which it was born, there to die) to see the place familiar to her innocence, yet once again before her death.

She dies and they bury her in the same grave as John Barton, whom she has looked on as an accusing angel. As murderer and prostitute 'they lie without name, or initial, or date' but there is a tombstone which carries the whole weight of Victorian sorrowful wrath: 'For He will not always chide, neither will He keep His anger for ever.'

The history of Lizzie Leigh, in the short story of that name, though naturally less developed, brings out many of the same points. Lizzie, too, has been seduced – we are not told in what circumstances – and duly cursed and cast off by her father, whose forgiveness of her on his deathbed begins the story. Her mother, accompanied by her brothers, goes to live in Manchester to look for her, undissuaded by the assertions of Will, the elder brother, that she must be dead: she was pregnant at the time of her disappearance and as Will blurts

16 Ibid., ch. 38.

out, 'Many a one dies in —'. By a series of wild coincidences Mrs Leigh finds Lizzie's baby which has been informally adopted and we infer, from the fostermother's account of how money is left regularly but furtively at the house, that Lizzie has turned to prostitution.

When Lizzie appears she has degenerated physically in the same way as Esther.

> This Lizzie was old before her time; her beauty was gone; deep lines of care, and, alas! of want (or thus the mother imagined) were printed on the cheek, so round, so fair, and smooth, when last she gladdened her mother's eyes. Even in her sleep she bore the look of woe and despair which was the prevalent expression of her face by day; even in her sleep she had forgotten how to smile.

Her behaviour has the same uncivilised intensity as Esther's and the same loss of ability to deal with human beings in a normal way: 'She looked so fierce, so mad, so haggard, that for an instant Susan was terrified.'

Again, in this story, the characters are sorted out according to the way in which they react to the sinner, and, again, it is the women who are charitable, headed of course by the author who even gives her her own name. The father, the brother and the employer's husband are the sternly censorious ones. The women believe that reformation is possible. Susan says, 'For all that's come and gone, she may turn right at last. Mary Magdalen did, you know.'

And so it proves. Lizzie, like Esther, is not allowed to keep her daughter, who dies, but she is allowed to live and to work for her eternal salvation and consequent reunion with her child. (It is not disinterested repentance.)

> I only know that, if the cottage be hidden in a green hollow of the hills, every sound of sorrow in the whole upland is heard there – every call of suffering or of sickness for help is listened to by a sad, gentle-looking woman, who rarely smiles (and when she does her smile is more sad than other people's tears), but who comes out of her seclusion whenever there is a shadow in any household. Many hearts bless Lizzie Leigh, but she – she prays always and ever for forgiveness – such forgiveness as may enable her to see her child once more.

142

This dreary, masochistic, superstitious life, as it is bound to seem to non-believers, is presented elsewhere in Mrs Gaskell's work if sometimes only in brief glimpses as in *The Well of Pen-Morfa*, a short story which begins with a description of the village of Pen-Morfa and of some of its inhabitants. One of them is a fallen woman.

> She had been the beauty of Pen-Morfa; had been in service; had been taken to London by the family whom she served; had come down, in a year or so, back to Pen-Morfa, her beauty gone into that sad, wild, despairing look which I saw, and she about to become a mother.

This woman, middle-aged now, is given no name and is merely glimpsed in her garden as the narrator passes, but we are told that her child is deformed, bedridden and in constant pain, that she nurses it devotedly, living in appropriate solitude (the narrator's friend does not particularly want to address her) and presumably in a state of penitence as the narrator is able to hope that 'that woman and her child are dead now and their souls above'. The story then passes on to its real heroine Nest Gwynn and remains with her to the end, but the tale of the seduced girl is not forgotten though it is alluded to no more. Nest does not sin in the sexual sense but – in significant parallel – she is cruelly rejected by a man after she becomes crippled in a fall and spends the rest of her life loving and caring for an idiot girl to atone for past resentment and unkindness. The last words, spoken by the idiot, tell us that Nest has gone to Heaven.

Of course the most sustained picture of female atonement comes in *Ruth*, and it is in this book that Mrs Gaskell is most scrupulous in assessing exactly how much there is to atone for. Ruth would probably never have become a prostitute, though her seducer later reflects complacently that this is what must have happened to her. It is suicide Mr Benson saves her from not prostitution. And she truly loved the appalling Mr Bellingham. Not that for one minute does Elizabeth Gaskell think that love justifies everything. We know from her letters that she was aware of the circumstances which made it necessary for Marian Evans and G. H. Lewes to live in sin, if they were to live together at all, and if circumstances were ever extenuating these were. Yet she could only deplore the situation, though, like Ruth's landlady at the Welsh inn, she found it impossible to work up the 'proper contempt'. But though love cannot justify, it *is* relevant, and an illicit union, entered on with love, is morally better than cold-bloodedly selling oneself, concludes Mrs Gaskell. Ruth's love for Mr Bellingham, the distracted love of someone who has nobody else, makes her seem almost innocent. She acts like a devoted dog, crouching outside her master's room while he is ill and, when he leaves her, following his coach along the road till she can run no more. And not even nineteenth-century moralists would censure the morals of dogs, only their habits. Esther, too, dearly loved her seducer. It is interesting that Mrs Gaskell should have given her a worse fate than Ruth for she had also been promised marriage which Ruth had not.

The train of events leading to Ruth's seduction, from the great, such as the terrifying arrival of her employer Mrs Mason, to the trivial, such as the social embarrassment of having no money to pay for the tea at the inn, is almost enough to excuse her; it is far more coercive than the happenings that drove Hardy's Tess on. The powers of evil close in on her as they did on Richardson's Clarissa. In joining the establishment of the dressmaker Mrs Mason, Ruth, orphaned and homeless, is transplanted from a country setting as idyllic as that of *Cousin Phillis*. She reacts like the heroine of Hood's *The Song of the Shirt*.

> Oh! but to breathe the breath
> Of the Cowslip and primrose sweet –
>   With the sky above my head,
>   And the grass beneath my feet,
> For only one short hour
>   To feel as I used to feel.

Mrs Gaskell repeatedly and skilfully evokes the lost Paradise, for example, with a description of the wallpaper opposite which Ruth had chosen to sit.

> On these panels were painted the most lovely wreaths of flowers, profuse and luxuriant beyond description, and so real-looking, that you could almost fancy you smelt their fragrance, and heard the south wind go softly rustling in and out among the crimson roses – the branches of purple and white lilac – the floating golden-tressed laburnum

144

boughs ... They conjured up visions of other sister-flowers that grew, and blossomed, and withered away in her early home.

One by one the horrors of Ruth's situation are borne in on her, and on us. We first see her toiling upstairs to the work-room at two o'clock on a snowy January night, having been sent to find out the time, faced like the rest of the girls with further hours of work and too weary to eat the supper provided in a brief interval. We see the crowded sleeping quarters, and hear Ruth's hysterical, though well-founded dread of the future:

> Oh! how shall I get through five years of these terrible nights! in that close room! and in that oppressive stillness! which lets every sound of the thread be heard as it goes eternally backwards and forwards.

Even more depressing is the consolation of Jenny the fore-woman: that you soon get not to notice it. We are told of the nightmares which show so clearly Ruth's unreadiness for an independent life.

> I thought I saw mamma by the side of the bed, coming as she used to do, to see if I were asleep and comfortable; and when I tried to take hold of her, she went away and left me alone – I don't know where; so strange![17]

She is contemptuously treated at the ball to which four of the apprentices are sent to repair such dresses as may get torn.

> Make haste – don't keep me an hour! ... Will it never be done? What a frightful time you are taking; and I'm dying to return in time for this galop! ... I had no idea any one could have spent so much time over a little tear. No wonder Mrs. Mason charges so much for dressmaking, if her workwomen are so slow.

As she returns home she and her companions are the only ones up and about in the winter dawn except the houseless beggars and with them she identifies herself.

> Here was cold, biting midwinter for her, and such as her – for those poor beggars almost a season of death.[18]

[17] *Ruth*, ch. 1.   [18] Ibid., ch. 2.

Perhaps worst of all are the Sundays, when Mrs Mason heartlessly chooses to assume that all her young ladies have friends to go to and so leaves such as have not, like Ruth, to a loneliness, cold and hunger which would drive almost anybody into the arms of Mr Bellingham. All possible support is withdrawn from Ruth. Jenny, the kind forewoman, has to go home with tuberculosis. Mary, the old servant and friend of Ruth's parents, who means to warn Ruth about Mr Bellingham and his intentions, plans to do it the following week and then it is too late. It is like the terrifying sequence in *The Woman in White* where everybody who is honest, well-intentioned and kind, quits Blackwater Park, leaving the heroine to the villains.

Not that Mrs Mason is really a villain, as Mrs Gaskell is careful to explain. 'Mrs. Mason was a very worthy woman, but, like many other worthy women, she had her foibles.'[19] But the most designing wretch in creation could hardly cause more harm. Her appearance to Ruth as she returns from her expedition with Mr Bellingham, though not presented in mock-heroic style as Fielding might have done it, is made by Ruth's inexperience and vaguely-felt guilt into a scene of such epic horror that we can no more reflect than could Ruth that this is merely a bad-tempered, unimaginative woman, worried by her own personal concerns, taking it out on a subordinate.

Nearly everybody who writes about *Ruth* points out its basic inconsistency: if Ruth is really an innocent victim of circumstances, why does she have to be so severely punished – by years of abject penitence, by the prospect of permanent dependence, by terrible suffering when her past becomes known, and with early death at the end? The answer seems to be that Elizabeth Gaskell regards sexual intercourse outside marriage as a kind of disease with after effects, rather like the fever that she uses with such heavy symbolism at the end of the book. It may not have been the heroine's fault that she caught it, or she may have been guilty of little worse than imprudence, but it cannot possibly be annulled and the results are automatic and inescapable.

Ruth is in fact lucky. Her child lives and will have a good future. He has a dangerous bout of sickness, significantly at the time when Mr Bellingham crosses Ruth's path again, but

[19] Ibid., ch. 1.

146

he recovers. Ruth has time to redeem herself (though from what?) and dies at last in a blaze of heroism, having nursed a hospitalful of fever victims and become, in a thoroughly reputable way, the talk of the town.

Unlike Esther and Lizzie, Ruth is allowed to come within striking distance of marriage, that is to say, marriage is spoken of in connection with her. It is not that Mr Bellingham eventually suggests making an honest woman of her. His proposal is predictable and is somehow made to sound as contemptible as the rest of his behaviour; it does him no more service in the eyes of the reader or indeed of the heroine than does Henry Carson's in *Mary Barton*. Ruth's refusal is important, in that she is seen to realise that environment – in this case close daily contact with a bad man – could be worse for a child than the slur of illegitimacy. As far as the moral law is concerned, she is upholding the spirit rather than the letter. It is Mr Farquahar's idea of marrying her that indicates the extent of her innocence and reclamation, but it is also at this point that we get the full force of Mrs Gaskell's adamant refusal to consider Ruth's full return to the land of the living. We realise from the first hint that Ruth would never even contemplate accepting Mr Farquahar, even if he were not the former suitor of her employer's daughter and even if he knew and condoned her past history, which of course he does not. It is simply out of the question. When Ruth's story becomes known, Mr Farquahar reflects that he has had a lucky escape, but Mrs Gaskell makes it clear that instead of disliking him for this reaction, we are supposed to think of him as on the whole a good and sympathetic man. Fallen women must not get married.

That is to say, in the novels of that particular day. In real life of course they quite frequently did. Stephen Marcus in *The Other Victorians* quotes William Acton, a doctor who flourished in the middle of the nineteenth century and published, among other works, a long and illuminating book on prostitution. Dr Acton asserts that many prostitutes gave up their profession to marry and, in fact, as wives often had an easier time than their virtuous sisters as they had fewer children or none. (This, however, was a bonus that those who thought as Mrs Gaskell did about babies would not appreciate.)

Dr Acton denies that prostitution necessarily has deleterious effects on women; he would not at all agree with Elizabeth Gaskell's descriptions of Esther and Lizzie, and in fact, whereas she compares the physical appearance of the virtuous woman, Mrs John Barton, with that of the sinner, Esther, to the entire advantage of the former, he would absolutely reverse her conclusion.

> If we compare the prostitute at thirty-five with her sister, who perhaps is the married mother of a family, or has been a toiling slave for years in the over-heated laboratories of fashion, we shall seldom find that the constitutional ravages often thought to be necessary consequences of prostitution exceed those attributable to the cares of a family and the heart-wearing struggles of virtuous labour.

Neither would he have felt that Esther's illness and death were a result of her calling; his experience has shown him

> that the downward progress and death of the prostitute in the absolute ranks of that occupation are exceptional, and that she succumbs at last, not to that calling, nor to venereal disease, but in due time, and to the various maladies common to respectable humanity.[20]

If we are to believe Dr Acton, and there is every reason to, these were the scientific facts. But the novelists were none too ready to accept them.

The seducers in Elizabeth Gaskell's novels are an unappetising set of men. It is fortunate for them that they are assisted by chance, fate and contributory circumstances of every sort; their charms, we feel, would not get them very far. The great Lovelace with all his evil allure has dwindled to a mother-fixated tailor's dummy. Mr Bellingham and young Mr Carson are not so much his descendants as they are the ancestors of Alec d'Urberville. The only one who sounds at all pleasant is a man we never see, Esther's seducer, and this is mainly because he is surrounded by the rosy glow of Esther's remembered affection; we know no good of him except that he paid her off with £50 which he could ill afford. £50, incidentally, seems to have been the standard sum in such emergencies.

[20] *The Other Victorians*, p. 5.

To begin with, they lack the charm of intelligence. (Lovelace was brilliant.) Mr Bellingham is not very bright and Henry Carson is downright stupid. His handling of the situation in which Mary Barton declares she will have nothing more to do with him is so inept as to draw protest even from the obtuse, though cunning, Sally Leadbitter:

> But if you did think of marrying her, why (if I may be so bold as to ask) did you go and tell her you had thought of doing otherwise by her? That was what put her up at last.[21]

It could be said in Mr Carson's defence, however, that he does not behave much worse than the noble Mr Darcy. The street scene in which Henry Carson is driven by the excess of his desire to offer marriage to a poor dressmaker has weird echoes of the scene in Hunsford Parsonage where Mr Darcy carefully explains to Elizabeth how the inferiority of her station has so far kept him from proposing to her. True, he has no idea of seducing her and he accepts her refusal in a less cocksure spirit than that of Henry Carson whose reaction is:

> She'll come round, you may depend upon it. Women always do . . . Mind, I don't say I shall offer her the same terms again.[22]

But in essentials the master of Pemberley and the jumped-up small-town dandy are brothers.

The vanity and conceit of Elizabeth Gaskell's seducers are bottomless. Henry Carson

> had no doubt of the effect of his own personal charms in the long run; for he knew he was handsome, and believed himself fascinating.[23]

Mr Bellingham is equally confident. That Ruth should, as he thinks, have died as a consequence of her love for him causes him no surprise.

Mr Bellingham is much more fully drawn than Henry Carson, who in any case has no opportunity actually to become the seducer he has planned to be. It is remarkable how few excuses Mrs Gaskell makes for Bellingham. She could hardly do enough for Branwell Brontë in this respect. In her

[21] *Mary Barton*, ch. 11.   [22] Ibid.   [23] Ibid., ch. 10.

Life of Charlotte Brontë she is emphatic about the handicap imposed on an only son.

> There are always peculiar trials in the life of an only boy in a family of girls. He is expected to act a part in life; to *do*, while they are only to *be*; and the necessity of their giving way to him in some things, is too often exaggerated into their giving way to him in all, and thus rendering him utterly selfish.[24]

She presents Branwell as she might one of her innocent misguided heroines for whose purity and frailty the wiles of wordly deceivers were altogether too much. In speaking of Mrs Robinson she takes the same tone as her own character, Mrs Bellingham, Henry's mother, talking of Ruth: 'It is right to repent, but I have no doubt in my own mind she led you wrong with her artifices.'[25]

Mr Bellingham had, in fact, handicaps comparable in seriousness with those of Branwell Brontë though of a different nature. He was an only child, spoilt and injudiciously brought up by his mother, a widow with limited human sympathies and an unlimited income, who by example taught him to be inattentive to the feelings of others. Though his father had left him some property, he was to a large extent financially dependent on his mother who loved power and was therefore capricious in her handouts.

But before we can really start feeling sorry for Mr Bellingham, Mrs Gaskell adds a detail which nips our sympathies very firmly in the bud.

> He would refuse to visit her [his mother's] schools; and when wearied into going at last, revenge himself by puzzling the children with the most ridiculous questions (gravely put) that he could imagine.[26]

We cannot forgive him for taking it out on underprivileged children; and it is a particularly well-chosen example of his general attitude, as he is so soon to behave abominably to another underprivileged child, Ruth. Mr Darcy, whose upbringing involved similar disadvantages to those of Mr Bellingham – he was an only son and positively trained to be

[24] *Life of Charlotte Brontë*, ch. 9.
[25] *Ruth*, ch. 8.   [26] Ibid., ch. 2.

arrogant – would never have behaved like this; he was always 'affable to the poor'.

Mr Bellingham's pursuit of Ruth is heartless to the point of sadism. At the moment when she is reduced to panic-stricken tears after her dismissal by Mrs Mason – justifiable panic as she has virtually no one in the world to turn to – he deliberately removes her one prop with a calculating lie.

> It is very unfortunate; for you see, I did not like to name it to you before, but, I believe – I have business, in fact, which obliges me to go to town to-morrow – to London, I mean; and I don't know when I shall be able to return.[27]

This reduces her even further, and with equally deliberate falsehoods he destroys any hope she may have had of Mrs Mason's relenting or of her guardian's coming to the rescue. As the victory is still not won, he turns the trip to London into a long visit to Paris with his mother.

We next see him in Wales with Ruth as his travelling-companion, behaving to her with all the petulance that we might have expected, heedless of her interests and impatient with her pleasures. But this is nothing compared with his desertion of her, a monstrous act, monstrously carried out.[28] Mrs Gaskell, presumably for artistic reasons, allows him as many extenuating circumstances as she can. He really does become seriously ill and such moral fibre as he has is completely undermined. The great extenuating circumstance is his mother, a gorgon, who arrives to nurse him and takes charge of the entire situation, including Ruth. To have her as a mother is like having Lady Macbeth as a wife. The culprit is still responsible; he can say no; but the odds are heavily against him. To Bellingham's credit he does make a feeble attempt to defend Ruth's character against his mother's self-righteous accusations, but after that he leaves all the dirty work to her, letting her write the cruel note of dismissal (enclosing the inevitable £50) in much the same way that Mr Willoughby in *Sense and Sensibility* allows his future wife to compose the insolent letter to Marianne. The creators of both these mad dogs of seducers make them, in emergencies, hide behind women's skirts like frightened puppies.

When Mr Bellingham, now called Mr Donne, reappears several years later, he seems much the same to the reader.

[27] Ibid., ch. 4.   [28] Ibid., ch. 8.

The crudity of his reaction when he recognises Ruth, his threat to undeceive the people of Eccleston about her past, and the sadistic way he seizes on the knowledge that she has a child in order to coerce her into meeting him alone – all this behaviour is completely in keeping with what he was before.

But Ruth has changed. She can now judge him. She has had opportunity to observe other people and especially the good Bensons who have rescued and protected her. The disillusionment is complete.

> That half-hour seemed to separate the present Mr. D nne very effectively from her imagination of what Mr. Bellingham had been. She was no analyser; she hardly even had learnt to notice character; but she felt there was some strange difference between the people she had lived with lately and the man who now leant back in his chair, listening in a careless manner to the conversation, but never joining in, or expressing any interest in it, unless it somewhere, or somehow, touched himself.[29]

The impression is intensified during the days that they are staying in the same house until when he finally asks her to marry him, she can say with perfect truth:

> I could never love you again. All you have said and done since you came with Mr. Bradshaw to Abermouth first has only made me wonder how I ever could have loved you.[30]

Already the cliché of the reformed rake, which was to break u completely in later Victorian fiction, is beginning to crack. When Bellingham says complacently: 'People who are no saints have made very good husbands before now', the words have a very hollow ring. Even more hollowly sounds the expression 'youthful folly' which Mr Bellingham uses about his early seduction of Ruth, as he stands by the bed where she has died of the fever she caught in nursing him. He does not talk about sowing wild oats but he might as well have done; the concept is present. Wild oats were being sown throughout the Victorian novel, at first in an atmosphere of half-approving tolerance or slightly amused disapproval, later in a climate of genuine condemnation. Mrs Gaskell was one of the first to bring whole-hearted severi y

[29] Ibid., ch. 23. [30] Ibid., ch. 24.

to bear on the subject. At the words 'youthful folly', the gentle Mr Benson at first sets 'his teeth hard together, to keep in words little short of a curse' and then 'with the stillness of ice' in his voice he pronounces the grand rebuke: 'Men may call such actions as yours youthful follies! There is another name for them with God.'[31]

Elizabeth Gaskell has an interesting line in near-seducers: the flirts, the triflers, who without actually doing anything wrong cause a great deal of misery. Such a one is Mr Holdsworth, the railway engineer and boss of the Paul Manning who relates the story of *Cousin Phillis*. Mr Holdsworth is suspiciously dashing.

> He was a young man of five-and-twenty or so, and was in a station above mine, both by birth and education; and he had travelled on the Continent, and wore mustachios and whiskers of a somewhat foreign fashion. I was proud of being seen with him.[32]

He falls in love with Phillis as sincerely as she falls in love with him, but not as steadfastly. When his work suddenly calls him to Canada for two years he goes away in honourable silence, as he is not yet in a position to propose, but with the serious though short-lived intention of returning to marry her. It is not his fault but Paul's that Phillis is told of his love and lives in ecstasies of anticipation until the day she hears he has married a girl in Canada, which news precipitates her into an almost fatal illness. The story ends on a dying fall with no hope of a second attachment for Phillis, only a rather dreary peace.

The best example is Charley Kinraid the specksioneer, hero of *Sylvia's Lovers*. His first appearance is accompanied at length and with eloquence by stories of his brave and violent deeds at sea, defending a whaler's crew against the press-gang, and of his fickleness with girls. There are both glorious and ugly accounts abroad about him, from the near-legend of his defiance of the press-gang to William Coulson's bitter testimony:

> He kept company with my poor sister as is dead for better nor two year, and then left off coming to see her and went wi' another girl, and it just broke her heart.[33]

---

[31] Ibid., ch. 36.   [32] *Cousin Phillis*, pt. 1.   [33] *Sylvia's Lovers*, ch. 7.

William in fact equates the two activities: 'He killed her as sure as he shot down yon sailors.'

Kinraid's courtship of Sylvia is straightforward and successful and in all the miserable events that follow we can say nothing rational to his discredit. He cannot help being taken off by the press-gang; he does his best to get a message to Sylvia of the fate that has befallen him and of his constancy to her, though unfortunately the only messenger available is his rival Philip Hepburn, who suppresses the knowledge. He comes back to Sylvia as soon as he can, with the intention of marrying her, only to find her the wife of Philip. All perfectly sincere and honourable behaviour; yet Elizabeth Gaskell manages to surround him with an atmosphere of suspicion throughout. It is not for nothing that she introduces an obvious parallel with Othello's technique of winning women by story-telling.[34] Philip always regards him as untrustworthy and it may not be only jealousy that makes him think so. And there *are* those stories about the other girls. After Charley's discovery of Sylvia's marriage and her refusal to elope with him, he finds a wife with indelicate haste. Again, why should he not, and why should he not choose, advantageously, a girl above him in station? And why should he not be very happy with her? But the suspicion is always there.

'Thou wast a delightful fellow! Ay, and a good one too; though much sorrow was caused by thee!' Paul Manning's valedictory words about Edward Holdsworth seem to express Elizabeth Gaskell's own feelings about these fascinators and she clearly means that they are sexually attractive, as opposed to Paul himself and to Philip Hepburn who do not begin to stir the pulses of the lovely heroines. The portrait of Philip is masterly in its evocation of the worthy, serious, priggish young man who is repulsive to the pretty, flighty girl whom he inevitably desires, and the description of Sylvia's complete lack of response in their married life is thoroughly chilling. As an unaffected married woman and the experienced helpmeet of a parish clergyman in a tough district, Mrs Gaskell can hardly have subscribed to the Victorian belief that women do not feel sexual desires in the way men do. Certainly she conveys a very different message in her novels.

[34] Ibid., ch. 9.

Particularly in *Cranford*. It was not until she wrote *Wives and Daughters* that Elizabeth Gaskell showed thorough interest in the eternal who-marries-whom, which was the essential subject matter of so many previous novelists, including of course Jane Austen. Up to then she had worked on the assumption that women have difficulties and challenges to meet beyond the acquisition of a husband, though some of the problems might arise from not having acquired one.

Cranford is a community of women, who though the word 'Amazons' in the first sentence is used ironically, do seem able to manage without men in the same way that they are able to manage without money; in fact, poverty and lack of men are equated as facts of life which can be combated by gentility and proper organisation. Sexually it is the middle class that is deprived.

> If gentlemen were scarce, and almost unheard of in the 'genteel society' of Cranford, they or their counterparts – handsome young men – abounded in the lower classes.[35]

Financially, too, it is the middle class that has fallen from a previously high estate and might be said to have suffered. The poor of Cranford are as they would have been anywhere else.

Sexual deprivation, in Cranford, results in the traditional dishonesties that the situation tends to call forth: sour grapes, for example ('We had almost persuaded ourselves that to be a man was to be "vulgar");[36] the assumption of superiority ('She [Miss Jenkyns] would have despised the modern idea of women being equal to men. Equal, indeed! she knew they were superior');[37] or simply the enumeration of masculine deficiencies:

> Men will be men. Every mother's son of them wishes to be considered Samson and Solomon rolled into one – too strong ever to be beaten or discomfited – too wise ever to be outwitted. If you will notice, they have always foreseen events, though they never tell one for one's warning before the events happen. My father was a man, and I know the sex pretty well.[38]

But honesty keeps breaking through, from the hanging up of

[35] *Cranford*, ch. 3.   [36] Ibid., ch. 1.
[37] Ibid., ch. 2.   [38] Ibid., ch. 10.

a man's hat in t e lobby to scare burglars to Miss Matty's speech about Lady Glenmire's engagement.

> I don't mean to deny that men are troublesome in a house. I don't judge from my own experience, for, my father was neatness itself, and wiped his shoes on coming in as care-fully as any woman; but still a man has a sort of know-ledge of what should be done in difficulties, that it is very pleasant to have one at hand ready to lean upon.[39]

It is against this background of frustration that Elizabeth Gaskell presents her brightest portrait of sexual fulfilment in the unlikely form of the romance of Lady Glenmire and Mr Hoggins. In all her accounts of seduction and wedded love she comes nowhere as near to indicating a woman's sexual needs as she does in this sweet rather absurd little story. Lady Glenmire, widow of a Scottish peer, comes to stay with her sister-in-law, the Hon Mrs Jamieson, doyenne of Cranford, and her advent is heralded by a great deal of snobbish fluster, and a resentment on the part of the less well-born inhabitants who have not been asked to meet her ladyship, which makes them dependent on the description of her given by the servant Martha.

> Very bright, black eyes she had, ma'am, and a pleasant, sharp face;. not over young, ma'am, but yet, I should guess, younger than Mrs. Jamieson herself. She looked up and down the church, like a bird, and nipped up her petti-coats, when she came out, as quick and sharp as ever I see.[40]

This impression of vitality, indeed of friskiness, is confirmed when the Cranford ladies do eventually meet Lady Glenmire, and she becomes very popular. The story of her love affair is most skilfully told, with all manner of clues planted, to be interpreted retrospectively. That bird-like survey of the congregation, for example, must have included Mr Hoggins, a noticeable man, and the brisk nipping-up of petticoats may well have been a reaction to his manly presence.

As the local doctor Mr Hoggins has been in and out of the story from the beginning. He stands for a virility alien to Cranford, a sort of farmyard quality. His boots smell of the stable. We are conscious of his body: his back is broad; he

[39] Ibid.   [40] Ibid., ch. 8.

crosses his legs as he sits which upsets the ladies. It is his hat that Miss Pole hangs up in her hall to keep the burglars away. And when all is finally revealed, his successful courtship is described in animal terms. Mrs Jamieson goes to Cheltenham and Lady Glenmire remains in charge of the house, ostensibly to stop the maid-servants from picking up followers.

> It turned out that a servant of Mrs. Jamieson's had been ill, and Mr. Hoggins had been attending her for some weeks. So the wolf had got into the fold, and now he was carrying off the shepherdess.[41]

The description of the engaged couple at church glows with sex.

> Her face seemed to have almost something of the flush of youth in it; her lips looked redder and more trembling full than in their old compressed state, and her eyes dwelt on all things with a lingering light, as if she was learning to love Cranford and its belongings. Mr. Hoggins looked broad and radiant, and creaked up the middle aisle at church in a brand-new pair of top-boots.[42]

The same unequivocal radiance suffuses the account of their first visit to church as Mr and Mrs Hoggins, with 'the smiling glory of his face, and all the becoming blushes of hers'.[43] And they live happily ever after.

The effect of the marriage on the spinsters of Cranford is as carefully worked out as the story itself. The chief public reaction is one of relief that the lightning has struck elsewhere, mingled with alarm that it should have got so close.

> 'Marry!' said Miss Matty once again. 'Well! I never thought of it. Two people that we know going to be married. It's coming very near!'
> 'So near that my heart stopped beating when I heard of it, while you might have counted twelve,' said Miss Pole.
> 'One does not know whose turn may come next. Here, in Cranford, poor Lady Glenmire might have thought herself safe,' said Miss Matty with gentle pity in her tones.'

But the ladies see in the affair elements not only of danger

[41] Ibid., ch. 12.   [42] Ibid.   [43] Ibid., ch. 15.

but of degradation, and this not merely because of Mr Hoggins's inferior rank.

'You and I, Miss Matty, would have been ashamed to have known that our marriage was spoken of in a grocer's shop, in the hearing of shopmen!'
'But,' said Miss Matty, sighing as one recovering from a blow, 'perhaps it is not true. Perhaps we are doing her injustice.'

And there are even worse elements. Miss Pole goes as far as any Victorian lady would dare in commenting on Lady Glenmire's sexiness.

Well, there is a kind of attraction about Lady Glenmire that I, for one, should be ashamed to have.[44]

But private reaction is different and more complicated. It is inextricably linked with the story of Signor Brunoni which Mrs Gaskell so scrupulously interweaves with the Hoggins–Glenmire story. A wave of burglary – though greatly exaggerated, the reports have some truth in them – soon after the visit of Signor Brunoni, conjuror and foreigner, leads to the assumption that he must be at the bottom of it. The ensuing panic causes that very departure of Mrs Jamieson's to Cheltenham which opens the door to Mr Hoggins; it also causes the rumour that Mr Hoggins has been set upon by robbers, a rumour which he denies, as does Lady Glenmire – with suspicious vehemence, only nobody does suspect.

The burglar scare is scotched once and for all when Lady Glenmire and Miss Pole discover Signor Brunoni, who has been lying injured for six weeks at an inn three miles from Cranford after a road accident. Lady Glenmire is actively kind and goes personally to Mr Hoggins to beg for help and when the Signor is brought back to lodgings in Cranford she

undertook the medical department under Mr. Hoggins's directions, and rummaged up all Mrs. Jamieson's medicine glasses, and spoons, and bed-tables, in a free-and-easy way.[45]

Both Lady Glenmire and Mr Hoggins are unwearyingly kind in their attentions to Brunoni and his family, and what Emma Woodhouse hoped for in throwing Harriet and Mr

[44] Ibid., ch. 12.   [45] Ibid., ch. 11.

158

Elton together on an errand of mercy actually happens to the later couple.

In the course of all this the Brunonis are revealed as Mr and Mrs Sam Brown, a couple whose marital story is one of hardship, bereavement and mutual fidelity. It is their circumstances, common enough to married people, that bring a note of reality into the high-flown terrors of the Cranford spinsters. Miss Matty takes the ball she has been rolling under her bed at night in case there should be a man hiding there and covers it in rainbow stripes for little Phoebe Brown to play with. And when, about the same time, Miss Pole speaks disparagingly of the effects of matrimony, attributing Lady Glenmire's credulity (in backing up Mr Hoggins's denial of the burglars) to the fact that she has been married, Miss Matty in a burst of honesty confides to Mary Smith that night her own past dream of having a husband and children.

Cranford ends with the saving arrival of a man on the scene, Peter Jenkyns, Miss Matty's long-lost brother. It is as though her honesty, so much greater than that of the other single women, is rewarded. He is not a husband, it is true, but he is a protector, a companion, a financial support and a restorer of harmony to the whole of Cranford, even inducing Mrs Jamieson to speak to the fallen, radiant, impenitent Mrs Hoggins.

Throughout the book Mary Smith, the narrator, is presented, unobtrusively, as a foil to the self-deceiving frustrated spinsters. Her views on marriage are sane and for those days advanced. When confronted simultaneously with Miss Pole's dire warnings against wedlock and the history of the poor struggling Brunonis she comments:

> If I had been inclined to be daunted from matrimony, it would not have been Miss Pole to do it; it would have been the lot of poor Signor Brunoni and his wife.[46]

It is not easy to deduce from Mrs Gaskell's novels what kind of women she approved of, since she deals with her women characters on an ad hoc basis, which makes Jane Austen and Charlotte Brontë by comparison seem to write from a network of preconceptions. Mrs Gaskell's compassion and tolerance as a woman are two of her chief characteristics

[46] Ibid.

as a writer; she could present as attractive in a girl qualities which she personally shunned. On the subject of female education, for example; she proved in the upbringing of her own daughters what store she set by it, yet in Sylvia Robson she presents with sympathy and understanding a pretty girl who is not only completely illiterate but who wishes to remain so and repels all attempts at instruction that come her way. Of course the direction from which they principally come, that is, her cousin Philip, is a factor in her reluctance but not the whole story; without being lazy – in fact she is an energetic girl – she seems to have a pure and simple desire to be ignorant. 'Well! if I mun be taught, I mun; but I'd rayther be whipped and ha' done with it', sums up her general attitude.

When the lessons actually begin her recalcitrance continues.

'My fingers is stiff,' pleaded Sylvia, holding up her little hand and shaking it.
'Let us take a turn at spelling, then,' said Philip.
'What's t'use on't?' asked captious Sylvia.
'Why, it helps one i' reading and writing.'
'And what does reading and writing do for one?'[47]

She makes Catherine Morland seem like a Senior Wrangler. But she is not inept at everything; her housewifery is particularly good. And she is not stupid; she is quick to sense her father's danger after his fight with the press-gang, much quicker than he is. Her attitude to book-learning, however, quite reverses the teacher/pupil relation established by Charlotte Brontë and Jane Austen, where the woman learns from the man in an atmosphere of loving protection and dependence. Philip's reactions are perfectly normal: 'It was very delightful to stand in the relation of teacher to so dear and pretty, if so wilful, a pupil'; but Silvia will not play – or rather she will do nothing else.

That some men do not like well-educated women Mrs Gaskell would not deny. Dr Gibson in *Wives and Daughters* arranges for his daughter to have as little education as possible.

Don't teach Molly too much; she must sew, and read, and write, and do her sums; but I want to keep her a child,

[47] *Sylvia's Lovers*, ch. 8.

and if I find more learning desirable for her, I'll see about giving it to her myself. After all, I'm not sure that reading and writing is necessary. Many a good woman gets married with only a cross instead of her name; it's rather a diluting of mother-wit, to my fancy.[48]

In the event the passage is trebly ironical. Dr Gibson's powers of judgement and his worldly wisdom are soon shown to have a fatally blind spot; he chooses precisely the wrong woman as his second wife. Yet Mrs Gibson almost proves him right in his condemnation of literacy in women; one of her most aggravating characteristics is her parade of ill-digested reading with its misquotations and failures of memory. And Molly will grow up to marry one of the most intelligent men in England and will need every bit of education she can get if only, according to the Victorian ideal for women, to keep up with him.

Cousin Phillis, so subtle a story in every way, presents this subject with delicate irony and some ambiguity. Minister Holman is a learned man; his wife is

a purely motherly woman, whose intellect had never been cultivated, and whose loving heart was entirely occupied with her husband, her child, her household affairs and, perhaps, a little with the concerns of the members of her husband's congregation because they in a way belonged to her husband.

She is sensitive about her shortcomings in spite of her husband's tact.

I had noticed before that she had fleeting shadows of jealousy even of Phillis, when her daughter and her husband appeared to have strong interests and sympathies in things which were quite beyond her comprehension. I had noticed it in my first acquaintance with them, I say, and had admired the delicate tact which made the minister, on such occasions, bring the conversation back to such subjects as those on which his wife, with her practical experience of everyday life, was an authority.[49]

Mrs Holman tries to make affection compensate for lack of understanding.

[48] *Wives and Daughters*, ch. 3.   [49] *Cousin Phillis*, pt. 3.

'Go on, minister,' she said; 'it is very interesting what you are reading about, and when I don't understand it, I like the sound of your voice.'

But how successful this unequal marriage really is we are left to decide for ourselves. Certainly there is something claustrophobic about the ménage and even a suggestion of abnormality in the way the daughter Phillis, aged seventeen, is treated as a baby in emotional matters. When her father discovers her love for Mr Holdsworth, he seems utterly bewildered, though in fact it is the most natural thing in the world.

> Phillis! did we not make you happy here? Have we not loved you enough? ... You would have left us, left your home, left your father and mother, and gone away with this stranger, wandering over the world.[50]

Intellectually she is credited with being her age; her father, no doubt trying to provide himself, in the daughter, with an intellectual companionship which the wife cannot supply, has taught her Latin and Greek, and, quite unlike Sylvia Robson, she has a natural taste for learning and enjoys it. When Mr Holdsworth comes on the scene it is love not only of him but of education that makes her gladly accept him as a kind of supplementary teacher.

> He directed her studies into new paths, he patiently drew out the expression of many of her thoughts, and perplexities, and unformed theories.[51]

Phillis is the archetypal bluestocking, humourless and deadly literal, as in this dialogue after her first meeting with Holdsworth.

> 'Don't you think him handsome?' asked I.
> 'Perhaps – yes – I have hardly looked at him,' she replied.
> 'But is not he very like a foreigner?'
> 'Yes, he cuts his hair foreign fashion,' said I.
> 'I like an Englishman to look like an Englishman.'
> 'I don't think he thinks about it. He says he began that way when he was in Italy, because everybody wore it so, and it is natural to keep it on in England.'

[50] Ibid., pt. 4.   [51] Ibid., pt. 3.

'Not if he began it in Italy because everybody wore it so. Everybody here wears it differently.'[52]

The narrator, Paul Manning, is an unattractive boy. Those in his own walk of life are all too polite to say so, of course, but the outspoken servant Betty – Elizabeth Gaskell often ropes in the staff when a few home truths are artistically necessary – tells him, and us:

It's a caution to a man how he goes about beguiling. Some men do it as easy and innocent as cooing doves. Don't you be none of 'em, my lad. Not that you've got the gifts to do it, either; you're no great shakes to look at, neither for figure, not yet for face, and it would need be a deaf adder to be taken in wi' your words, though there may be no great harm in 'em.[53]

There we are, and it is as well to be sure, but much earlier in the book we have suspected it, from the following conversation between Paul and his father, who wants him to marry her.

'You see she's so clever – she's more like a man than a woman – she knows Latin and Greek.'
'She'd forget 'em, if she'd a houseful of children' was my father's comment on this . . .
'I don't think I should like to have a wife taller than I am, father,' said I smiling.[54]

So on this point Elizabeth Gaskell leaves us in a state of fruitful uncertainty as to what she or anyone in the novel really thinks about this particular educated woman, the heroine.

The situation of woman in the home, obviously a topic closely related to female education, she displays with her usual accuracy, not at particular length, but as a necessary part of the background. To take the Robson household, for example: Daniel Robson is an obtuse, stupid and childish man, who despises the company and conversation of women: 'They talk so foolish it gets int' bones like.' Bell, his wife has been conditioned to the extent that

she really believed her husband to have the serious and important occupation for his mind that she had been taught

[52] Ibid., pt. 2.   [53] Ibid., pt. 4.   [54] Ibid., pt. 2.

to consider befitting the superior intellect of the masculine gender.[55]

And it was not only her upbringing as a girl; her husband continued the indoctrination. Mrs Gaskell distinctly states that Bell 'was in fact superior to him' but he imagined he ruled her with 'a wise and absolute sway',[56] and he had from the beginning of his marriage 'made his place and position clear as the arbiter and law-giver of his household',[57] with the disastrous result that after his execution the household did in fact collapse, though the ones who were left were perfectly capable of running it, had they ever been allowed any co-operation in the past.

Mrs Gaskell, as we know, was against husband-worshipping. (She saw the dangers of wife-worshipping with equal clarity; after all *Sylvia's Lovers* was originally going to be called *Philip's Idol*.) *Mr. Harrison's Confession*, a slight tale in itself, introduces the point, forcefully though in passing. *Lizzie Leigh* shows at somewhat greater length how a woman can, and indeed should, differ from her husband on a question of right or wrong if she does so from genuine principle. But in *Ruth* we have a sustained account of how not only one woman but two, wife and daughter, rebel against the head of the household and set their own judgement up against his and are approved of for doing so. When Mr Bradshaw hears of Ruth's past his coarse and savage indignation bursts out uncontrollably, but Jemima, though for so many months she has disliked Ruth through jealousy, now as a matter of justice supports her with the greatest courage, standing beside her and holding her hand in the full path of her father's wrath.[58] Mrs Bradshaw's turn comes later, when Mr Bradshaw casts off their son Richard for forgery and embezzlement. Her reaction is an entirely emotional one. She comes to Mr Benson in a state of collapse and makes the following declaration:

> I have been a good wife till now. I know I have. I have done all he bid me, ever since we were married. But now I will say to everybody how cruel he is – how hard to his own flesh and blood! If he puts poor Dick in prison, I will

[55] *Sylvia's Lovers*, ch. 11.
[56] Ibid., ch. 22.   [57] Ibid., ch. 25.
[58] *Ruth*, ch. 27.

go too. If I'm to choose between my husband and my son, I choose my son.[59]

The two acts of rebellion are very different from each other. Jemima's is the result of long thought and close observation; and when the immediate emergency is over she decides that she must obey her father's decree that she should not visit Ruth, though she keeps in touch with her through a third party. Mrs Bradshaw's rebellion is the turning of the worm. It is interesting to compare her with the Jane Austen mothers in the hour of their children's disgrace. Mrs Bennett supports Lydia simply because she cannot take in that she has done anything wrong. Lady Bertram, 'guided by Sir Thomas', gives up Maria for lost; it is the odious Mrs Norris who stands by her.

Mrs Gaskell can admire women who are strong-minded and self-reliant in physical as well as moral issues. In Mary Barton we have a heroine who, in her venturesome pursuit of the ship on which the witness who can save Jem's life is sailing way, is almost an anticipation of the tomboy heroine of later Victorian fiction. But the case is complicated by the fact that Mary is a working-class girl and moreover a city dweller, and, though surprisingly naïve about some things, for example, Henry Carson's intentions, she can be supposed not to need the sheltering and protection that a lady would. Even so, over the whole pursuit sequence there hangs a sense of her frailty. 'I am so helpless, so weak, but a poor girl after all.' And after the strain of the trial she falls ill with the brain fever so dear to Victorian novelists as a symbol of feminine delicacy. Jem, the accused, recovers at a bound and is anxious to stress her weakness.

'Thou'rt not fit to be trusted home by thyself,' said he, with fond exaggeration of her helplessness.[60]

It is an interesting remark: if she had really been so feeble, he would already have been hanged.

Margaret Hale is a lady and cannot be expected to thread her way through strange rough cities, accost tough sailors at the quayside and get herself rowed down the river in an open boat as Mary Barton does, but in a way more appro-

priate to her station she seems just such a heroine, braving

[59] Ibid., ch. 31.   [60] *Mary Barton*, ch. 35.

physical danger to protect the man she loves. The central incident in *North and South* is the riot where Margaret throws herself in front of Mr Thornton the mill-owner and is hit by the stone aimed at him by one of the strikers. The beautiful girl deliberately taking the arrow, bullet or other missile meant for the hero is a commonplace of fiction, whether in the form of film, opera, novel or poem. Mrs Gaskell liked it well enough herself to use it elsewhere, in the short story *The Heart of John Middleton*, though the circumstances there are different: for example, the event is precipitated by the man's going to the rescue of the girl.

Margaret's heroism has many interesting ambiguities. In the first place it is partly the product of a guilty conscience: it is her bossy, bullying speech to Thornton, to the effect that it is his manly duty to go down to speak to the rioters, that puts him in danger to begin with.[61] Secondly, she quite deliberately exploits her sex: her bravery is founded on her belief that the mob will not hurt a woman. She says as much to Mr Thornton later:

> We all feel the sanctity of our sex as a high privilege when we see danger ... Any woman, worthy of the name of woman, would come forward to shield, with her reverenced helplessness, a man in danger from the violence of numbers.[62]

And, thirdly, she declares she would have done as much for anyone. But even Thornton's stupid sister Fanny sees through that, and Thornton himself thinks otherwise, to the extent of coming round to propose, and though he allows himself to be put down at the time he is proved right in the last chapter when she comes to the rescue again, financially, and this time faces her own motives.

But the relief of heroism cannot be allowed to many of Mrs Gaskell's women. Their rôle is still the traditional one of helpless waiting. Even Mary Barton endures some periods of it at the time of Jem's trial, in the same way that earlier in the book she and Margaret have watched the mill fire in impotent agony while Jem performs his daring rescues high in the air above them. But the most excruciating account of what women suffer because of the passivity which has been assigned to them comes in *Sylvia's Lovers*. When Daniel

[61] *North and South*, ch. 22.   [62] Ibid., ch. 24.

Robson is taken off to the Assizes at York to be tried for his actions against the press-gang, the forty-mile journey seems quite impracticable to his wife and daughter and they wait at home. The relevant chapters are aptly called *A Dreary Vigil* and *Gloomy Days*. As the possibility that Daniel may be hanged steals over Sylvia and eventually over her mother, a darkness full of nightmares falls on Haytersbank Farm. Mrs Robson decays mentally and physically from week to week, the cold March wind blows and the hours drag on till the day of the trial and then seem to stop altogether as Bell and Sylvia wait for news of the verdict to be brought from York.

> 'Will this day niver come to an end?' cried Bell plaintively.
> 'Oh, mother! it'll come to an end some time, niver fear. I've heerd say –
>
> > Be the day weary or be the day long,
> > At length it ringeth to evensong.'
>
> 'To evensong – to evensong', repeated Bell. 'D'ye think now that evensong means death, Sylvie?'
> 'I canot tell – I cannot bear it. Mother,' said Sylvia, in despair, 'I'll make some clap-bread: that's a heavy job, and will while away t'afternoon.'
> 'Ay do, do!' replied the mother. 'He'll like it fresh – he'll like it fresh.'[63]

This is harrowing enough, but at least Sylvia does have bread-making to turn to. The situation of idle rich ladies presents no such relief and when trouble overtakes them, as in the case of Mrs Carson, their lot is pitiable indeed. Even before the murder of her son, she is represented as being in a state of chronic malaise, due to not having enough to do. She was a factory girl before her marriage, and now

> without education enough to value the resources of wealth and leisure, she was so circumstanced as to command both. It would have done her more good than all the ether and sal-volatile she was daily in the habit of swallowing, if she might have taken the work of one of her own house-maids for a week.

Not that her daughters, who have been brought up to wealth

---

[63] *Sylvia's Lovers*, ch. 27.

and leisure, seem to have a much more exciting way of employing it. Here they are whiling away the time until the tea-hour:

> One tried to read 'Emerson's Essays' and fell asleep in the attempt; the other was turning over a parcel of new songs, in order to select what she liked. Amy, the youngest, was copying some manuscript music.[64]

All this is not so far from John Barton's bitterly satirical picture of

> a do-nothing lady, worrying shopmen all morning, and screeching at her pianny all afternoon, and going to bed without having done a good turn to any one of God's creatures but herself.[65]

Even the much gentler observations of Ruth bear him out; while she is staying in the Welsh village with Mrs Bellingham she notices the complete inability of the gentry to amuse themselves on a wet day though the village women are as busy as in fine weather.

We have already seen, from Mrs Gaskell's letters, that she considers genuine work of some kind to be essential to well-being. When Margaret Hale at the end of *North and South* inherits a fortune all her friends and relations expect her to sit back decoratively and wait for a husband. The strenuous social work on which she in fact embarks is admittedly rather frenetic, because she is not happy, but Mrs Gaskell always presents energy attractively, even if it is overdone. The laziness of Mrs Kirkpatrick in *Wives and Daughter* is one of the bad marks against her, assigned quite early in the book. She marries Dr Gibson principally in order to stop working and indeed cleverly hastens on the date of the wedding so as to avoid even a few more weeks of running her school, a task at which, through sheer lack of effort, we gather, she has conspicuously failed. Throughout the book she is always having little naps and putting her feet up, and her last recorded words are:

> And now cover me up close, and let me go to sleep, and dream about my dear Cynthia and my new shawl![66]

[64] *Mary Barton*, ch. 18.   [65] Ibid., ch. 1.
[66] *Wives and Daughters*, ch. 60.

168

But Mrs Gaskell is realistic in presenting the kinds of work available to women; realistic in two ways. She is fully aware of the daunting limitations of choice and prospects that they face: in *Sylvia's Lovers* when John and Jeremiah Foster are planning their retirement they decide to make their very prosperous shop over to Philip Hepburn and William Coulson, who have been serving in it; there is no question of taking Hester Rose into partnership though she has been working alongside the two men; her only chance is to marry one of them. But Mrs Gaskell is not always so tragic about the work itself. Governessing, for example: Mrs Kirkpatrick had a delightful life as governess at The Towers. True it would only have been delightful to a sycophantic snob, but as she was a sycophantic snob, it suited her excellently, and though she was patronised by the Cumnors she met with none of the disdain and mental cruelty that Charlotte Brontë describes so harrowingly, and long after she has left her post she is still remembered and treated with something like affection by the family. Her daughter Cynthia has positively romantic ideas about governessing – only it would have to be in Russia – as a way of escape from the self-imposed complications of her own life. Miss Matty asserts that she would have enjoyed being a governess because of her love of children.

Mrs Gaskell is also conscious that not all sempstresses have the terrible time experienced by Ruth and, in real life, by the many exploited girls whose cause she supported. Miss Jessie Brown, in *Cranford*, left destitute and unaware that Major Gordon is on his rescuing way, contemplates earning her living by her needle and is not indignantly headed off the idea by Miss Jenkyns as she is when she considers serving in a shop; and Miss Jessie is a lady. Mary Barton, who is not, facing the possibilities of either factory work, or domestic service or becoming a dressmaker's apprentice, choses the last, on the grounds that it gives her greater independence, as it clearly does, and is not as dirty as housework. Libbie Marsh, heroine of the short story *Libbie Marsh's Three Eras*, is a sempstress and quite likes her work. And even factory work is seen to have some compensations. The bold, independent bearing of the mill girls in *Mary Barton*, coarse and raucous as they sometimes are, seems to be a step in the right direction.

It is hardly surprising that Mrs Gaskell's ideas about working women show, by modern standards or even by later Victorian standards, certain lacunae. She dislikes the idea of working wives. She does not expect working girls to be interested in the ideals and activities of the Unions. And her completest picture of a working woman, that of Miss Galindo in *My Lady Ludlow*, almost betrays the cause as it is so much of a caricature as to rob the subject of much of its seriousness. And finally, there is her far from progressive idealisation of woman as nurse, which recalls Elizabeth Barrett Browning's comment: 'Every man is on his knees before ladies carrying lint.' In *Ruth* she regards nursing in the traditional light of some kind of saintly ministration, yet she knew both the Mrs Gamps of her world and also the attempts of Florence Nightingale to turn nursing into a proper profession. Ruth, whom we have seen in two types of work – miserable as a sempstress, happy as a governess – seems as a nurse to be not so much working as blessing and redeeming.

If one had to decide which quality in women Mrs Gaskell most admired it would be honesty, though perhaps 'wished to admire' or 'wished to understand' would be more accurate. Obviously the subject intrigued her, but obviously she was confused by it. We get the impression that in her novels she is grasping for a definition of female honesty; she certainly has trouble in reconciling it with the devious behaviour necessary to the coquetry which was thought proper, even by herself, to marriageable young women. (She was less lenient to middle-aged widows such as Mrs Kirkpatrick.) Nowhere has her confusion been better explored than by Mr P. N. Furbank in his essay 'Mendacity in Mrs. Gaskell'[67] where he shows her in *North and South* tying up both herself and her heroine Margaret Hale in knots of duplicity, all in the artistic and moral cause of trying to present Margaret as an open and unaffected girl. It is as though, he says, the ladies of Cranford with all their subterfuges and dishonesties have edited this other book, the great difference being that here the insincerities are not acknowledged to be such. 'Miss Matty seems to have taken a hand in *North and South*.'

Mr Furbank stresses that the upbringing to which girls of that time were subjected was at the root of the problem and he is right to do so. We find other examples in *Wives*

[67] *Encounter*, May 1973.

170

and Daughters, and they cut both ways. Molly Gibson, the sweetest and most unaffected of girls, behaves to Roger Hamley, a kind and straightforward man, in a woundingly off-hand way for a whole week while she is staying at his father's house, because she has overheard their names being coupled together by the town gossip. She loves him and, now that his previous engagement has been broken off, is free to do so, but the maidenly modesty in which she has been trained makes her behave in this stupidly insincere and self-defeating way. Her step-sister Cynthia Kirkpatrick, on the other hand, is a double-crosser by temperament and inclination who, while she is still in her teens, has established quite a pattern of getting engaged to one man before she has thoroughly broken off with his predecessor. She is one of the most efficient and heartless flirts in the Victorian novel. The following is a typical incident in her career. One lover, who has called on her, is looking out of the window into the garden when 'a sudden deep colour overspread him':

> Cynthia and Mr. Henderson had come in sight; he eagerly talking to her as he bent forward to look into her face; she, her looks half averted in pretty shyness, was evidently coquetting about some flowers, which she either would not give, or would not take.[68]

All perfectly acceptable, indeed obligatory, feminine behaviour. Yet the remarkable fact is that Cynthia is perhaps the least hypocritical girl, and the one with most self-knowledge, that we meet before the twentieth-century novel. In an age when filial affection was a dutiful cliché, she admits she does not love her mother and explains accurately why not, without unnecessarily blaming either her mother or herself. She knows her own failings precisely, enumerates them when it is relevant to do so but without exhibitionism, and is surprisingly aware of their origin and probable outcome. She has not lost the power to love, as is proved by her affectionate behaviour to Molly when she is ill; leaving a smart London party and travelling down to the country by the overnight coach is no light proof of warm-heartedness. But she has lost sight of the moral rules. Her touching speech to Molly sums it all up:

[68] *Wives and Daughters*, ch. 56.

Don't you see I have grown up outside the pale of duty and 'oughts'. Love me as I am, sweet one, for I shall never be better.[69]

Cynthia is charming and good-mannered to everybody, except her mother, but even when a pretty girl such as Sylvia Robson behaves pettishly and ungratefully – as in her reception of the polite old Foster brothers' offer of refreshment[70] – Mrs Gaskell somehow manages to excuse her by making her response seem at least more honest than the eternally controlled and correct reactions of Hester Rose.

Elizabeth Gaskell's fascination with female honesty can be seen even more clearly when contrasted with the attitude of Jane Austen. For both novelists inferior women are automatically dishonest – Lucy Steele, Mrs Bennet, Mrs Gibson. But Jane Austen often tolerates crass dishonesty from a heroine without apparently noticing it. When Emma is told of the secret engagement of Frank Churchill and Jane Fairfax, her distress is real enough, because of what she has said to one about the other, but both Mrs Weston and Mr Knightley attribute it to the dashing of her hopes of marrying Frank herself. She reassures them, on separate occasions, but by means of two different stories which cannot both be true. To convince Mrs Weston she says that there was a time when she did love Frank but that time has long since passed away. To Mr Knightley she declares she has never loved Frank. The reader knows that the story she tells Mrs Weston is more accurate than the story she tells her future husband. No one could blame her, but Jane Austen seems not to notice the discrepancy.

It is hardly necessary to add that Elizabeth Gaskell could not go as far as to allow feminine frankness to declare love. (We are still waiting for George Eliot.) When Mary Barton realises after having rejected Jem's proposal that she does love him, there follows the usual protracted and ridiculous situation where 'the whisperings of a womanly nature' prevent Mary from even hinting to Jem what he would be so delighted to hear. But in this case Elizabeth Gaskell excels even Jane Austen in resourcefulness. When Mary is in the witness box at Jem's trial she can and does make an eloquent avowal of her love, for, of course, when you are giving

[69] Ibid., ch. 20.   [70] *Sylvia's Lovers*, ch. 3.

evidence you *must* tell the truth, the whole truth and nothing but the truth, and the prosecuting counsel, 'a pert young barrister', *happens* to question her about her personal feelings. So out it all comes.[71] Poor Hester Rose, of *Sylvia's Lovers*, who is in love with Philip Hepburn remains the unwilling companion of patience on the monument and is given no such opportunity as Mary; true, Philip had no active wish to hear such an avowal from her, but it might have affected him (as Benedick was affected), to the happiness of all.

The Lie was as great a standby to Victorian fiction as the Will or the Secret. Most of Mrs Gaskell's plots contain an important Lie. Some are white, some black. Job Legh is surely meant to be forgiven for telling Jem's mother the night before the trial that the crucial witness has been found, so that she may get some rest. Mr Benson, though he blames himself, is probably not blamed by the readers for concealing Ruth's past and presenting her to his friends and congregation as a young widow, and he is certainly more sympathetic than Mr Bradshaw, who refuses to hush up his son's forgery and embezzling, and indeed goes round imploring the young man's victims to prosecute him. The unforgivable lie, which takes the form of the deliberate concealment of a vital piece of knowledge, is Philip Hepburn's suppression of Charley's message to Sylvia as his rival is dragged off by the press-gang.

But these lies are uttered by men and are judged simply by their motivation and the degree of harm they cause. For lying women the situation is complicated by the fact of their sex. Margaret Hale's lie in *North and South* – a serious but necessary one as the life of her brother seems to depend on it – leads to a long train of emotional developments solely because of the maidenly modesty which prevents her from explaining matters to a young man who is in love with her. Perhaps the most interesting lie of all is that of Mrs Kirkpatrick, later to be Mrs Gibson, at the very beginning of *Wives and Daughters*.[72] Little Molly Gibson who has turned faint in the park on an expedition to The Towers, has a tray of food brought out to her by Mrs Kirkpatrick who, when Molly is too weak to eat anything, clears the whole lot herself – quite reasonable if mildly greedy behaviour. But when the Countess's daughter, seeing the empty tray comments rather

---

[71] *Mary Barton*, ch. 32.
[72] *Wives and Daughters*, ch. 2.

nastily that probably all that is wrong with the child is over-eating, Mrs Kirkpatrick serenely gives no word of explanation and Molly is greatly distressed. We know Mrs Kirkpatrick from that moment onwards. Ladies are supposed to pick at their food, so in front of a Countess's daughter she does not hesitate to let the blame rest on a child who is too young and scared and unwell to speak up for herself. Trivial as this example may seem it sums up the sort of female dishonesty that Mrs Gaskell despised. The ladies of Cranford, by contrast, with their polite pretences which deceive nobody and harm nobody, seem a very straightforward set, like schoolboys, or indeed grown men, acting according to some accepted code.

Chapter V

Of the four writers in question George Eliot has the highest faith in the potential of women and the deepest distrust in the likelihood of its realisation. The English domestic setting is most often the enemy. The strivings of Maggie Tulliver in *The Mill on the Floss* (1860) to do and be something more than her womanhood seems to allow her are doomed from the start by the nature of the background. So are Dorothea's in *Middlemarch* (1871–2): 'How can one ever do anything nobly Christian, living among people with such petty thoughts ?'[1] *Romola* (1862–3) gives its heroine more scope, as the action takes place far away and long ago, and moreover the novel as a whole, with the totally unconvincing pastiche that passes for dialogue and its ton-weight of erudition about, for example, the sort of hats and belts that people wore then, has a place for the unrealistic gestures of high, romantic endeavour which would hardly seem natural in St Ogg's, or in Tipton and Lowick. Romola can become the sainted lady who does 'beautiful loving deeds' of rescue and relief. But the idea of the high quest, the lofty important mission that can be carried out by a woman, is most thoroughly declared in a long poem, *The Spanish Gypsy* – and it is relevant to remember Maggie's childish attempt to be leader of a gypsy band – first written in 1864–5 and amplified a few years later.

In fact, Romola's mission, though differently motivated, is not really much more dashing than that of Mrs Gaskell's Ruth. But Fedalma, heroine of *The Spanish Gypsy,* is a real high-flier, with a rôle to play as grand as that of any of Racine's heroines, though expressed in decidedly less lofty poetry. But however much we may deplore George Eliot's verse, we can still be grateful that the story is told in this medium, as it is presumably why she feels free to show the heroic spirit of woman demonstrating itself in actions that do not have to be adapted to the limitations of polite provincial

[1] *Middlemarch*, ch. 4.

society, but can be openly and indisputably heroic on a grand scale.

Fedalma, though her future as the wife of Duke Silva, whom she dearly loves, seems so bright, feels trapped from the beginning in the feminine part she has to play. She has recurrent dreams of flying off the battlements of the castle and escaping, and when, on the night before their intended marriage, the Duke dresses her up in all the jewels she will inherit as his wife, she feels sympathy with the gems.

> Their prisoned souls are throbbing like my own.
> Perchance they loved once, were ambitious, proud;
> Or do they only dream of wider life,
> Ache from intenseness, yearn to burst the wall
> Compact of crystal splendour, and to flood
> Some wider space with glory? Poor, poor gems!
> We must be patient in our prison-house
> And find our space in loving.[2]

Opportunity knocks, however, and disconcertingly soon, with the appearance of Zarca, the captive gypsy leader, who claims Fedalma as his daughter, stolen from him in childhood by the Spaniards, and destined to lead the tribe after his death. Fedalma responds to his claim, but her first idea is that she will marry the Duke and then coax him into releasing the gypsies. Zarca fiercely condemns these feminine methods as 'almsdeeds fit for holidays' and reproaches her for the dishonesty of such wiles.

> A woman's dream – who thinks by smiling well
> To ripen figs in frost. What! marry first
> And then proclaim your birth? Enslave yourself
> To use your freedom? Share another's name,
> Then treat it as you will?

Fedalma is convinced by this rebuke, but is still uncertain that the good he proposes for their tribe will be a genuine benefit.

> O father, will the women of our tribe
> Suffer as I do, in the years to come
> When you have made them great in Africa?
> Redeemed from ignorant ills only to feel
> A conscious woe?[3]

[2] *The Spanish Gypsy*, bk. 1.　　　[3] Ibid.

However, she finally leaves the castle with him. Her dream of escape has become reality; ironically, because she is heartbroken at having to leave Silva. Nevertheless, it is escape, as Silva, even in his distress on reading her farewell letter, acknowledges by saying, 'she has gone into free air'.

The course of Fedalma's life from now on is neither happy nor straightforward. The gypsies accept her as their queen and future leader; the fact that she is a woman presents no problem. But her own womanly feelings do: she cannot respond whole-heartedly to her mission. Zarca is for ever making grandiloquent speeches about the greatness of her vocation and keeps congratulating her on her fortunate release from a life of comfort and repose.

> The worst of misery
> Is when a nature framed for noblest things
> Condemns itself in youth to petty joys,
> And, sore athirst for air, breathes scanty life
> Gasping from out the shallows. You are saved
> From such poor doubleness. The life we choose
> Breathes high, and sees a full-arched firmament.
> Our deeds shall speak like rock-hewn messages
> Teaching great purpose to the distant time.[4]

But though she will, we gather, always be loyal to her destiny, she regards it in much the same spirit that impels Dorothea as she approaches the summer-house to make her promise to Casaubon: a sad, dutiful, unenthusiastic acceptance, not in the least like the attitude of Daniel Deronda setting out on his mission.

It is interesting that George Eliot, who laments so eloquently in *Middlemarch* that women have no opportunity for heroic deeds, when she does give a heroine such an opportunity hedges it with ambiguities. For it is not only Fedalma's attitude that taints the glory of the enterprise, but also the suggestion that it is doomed to failure. Fedalma is not going to be able adequately to carry out her father's project any more than Dorothea could have made something coherent or useful out of Casaubon's *Key*.

In some ways the picture of what the heroines settle for is less melancholy in the novels of English provincial life. No really worthwhile fulfilment of their aspirations is ever

4 Ibid., bk 3.

offered to them, consequently they have none of Fedalma's disillusionment to cope with. One by one they relapse quite gracefully into states of negation. Janet Dempster, as she walks calmly round the garden after the funeral of Mr Tryan,

> thirsted for no pleasure; she craved no wordly good. She saw the years to come stretch before her like an autumn afternoon, filled with resigned memory. Life to her could never more have any eagerness; it was a solemn service of gratitude and patient effort.[5]

Dinah Morris gives up the preaching which has been so much the driving force of her life as almost to prevent her marrying Adam. It is true that the decision of the Methodist Conference to forbid women preaching is the immediate cause of her sacrifice but, as her brother-in-law Seth points out, she could have joined another religious body that did allow them to. But 'she thought it right to set the example of submitting'. Altogether she sounds rather like Mrs Elton and Lady Middleton giving up music on the occasion of their marriages. The last we see of Romola is her making a home for her husband's mistress and illegitimate children apparently free of any wish for herself. Esther Lyon gives up wealth and position to marry Felix Holt; we are told she never repents doing so, but her life must have been limited and unexciting.

Immediately after Deronda's defection, Gwendolen Harleth's only hope and determination are simply to survive. On the morning of his wedding day, however, he receives a sad letter from her – all the sadder because she keeps urging him not to grieve – which makes it clear that she has sunk into a condition of self-denial and limp yearning to be a better person. And so her story ends. The faint hint that perhaps one day she and her cousin Rex may be united is not very attractive, from either of their points of view.

The fate of Maggie Tulliver is too overtly tragic to be called negative, but there are strong elements of negation in it. She turns away from the love of two adult men and from any hope of future personal happiness to die, ecstatically, in the arms of a loutish cruel brother. Earlier in the book she has said that her first memory was of standing beside the Floss

[5] *Janet's Repentance*, ch. 28.

with her hand in Tom's. George Eliot echoes this in the famous sentence:

> The boat reappeared – but brother and sister had gone down in an embrace never to be parted: living through again in one supreme moment the days when they had clasped their little hands in love, and roamed the daisied fields together.[6]

We have never seen them doing this. In any daisied field that we are shown them roaming in, Tom is bullying and tormenting Maggie. But the sentence is not entirely sentimental. This is Maggie's view of childhood affection and she turns back to it in death with no thought of Stephen Guest or of Philip Wakem.

In terms of melancholy rather than tragedy the worst fate of all is surely that of Dorothea, happy wife of Will Ladislaw and happy mother of his children. How little she settles for. Critics have hopefully pointed out that George Eliot herself glorifies Will in her own imagination and sees something in him as a creature which readers cannot see. But, in fact, she seems to go out of her way to make him as like the idiotic, dilettante Mr Brooke as she can: the resemblance between them is marked and must have been consciously established. Dorothea knows what she is doing.

> It is quite true that I might be a wiser person, Celia, and that I might have done something better, if I had been better. But this is what I am going to do. I have promised to marry Mr. Ladislaw; and I am going to marry him.[7]

George Eliot is perfectly clear-sighted, too, about what her heroine is up to. She calls the act of marrying Ladislaw a 'not ideally beautiful' one. She shows Dorothea resigning all her own plans for cottages and communes and giving 'wifely help' to her husband.

> Many who knew her thought it a pity that so substantive and rare a creature should have been absorbed into the life of another, and be only known in a certain circle as a wife and mother.[8]

Among these many people most of the readers are included.

[6] *The Mill on the Floss*, bk. 7, ch. 5.
[7] *Middlemarch*, ch. 84.   [8] Ibid., finale.

The final sop about the good influence of those who 'lived faithfully a hidden life, and rest in unvisited tombs' almost makes matters worse.

The whole concept of renunciation, as entertained and practised by women, is one which George Eliot analyses very carefully. It takes place in two stages: at first the unsatisfactory nature of a woman's life leads her to renunciation in an unrealistic and almost pleasurable way; later experience also leads her to it, but this time it is painful. The case of Maggie Tulliver shows the two stages very clearly. In the year of harrowing frustration which follows Mr Tulliver's bankruptcy, she comes across Thomas à Kempis's *Imitation of Christ* and instantly feels she has found the secret.

> With all the hurry of an imagination that could never rest in the present, she sat in the deepening twilight forming plans of self-humiliation and entire devotedness; and, in the ardour of first discovery, renunciation seemed to her the entrance into that satisfaction which she had so long been craving in vain. She had not perceived – how could she until she had lived longer? – the inmost truth of the old monk's outpourings, that renunciation remains sorrow, though a sorrow borne willingly.[9]

Philip, whom she meets again soon after, attacks her course of self-sacrifice as pernicious and puts mental interests in her way, which do in fact give her a more balanced attitude. Later, at an even worse crisis of her life, when she is trying to fight her love for Stephen, she discovers the true difficulties of renunciation.

> O aunt Gritty, I'm very wretched. I wish I could have died when I was fifteen. It seemed so easy to give things up then – it is so hard now.[10]

Later still, when she is disastrously involved, she recalls Philip's words:

> Philip had been right when he told her that she knew nothing of renunciation: she had thought it was quiet ecstasy; she saw it face to face now – that sad patient loving strength which holds the clue of life – and saw that the thorns were for ever pressing on its brow.[11]

[9] *The Mill on the Floss*, bk. 4, ch. 3.
[10] Ibid., bk. 6, ch. 11.   [11] Ibid., bk. 6, ch. 14.

It is the same with Dorothea Brooke. Her adolescent schemes of renunciation are treated by George Eliot as an open joke.

Riding was an indulgence which she allowed herself in spite of conscientious qualms; she felt that she enjoyed it in a pagan sensuous way, and always looked forward to renouncing it.[12]

The element of self-seeking which is a part of Maggie's early self-denial is present, too, in Dorothea's:

She had not reached that point of renunciation at which she would have been satisfied with having a wise husband; she wished, poor child, to be wise herself.[13]

But as the story proceeds and real troubles come to her, she sadly and earnestly does suppress her own wishes. When her husband hears that the illness he is suffering from is a fatal one he repulses her and her sympathy, but she chokes back her grief and resentment in the presence of a sorrow greater than her own. She furthermore decides to promise to do what he asks and she most dreads: that she will finish the *Key* after his death.

What is fatally hampering to George Eliot's heroines is not society, not even provincial society, but their own lack of creativity, which includes creative intellectual powers. Obstacles of all kinds are put in their way, it is true, and George Eliot makes us feel so sorry for them that we overlook the fact that in real life, given the motivation and the talent, women could and did overcome them. George Eliot herself triumphed over greater handicaps than any of her women characters are faced with.

Nowhere in the nineteenth-century novel do we get a more chilling picture of the education provided for young women. George Eliot presents it to us not so much by explicit description as by showing us its products. To know Rosamond Vincy is almost enough.

She was admitted to be the flower of M s. Lemon's school, the chief school in the county, where the teaching included all that was demanded in the accomplished female – even to extras, such as the getting in and out of a carriage.[14]

[12] *Middlemarch*, ch. 1.   [13] Ibid., ch. 7.   [14] Ibid., ch. 11.

To know Gwendolen Harleth completes the picture. Her reading has done nothing but make her pert and her accomplishments wither away when exposed to professional standards. Even her vaunted manners are not good enough for London society: Grandcourt is right in suggesting that she makes 'a gawky' of herself with her would-be private communications to Daniel Deronda.

It is natural that those of the heroines who do have aspirations – Rosamond is entirely pleased with herself – feel that the answer lies in the studies provided for men. With something clearly lacking in their own upbringing, the forbidden knowledge, which they are constantly being told is too much for them, is bound to seem like a panacea. Maggie, in despair, turns to Tom's old school books.

> Latin, Euclid and Logic would surely be a considerable step in masculine wisdom – in that knowledge which made men contented, and even glad to live.

She overlooks the fact that they have had the opposite effect on Tom and begins to apply herself.

> And so the poor child, with her soul's hunger and her illusions of self-flattery, began to nibble at this thick-rinded fruit of the tree of knowledge, filling her vacant hours with Latin, geometry, and the forms of the syllogism, and feeling a gleam of triumph now and then that her understanding was quite equal to these peculiarly masculine studies. For a week or two she went on resolutely enough, though with an occasional sinking of heart, as if she had set out toward the Promised Land alone and found it a thirsty, trackless, uncertain journey.[15]

It is not so much Gwendolen Harleth herself, who has something of Rosamond's complacency, as Daniel Deronda who thinks her poor education unfits her for the difficulties she is meeting as Grandcourt's wife.

> It seems to me that she has a dreary lack of the ideas that might help her . . . But what do I know of her? . . . She was clearly an ill-educated, worldly girl; perhaps she is a coquette.[16]

15 *The Mill on the Floss*, bk. 4, ch. 3.
16 *Daniel Deronda*, ch. 35.

When she consults him his advice is forceful:

> Some real knowledge would give you an interest beyond
> the small drama of personal desires. It is the curse of your
> life – forgive me – of so many lives, that all passion is spent
> in that narrow round, for want of ideas and sympathies to
> make a larger home for it. Is there any single occupation
> of mind that you care about with passionate delight or
> even independent interest?[17]

But she misinterprets his advice, carrying up to her room a
selection of books –

> Descartes, Bacon, Locke, Burke, Guizot – knowing, as a
> clever young lady of education, that these authors were
> ornaments of mankind, feeling sure that Deronda had read
> them, and hoping that by dipping into them all in succes-
> sion, with her rapid understanding she might get a point
> of view nearer to his level.[18]

These efforts are of course in vain. Any enlightenment she
experiences comes from learning to like her relatives rather
better than before, not from 'her occasional dashes into
difficult authors, who instead of blending themselves with her
daily agitations required her to dismiss them'.

The completest trust in books and masculine studies is that
of Dorothea Brooke. We know nothing of her education
except that it had taken place first in an English family and
afterwards in a Swiss family at Lausanne, where she had been
in the habit of listening eagerly to a certain ugly and learned
Monsieur Liret, but we can assume it was as unsatisfactory
as that of Gwendolen. Dorothea feels its inadequacy even
before trouble touches her.

> It was not entirely out of devotion to her future husband
> that she wished to know Greek and Latin. Those provinces
> of masculine knowledge seemed to her a standing-ground
> from which all truth could be seen more truly. As it was,
> she constantly doubted her own conclusions, because she
> felt her own ignorance: how could she be confident that
> one-roomed cottages were not for the glory of God, when
> men who knew the classics appeared to conciliate indiffer-
> ence to the cottages with zeal for the glory? Perhaps even

---

[17] Ibid., ch. 36.   [18] Ibid., ch. 44.

Hebrew might be necessary – at least the alphabet and a few roots – in order to arrive at the core of things, and judge soundly on the social duties of the Christian.[19]

And to begin with, it really seems to work.

> To Dorothea, after that toy-box history of the world adapted to young ladies which had made the chief part of her education, Mr. Casaubon's talk about his great book was full of new vistas and this sense of revelation, this surprise of a nearer introduction to Stoics and Alexandrians, as people who had ideas not totally unlike her own, kept in abeyance for the time her usual eagerness for a binding theory which could bring her own life and doctrine into strict connexion with that amazing past, and give the remotest sources of knowledge some bearings on her actions.[20]

In this passage and others George Eliot stresses that Dorothea, even in her untried youth, does not make the dangerous mistake of isolating knowledge. For her, cultivation of the mind is integrally connected with development of the personality as a whole, including the emotions and affections. It is a point of view which her creator frequently emphasises in her own letters. Dorothea wants to know not what to think but how to behave. It is not wrong-headedness on this important issue which makes the life of the intellect less satisfactory than in the early days of her relationship with Casaubon she hopes it will be. It seems to be her inability to think creatively, and if we protest that no girl brought up as she was could be expected to, we have Mary Garth as a contrast. As Mary sits watching by Mr Featherstone's sickbed in the small hours, she does not indulge in 'notions' and warm-hearted fantasies as Dorothea might, but amuses herself for hours by a reconstruction of the scenes of the day, analysing her own observations and building them up into a coherent picture. It is no surprise to us to be told in the Finale that she writes a book: a compilation for children called *Stories of Great Men, taken from Plutarch*, not a great literary endeavour, perhaps, but more than Dorothea could have done; at all events more than she did.

Though George Eliot systematically refuses to make any of

[19] *Middlemarch*, ch. 7.   [20] Ibid., ch. 10.

her chief women characters creative, she has a great deal to say about creativity in other ways, not only by contrast with less important women characters as in the case of Mary Garth, but also by a careful presentation of the lack of this quality. Gwendolen Harleth is a brilliant study in anti-creativity, exemplifying to perfection the conceit of the un-gifted, badly taught amateur which cannot, except in occa-sional lip-service, recognise any higher standard, and, much more important, such a person's complete inability to under-stand the dedication and perseverance necessary to creativity. In contrast we have the genuinely creative girl, Catherine Arrowsmith (who marries the only creative man in the book), and, incidentally, it is she who manifests a development of the sympathies far beyond the capacity of Gwendolen.

An interesting example of uncreativity masquerading as its opposite is Rosamond Vincy's music. She was a highly imitative schoolgirl and by sheer chance at Mrs Lemon's had an excellent musician as master. She

> had seized his manner of playing, and gave forth his large rendering of noble music with the precision of an echo . . . A hidden soul seemed to be flowing forth from Rosamond's fingers; and so indeed it was, since souls live on in per-petual echoes, and to all fine expression there goes some-where an originating activity.[21]

It was no wonder that, hearing her for the first time, Lydgate is startled into thinking of her as 'something exceptional'. Only a close relationship reveals her essential emptiness.

The main feeling which George Eliot directs towards the women characters she has herself created is compassion. In this respect she condescends to all of them. Professor Barbara Hardy has pointed out how consistently she uses the adjective 'poor' in speaking of them, and has analysed the imagery which invests them with pathos in likening them to wounded animals, caged birds, vulnerable flowers and unhappy chil-dren.[22]

In some ways George Eliot's heroines have greater liberty than their predecessors in the nineteenth-century novel for, though the action often takes place, as in *Middlemarch*,

[21] Ibid., ch. 16.
[22] *The Novels of George Eliot*, ch. 10.

several decades earlier than the time of writing, the century as far as women were concerned was advancing in ways which George Eliot, who as we see in *Romola* was not particularly gifted at recapturing the spirit of a past age, could hardly help reflecting, brilliant as was her observation of her own age. The heroines have greater mobility: Gwendolen Harleth travels, on one occasion alone, to European spas – a far cry from Emma Woodhouse who saw the sea for the first time on her honeymoon – and she travels as a marriageable lady with a reputation to preserve, unlike Lucy Snowe and Jane Eyre who, their object being survival, had no energy to spare on such niceties. George Eliot's heroines have much of the boldness and independence which begins to infiltrate correct feminine behaviour in the novel as the century goes on. They can express their feelings for men if necessary without detracting from their own modesty. Catherine Arrowsmith bravely proposes to Herr Klesmer with a straightforwardness which springs from a true sense of proportion, that dares to recognise itself: 'I am afraid of nothing but that we should miss the passing of our lives together'.[23] Elizabeth Bennet feared a great many things more than the possibility of losing Darcy for ever, or rather she realised that straightforwardness, in her day, would defeat its own ends. Dorothea persuades Will that their marriage is, in spite of all difficulties, a possibility and we like her the better for such frankness, a great deal better probably than we like the conventional cunning of Gwendolen in her pursuit of Grandcourt, a cunning incidentally which puts her on a level with the despised Mr Lush, who admires her for it. Catherine Arrowsmith's and Dorothea Casaubon's declarations are made to sound not only noble but normal; they have none of the freakiness and eccentricity of Jane Eyre's passionate words to Rochester. Openness is becoming the fashion: when Gwendolen, after Grandcourt's death, makes her feelings for Deronda very apparent, Sir Hugo, far from despising her for it, resolves that he will protect her from her heedlessness in this respect.

But such gains as these do not really undermine the word 'poor'. The heroines labour under dreadful and time-honoured disadvantages and with George Eliot we have opportunities to study one of them which have been denied to us by novelists who end the story with wedding bells or

[23] *Daniel Deronda*, ch. 22.

death. We see the domestic tyranny of the husband. Grandcourt is the most egregious example. After a courtship where Gwendolen is made to feel she is complete mistress of the situation, a complete reversal of the balance of power takes place, so that within a few weeks she not only comes to obey Grandcourt but to fear him. His stranglehold over her is something we almost physically feel, as she herself does.

> That white hand of his which was touching his whisker was capable, she fancied, of clinging round her neck and threatening to throttle her.

It is most cleverly done. In every incident when he asserts his mastery over her she has to a large extent asked for it, and yet he is seen to go far beyond judicious remonstrance or rebuke. When she rather stupidly appears wearing emeralds rather than the diamonds which have such poisoned association for her and Grandcourt insists she puts them on, she struggles to right the situation: 'Oh, please not. I don't think diamonds suit me.'

> 'What you think has nothing to do with it', said Grandcourt, his *sotto voce* imperiousness seeming to have an evening quietude and finish, like his toilet. 'I wish you to wear the diamonds.'[24]

After the scene where she has worn the turquoise necklace Deronda once redeemed for her and drawn his attention to it in a way which Grandcourt is fairly accurate in describing as 'damnably vulgar', Grandcourt says:

> 'You are my wife. And you will either fill your place, properly – to the world and to me – or you will go to the devil'.
> 'I never intended anything but to fill my place properly', said Gwendolen, with bitterest mortification in her soul.
> 'You put that thing on your wrist, and hid it from me till you wanted him to see it. Only fools go into that deaf and dumb talk, and think they're secret. You will understand that you are not to compromise yourself. Behave with dignity. That's all I have to say.'[25]

Even her later impropriety in making an assignation with Deronda, at a time when she thinks her husband will be out

²⁴ Ibid., ch. 35.   ²⁵ Ibid., ch. 36.

of the house, meets with greater tyranny than it deserves. Without the slightest consultation of her wishes he announces that she will go with him on a yachting trip to the Mediterranean.

Grandcourt is of course such a monster that he may seem to exemplify nothing more particular than monstrosity. The point about marital tyranny may be better illustrated from a marriage where not only is the husband more normal but where the wife herself is something of a monster, that is, the Lydgate household. At Rosamond's classic remark when her husband tells her of their financial difficulties – 'What can *I* do, Tertius?' – we are certainly meant to recoil with horrified exasperation, but there is more to it than that. Lydgate has never given her a chance to act more responsibly. When things have really gone wrong between them he recalls

> his old dreamland, in which Rosamond Vincy appeared to be that perfect piece of womanhood who would reverence her husband's mind after the fashion of an accomplished mermaid, using her comb and looking-glass and singing her song for the relaxation of his adored wisdom alone.[26]

And we may reflect that if this is his idea of marriage it is just as well that it has been shaken up. Lydgate's tyranny partly takes the form of protectiveness. When the first insistent bills begin to come in, he refuses to confide in her (though she gives him an opening by questioning him quite closely about his worried look), on the grounds that she is pregnant. This seems at first glance considerate, at a second view unrealistic; the Rosamond we know is not going to miscarry at the sight of a furniture bill. When he lets their affairs become so desperate that she has to be told, it is a shock for which she has not been allowed to prepare herself. What could she do, indeed? When now she tries to act, by appealing to her father (which she has a right to do and Lydgate little right to forbid her) and by approaching his relations, her actions seem stupid because they fail; but they might have succeeded. When she cancels Lydgate's orders to the agent about finding a buyer for their house, her words, 'I think I had a perfect right to speak on a

26 *Middlemarch*, ch. 58.

subject which concerns me at least as much as you', carry some conviction, and in the quarrel that follows we may feel inclined to answer Lydgate back. 'You had no right to treat me as if I were a fool,' he says. But that is exactly how he treats her. 'And suppose I disregard your opinion as you disregard mine?'[27] Why is her disregarding his made to sound so much the more unreasonable attitude of the two? George Eliot's presentation of the clash between the couple is particularly skilful because of such ambiguities as these. The old protective tyranny is present when Lydgate tells Rosamond not to go riding while she is pregnant. He is right on medical grounds, but when he adds, 'Surely I am the person to judge for you. I think it is enough that I say you are not to go again', we should like to be sure he is speaking as a doctor and not just as a husband. Of course Rosamond is meant to be maddening, but there is something admirable – admittedly more to twentieth-century readers than to nineteenth – about her refusal 'to allow any assertion of power to be final'. Lydgate could have done with some of her obstinacy in his career, only he would have then called it perseverance.

A direct predecessor of Rosamond Lydgate is Bessie Tulliver. Mr Tulliver chose her because he considered her to be his inferior in intellect ('I picked her from her sisters o' purpose, 'cause she was a bit weak like; for I wasn't agoin' to be told the rights o' things by my own fireside')[28] and treats her accordingly whereas, in point of fact, they are about equally stupid. When money troubles assail this couple the same pattern emerges, even the same words are used. 'What could I do?' says poor Mrs Tulliver to Lawyer Wakem when, acting at last on her own initiative, she goes to beg him not to buy Dorlcote Mill, which immediately prompts him to do so.[29] But though her plan miscarries, it might have succeeded, and any woman with as little practice as herself in acting independently can hardly be blamed, certainly not by the man who has cynically deprived her of it.

The Mill on the Floss is a positive compendium of the handicaps imposed on women; they are seen all the more clearly because the lack of sophistication of most of the characters shows the prevalent attitudes in all their crudity.

[27] Ibid., ch. 64.   [28] *The Mill on the Floss*, bk. 1, ch. 3.
[29] Ibid., bk. 3, ch. 7.

Not only must the wife be inferior (and Stephen Guest's notions of what a man should look for in a wife are not much subtler than Mr Tulliver's), but so must the sister and the daughter. Fatherly and brotherly tyranny condition even a spirited and intelligent girl into accepting their viewpoint. Maggie feels she cannot go on seeing Philip because of the feud between his father and hers, though Philip tries to persuade her it is wrong to be ruled by the dislikes of others. And her brother Tom has an even completer ascendancy over her than her father has. It is almost unbelievable that she should allow him to drag her to the spot where she is to meet Philip and to make her listen to his cruel and vulgar abuse of a man whom she has reason to love and be grateful to. The book is eloquent, too, about the inequality with which girls are treated where education is concerned, an inequality so pervasive that we hardly need the dictum of Mr Stelling, the schoolmaster, that girls

> can pick up a little of everything, I daresay. They've a great deal of superficial cleverness; but they couldn't go far into anything. They're quick and shallow.[30]

Perhaps even harder to bear is the assumption that when domestic disaster strikes, men can exert themselves to do something about it whereas women have to stay mournfully in the stricken home. Tom not only has the outlet of striving with the world, but adopts the 'manly' attitude that his sister must do nothing as he can provide for her.

In *Middlemarch* Dorothea comes up against the sheer practical difficulty of getting anything done except through the good offices of a man. Before her marriage she designs cottages, but she can draw plans all day and every day without getting a single cottage built; for that she is dependent on Sir James Chettam, and she is extremely put out when she finds he is in love with her as now she cannot use him in this way. It is all bound up with grace and favour and the emotons. On her honeymoon she cannot explore Rome except by her husband's arrangement, a fact which accounts for much of the tension between them; he chooses the sights, hires the carriage and the courier, and then goes off to the library resenting the time he has had to spend. Casaubon could have gone on his honeymoon alone, as Dorothea

[30] Ibid., bk. 2, ch. 1.

realises only too soon. In her widowhood she plans to found a commune with the money he has left her, but to further her plans she has to go on an exploratory tour with Sir James and Celia, and Sir James decides it will not do.

Jane Austen's comment, when discussing Charlotte Lucas's engagement to Mr Collins, that for penniless girls marriage must be their pleasantest preservative from want, not only still holds good but is expanded into one of the principal themes of *Daniel Deronda*. The financial considerations that impel Gwendolen into marrying Grandcourt are felt to be inexorable. Genuinely the only alternative for her is to take a post as governess with Mrs Mompert, the Bishop's wife, and this is made to seem as impossible to us as it does to her, though we may perhaps feel that Mrs Mompert might have been the greater sufferer had the arrangement gone through. The theme is not dropped at the altar. Gwendolen, being made of less stern stuff than Charlotte Collins, cannot endure her loveless marriage. But she realises there is no turning back. At one point she seriously contemplates leaving Grandcourt but dismisses the idea on entirely practical grounds.

Women are to be pitied not only on account of what they cannot do but for what they have to do. They must be homemakers whether they have any inclination or aptitude for it or not. In *Amos Barton*, first of the *Scenes of Clerical Life*, we are presented, in the person of Milly Barton, with the 'soothing, unspeakable charm of gentle womanhood! which supersedes all acquisitions, all accomplishments',[31] and we see it taking the form of mending stockings, warming slippers, hanging up and proffering hats, and placing cool hands on hot foreheads. Love alone is thought to be not enough. Janet Dempster, the heroine of *Janet's Repentance*, is not very good at these ministrations, and to this shortcoming her mother-in-law attributes the difficulties of her marriage.

> What use is it for a woman to be loving, and making a fuss with her husband, if she doesn't take care and keep his home just as he likes it; if she isn't at hand when he wants anything done; if she doesn't attend to all his wishes, let them be as small as they may?[32]

[31] *Amos Barton*, ch. 2.   [32] *Janet's Repentance*, ch. 13.

It is often hard to catch George Eliot's tone in *Scenes*. In the following passage, for example, she sounds not only artistically sincere but as though she actually approves.

A loving woman's world lies within the four walls of her own home; and it is only through her husband that she is in any electric communication with the world beyond.[33]

We know she did not in fact approve, but perhaps she always kept a lurking belief that the ministering rôle she describes *is* woman's and ought not to be man's. There is a revealing comment in *Middlemarch* when Rosamond asks Lydgate to fasten up her hair:

He swept up the soft festoons of plaits and fastened in the tall comb (to such uses do men come!)[34]

The offering of personal attentions suits Milly Barton but degrades Tertius Lydgate.

Whatever George Eliot felt about homemaking in her own life – she says she hated it – she leaves us in no doubt of the value placed on it by society, as in her description of Squire Cass's household in *Silas Marner*:

The Squire's wife had died long ago, and the Red House was without that presence of the wife and mother which is the fountain of wholesome love and fear in parlour and kitchen; and this helped to account . . . for the frequency with which the proud Squire condescended to preside in the parlour of the Rainbow rather than the shadow of his own dark wainscot; perhaps also for the fact that his sons had turned out rather ill.

One of the sons, Godfrey, firmly attributes his moral failings to the lack of a ministering angel in the home, and when he contemplates marriage his sense of this lack causes

the neatness, purity and liberal orderliness of the Lammeter household, sunned by the smile of Nancy, to seem like those fresh, bright hours of the morning when temptations go to sleep and leave the ear open to the voice of the good angel, inviting to industry, sobriety and peace.[35]

[33] *Amos Barton*, ch. 7. [34] *Middlemarch*, ch. 58.
[35] *Silas Marner*, ch. 3.

When eventually he marries Nancy, the Cass house improves under her régime as a little earlier Silas's cottage has improved under Eppie's.

The womanless house appears again in *Mr. Gilfil's Love Story*; in the widower's sitting room we find 'no piece of embroidery, no faded bit of pretty triviality, hinting of taper-fingers and small feminine ambitions'. Upstairs, however, in the dead wife's room, there is an abundance of 'pretty triviality'.

> On the little dressing-table there was a dainty looking-glass in a carved and gilt frame; bits of wax-candle were still in the branched sockets at the sides, and on one of these branches hung a little black lace kerchief; a faded satin pincushion, with the pins rusted in it; a scent-bottle, and a large green fan, lay on the table . . . a pair of tiny red slippers, with a bit of tarnished silver embroidery on them, were standing at the foot of the bed.[36]

As George Eliot's work developed we hear much less about woman as homemaker, and with the last two heroines the subject is irrelevant in any case: Dorothea and Gwendolen marry into wealthy homes that are already thoroughly, indeed rigidly, made. To imagine them fluttering about administering womanly touches to the furniture and fittings is ludicrous. Their presence is needed, but for psychological reasons. Grandcourt wants the fun of dominating a spirited girl who is to be a kind of supernumerary and more complex horse or dog. Casaubon's requirements are clear in his own head and clearly conveyed to the reader. He had

> made up his mind that it was now time for him to adorn his life with the graces of female companionship, to irradiate the gloom which fatigue was apt to hang over the intervals of studious labour with the play of female fancy, and to secure in this, his culminating age, the solace of female tendance for his declining years.[37]

The idea of female fancy irradiating gloom recalls Helen Schlegel's exasperated remark in *Howard's End* about 'ladies': 'The darlings are regular sunbeams.' It must be even worse to be married as a sunbeam than as a sicknurse, and

[36] *Mr. Gilfil's Love Story*, ch. 1.
[37] *Middlemarch*, ch. 7.

tragic indeed when having tried most conscientiously to be both, as Dorothea does, your efforts are rejected, like hers.

George Eliot's attitude to her heroines and to the woman characters of whom she approves is a great deal more dispassionate than that of Jane Austen, Charlotte Brontë and Elizabeth Gaskell to theirs. The identification and partisanship that these three writers display is single-minded beyond anything George Eliot intends, except perhaps in the portrait of Maggie Tulliver. We have already seen that by pitying her heroines she condescends to them, and that by refusing to allow them creative gifts she stoops even further. But what really puts them in their place are the terrifying blind spots that she imposes on their intelligence. Dorothea is shown from the beginning, in mild social terms, as a girl who cannot see what is before her nose, either literally or metaphorically, but as the plot develops there is an almost Shakespearean quality about the way in which she harps on the subject of Will Ladislaw at every moment when her husband is particularly suspicious and resentful of him. Her subconscious mind is keen enough; it must be, for her to choose so unerringly the wrong time to speak and the wrong terms to use. But consciously she is quite unaware of the harm she is doing. It is just like Desdemona dragging Cassio into the conversation with an inspired perversity which eventually destroys herself.

Gwendolen, too, is blind to the effects of her social behaviour, though throughout her life it has been a subject to which she has devoted her utmost concentration. In company she underestimates the intelligence of others and the extent to which they can understand her gibes (rather like Emma and Miss Bates on Box Hill). Mrs Arrowpoint is no genius, but she is not such a fool as Gwendolen thinks and can sense the impertinence which Gwendolen, who administers it, thinks she is the only one to appreciate. This blindness leads the way to the most fraught scenes of her life with Grandcourt. It is very strange that she cannot see how obvious she is being in her communications with Deronda. It is not only Grandcourt who notices it but casual and not especially astute observers like Hans Meyrick and Sir Hugo Mallinger. The delusion that people see only such of our behaviour as we wish them to is common enough, but Gwendolen seems to think she is a goddess who can make herself invisible at will.

George Eliot surely has a real affection for her heroines, often perhaps, as in the case of Gwendolen, more than the readers can summon up. Yet she says dreadful things about them. Jane Austen, in accusing Elizabeth Bennet of prejudice, makes it seem a rather lovable peccadillo that passes off as easily and naturally as a head cold, leaving no trace. But the flaws that George Eliot depicts, even in her favourite girls, are both ugly and lasting. The much-praised open ending of the plot of *Daniel Deronda* is usually assumed to be done for purely artistic reasons whereas it may well be that she sees Gwendolen's defects as irremediable (she is clearly going to be as selfish and wrong-headed in reformation as she has been in evil-doing), and can go no further than vague hints and hopeful promises of amelioration.

A study of two of her less important women characters shows the full extent of her impartiality. Nancy Lammeter, whom Godfrey Cass marries in *Silas Marner*, is called, it seems without satire, a sweet, good, and even noble-hearted woman. Yet she is seen to be bitchy, ignorant, pig-headed, snobbish and vain.

> Miss Nancy, whose thoughts were always conducted with the propriety and moderation conspicuous in her manners, remarked to herself that the Miss Gunns were rather hard-featured than otherwise, and that such very low dresses as they wore might have been attributed to vanity if their shoulders had been pretty.[38]

> It was as necessary to her mind to have an opinion on all topics, not exclusively masculine, that had come under her notice, as for her to have a precisely marked place for every article of her personal property: and her opinions were always principles to be unwaveringly acted on. They were firm, not because of the basis, but because she held them with a tenacity inseparable from her mental action. On all the duties and properties of life, from filial behaviour to the arrangements of the toilet, pretty Nancy Lammeter, by the time she was three-and-twenty, had her unalterable little code, and had formed every one of her habits in strict accordance with that code.[39]

[38] *Silas Marner*, ch. 11.   [39] Ibid., ch. 17.

Celia Brooke is the other example. George Eliot creates the general impression that she is a sympathetic character: the book begins and ends with her love for the heroine and this love is shown throughout as genuine. Yet her disclosure to her sister of the offensive clause in Casaubon's will is done unimaginatively and even cruelly, and on many occasions she uses the superficial quickness with which she is credited to wound Dorothea. She has a rare gift for the needling word, as when she calls Dorothea's heartfelt drawing of model cottages a fad. Her conversation, especially when she becomes a mother, is silly in the extreme. An explanation for her attacks on Dorothea could, of course, be found not only in normal sibling jealousy but in the fact that Sir James Chettham wanted to marry Dorothea before he wanted to marry her. This would be an interesting motive for her malice; if only we could be sure that George Eliot meant her to be malicious.

But though George Eliot makes nice women act meanly, she can also depict murderesses as being basically nice women. It is astonishing how frank and how detailed she is about her heroines' violent desires. Her understanding of what drives them to extremes – the frustration of their lives with men and the treatment they receive – results in a pity which makes it impossible for her to condemn. Romola, living in a more emancipated age than the Victorian, can express her resentment at Tito's treatment of her by deciding to leave him and actually setting out, but women in nineteenth-century society do not have this vent.

Woman as murderess appears very early in George Eliot's work, in the person of Caterina Sarti, heroine of *Mr. Gilfil's Love Story*. Her violence is partly explained by the fact that she is Italian by birth, though at the time of the story she is encapsulated in polite English society as the protégée of Sir Christopher and Lady Cheverel. From childhood, we are told, she has had 'a certain ingenuity in vindictiveness' and when she is grown up the taste for vengeance persists, though without the ingenuity, for it is not specially inventive to stab a faithless lover. The intended victim is Captain Wybrow, Sir Christopher's heir, who having flirted with Tina abandons her and becomes engaged to an heiress. Her impulse to murder him is premeditated and well-organised: she provides herself with a dagger and makes an appointment with him at an isolated spot in the grounds. When she gets there he is already dead, but in fact she has killed him: agitation about the approaching interview acting on his weak heart has brought on a fatal attack.

Mr Gilfil, the clergyman who loves her and to whom she later confesses everything, absolves her, on the shaky grounds that she would never have done it really. But Tina insists on her own guilt.

> I had had such wicked feelings for a long while. I was so angry and I hated Miss Assher so, and I didn't care what came to anybody, because I was so miserable myself. I was full of bad passions. No one else was ever so wicked.[40]

She faces the implications of her intention: 'When I meant to do it, it was as bad as if I had done it.' This is most orthodox, if we recall Christ's words about lecherous glances being the same thing as actual adultery; the clergyman, however, will have none of it and persists in his comforting and dismissive remarks. But Tina never fully recovers from the revelation of her own violence.

It is a problem to which George Eliot returns as her powers as a novelist develop, and the two novels of her maturity explore the theme of the murderous longings of both men and women at different moments in the plot and from varying points of view. What moral weight is to be put on intention? What *is* intention? What is murder? These events are posed by the events in *Middlemarch* leading up to the death of Raffles. Is Bulstrode, who certainly wishes him dead, a murderer, when without protest he allows someone else to give him the brandy which the doctor has told him could be fatal? On the whole we decide he is culpable, even as he is proved culpable in other matters. His wife lovingly shares his disgrace but nobody absolves him.

Towards the women in *Middlemarch* George Eliot is much more lenient. The English women are let off the most lightly. True, neither Rosamond nor Dorothea actually murders or contemplates murdering her unsatisfactory husband, but the desire is there, however well buried, under mountains of duty, as in Dorothea's case, or of respectability, as in Rosamond's. As neither girl is suicidally inclined the death of the

---

[40] *Mr. Gilfil's Love Story*, ch. 19.

oppressor is the only way out either in fantasy or fact, and Casaubon and Lydgate are undoubtedly oppressors.

Lydgate considers that Rosamond *has* murdered him.

> He once called her his basil plant; and when she asked for an explanation, said that basil was a plant which had flourished wonderfully on a murdered man's brains.[41]

Casaubon's distrust of Dorothea once he has seen that she has begun to criticise him – which happens on their honeymoon – makes him regard her as a danger and he shrinks from her sometimes as though she were holding a dagger, like Tina. And indeed, like Tina, she does contribute to his death; her anger at his reaction to Will Ladislaw's letter precipitates the first onset of his final illness, as she admits to herself. The resentment which she increasingly feels in her marriage as his tyranny threatens her more and more, to the extent of trying to shackle her for ever even after his death, finds expression in the note she writes on the paper he has left to direct her in the posthumous completion of his work.

> I could not use it. Do you not see now that I could not submit my soul to yours, by working hopelessly at what I have no belief in? – Dorothea.[42]

That the effort she has made for nearly two years to submit her soul to his has bred violence in her, is disclosed to us, if we have not already guessed it, on the night that Casaubon has repulsed her after being told the serious nature of his illness. She subdues her feelings and makes one more attempt to win his confidence by gentleness and affection. When for the moment he responds,

> she felt something like the thankfulness that might well up in us if we had narrowly escaped hurting a lamed creature.[43]

In the last months of their life together she knows what she has to face if he lives, and it is a fact that his death releases her, by only a minute or so, from the crushing promise which she has persuaded herself she should give him. She must have felt it as a release, and guilt at entertaining such a feeling, so against all her notions of devotedness, may well have been a factor in the prostration she suffered.

[41] *Middlemarch*, finale. [42] Ibid., ch. 54. [43] Ibid., ch. 42.

Though we should not wish Dorothea to recover from her bereavement with the crude almost joyful haste suggested by Celia, there is something in Celia's view that the intensity of her sister's mourning is inappropriate to the apparent circumstances.

The story of Laure, the strange flashback which is part of our early introduction to Lydgate, may at the time of telling seem both melodramatic and irrelevant. It continues to seem melodramatic, but its deadly relevance to Lydgate's choice of Rosamond as a wife becomes increasingly obvious. As time goes by it certainly does to Lydgate.

> His mind glancing back to Laure while he looked at Rosamond, he said inwardly, 'Would *she* kill me because I wearied her?' and then 'It is the way with all women.'[44]

This silly and disparaging generalisation, typical of Lydgate, is counteracted in his mind not by the thought that Rosamond would not do it but that Dorothea would not do it.

Laure is a Frenchwoman and an actress whom Lydgate loves as a young man in Paris, though at first only as a member of the audience. He takes time off from his experiments in galvanism to attend the play she is in, 'just as he might have thrown himself under the breath of the sweet south on a bank of violets for a while'. She is the graceful provider of the scientist's relaxation just as he later plans that Rosamond shall be. The drama requires that she shall stab to death the character who is played by her husband and one night she actually does it. A legal enquiry acquits her on the ground that her foot slipped. She leaves Paris, and Lydgate, more in love than ever, follows her with a proposal of marriage, which provokes the following conversation:

> 'I will tell you something,' she said in her cooing way, keeping her arms folded. 'My foot really slipped.'
> 'I know, I know,' said Lydgate, deprecatingly. 'It was a fatal accident – a dreadful stroke of calamity that bound me to you the more.'
> Again Laure paused a little and then said, slowly, '*I meant to do it.*'
> Lydgate, strong man as he was, turned pale and trembled:

44 Ibid., ch. 58.

199

moments seemed to pass before he rose and stood at a distance from her.

'There was a secret, then' he said at last, even vehemently. 'He was brutal to you: you hated him.'

'No! he wearied me; he was too fond: he would live in Paris, and not in my country; that was not agreeable to me.'

'Great God!' said Lydgate, in a groan of horror. 'And you planned to murder him?'

'I did not plan: it came to me in the play – *I meant to do it*.'[45]

Lydgate immediately relegates her to 'the throng of stupid criminals', quite wrongly: stupid she certainly is not and criminal she may well not be. Like Tina, she understands the guilt of intention, though in her case it is not premeditated but impulsive and bound up with the emotion generated by the play, and like Tina she refuses to justify herself. It is all too subtle and at the same time too straightforward for Lydgate, and he goes back, significantly, to torture his frogs and rabbits 'with their trying and mysterious dispensation of unexplained shocks'.

And so to Gwendolen Harleth. George Eliot makes it clear from the first paragraph of *Daniel Deronda* that there is evil in her. Daniel feels it as he watches her at the gaming table; Mr Vandervoordt likens her to a snake. In Chapter 3 the evil is narrowed down and defined: she is a killer, potentially of anything or anybody that crosses her will. We are given two examples of this propensity in her as a child. On one occasion she refuses to get out of bed to fetch her mother's medicine when she is seized with pain in the night. Mrs Davilow does not die for lack of it, but the attack has been severe enough to prevent her getting it herself and the neglect could have been fatal. On another occasion she does actually kill, the victim being her sister's canary which she strangles 'in a final fit of exasperation at its shrill singing which had again and again jarringly interrupted her own'.[46] George Eliot comments that she has never been 'thoughtlessly cruel, nay, delighting to rescue drowning insects and watch their recovery', – a kind of sentimentality not unknown in murderers – implying presumably that she can be deli-

---

[45] Ibid., ch. 16. [46] *Daniel Deronda*, ch. 3.

berately violent when crossed. The strangling of the canary she calls 'infelonious murder'.

Irretrievably warped as a child by Mrs Davilow's un-maternal dependence on her ('Scold me, darling'), unshake-ably conceited and arrogantly expectant of her own way in everything, Gwendolen seems the most unsuitable girl in England to be a wife for Grandcourt, which is why he chooses her. It is not surprising that within a few weeks she wants to dispose of him as she did of the canary; and here again her singing comes into it.

At the most important points of the story her singing has symbolical value. She has sung her way to fame in provincial drawing rooms and has everywhere been accepted at her own valuation, as an accomplished musician – on her arrival at Offendene she poses as Saint Cecilia – until the day when Herr Klesmer punctures her opinion of herself. 'Woman was dear to him but music was dearer', and when Gwendolen after one song appeals coquettishly and confidently to him: 'You cannot like to hear poor amateur singing', he replies, 'No truly; but that makes nothing. It is always acceptable to see you sing.' He follows up this classic snub with detailed comments about how badly she has been taught and what inferior music she has chosen to play.[47]

In spite of this (and with surprising obtuseness: what does she expect him to say?), it is to Herr Klesmer that she turns for advice when her family lose all their money and she decides to embark on a musical career on the stage, starting at the top of course. He tells her the painful truth – though not enjoying it – about the dedication, the unremitting hard work, the physical and mental stamina, as well as the talent, needed by the professional. She resents his words and cannot understand them, but she does act on them in giving up the idea. From this point she has a straightforward choice: be-tween Mrs Mompert and Grandcourt.

After her marriage, when her series of fraught conversa-tions with Deronda is well under way, he advises her not to give up her music. When she says she has not enough talent to make it worth while pursuing it, meaning that if she cannot win she will not contend, he replies:

But if you are fond of music, it will always be worth while

[47] Ibid., ch 5.

in private, for your own delight. I make it a virtue to be content with my middlingness; it is always pardonable, so that one does not ask others to take it for superiority.[48]

She takes his words to heart and when later in London she sees Mirah Lapidoth, as the highly gifted professional singer standing where she had once thought of standing herself, she decides to take singing lessons from her so that at least she can be cultivating some real interest of her own. When she puts her plan to Grandcourt his reply is, in the circumstances, one of the nastiest he ever makes to her.

I don't see why a lady should sing. Amateurs make fools of themselves. A lady can't risk herself in that way in company. And one doesn't want to hear squalling in private.[49]

It is as though Grandcourt likes arousing homicidal impulses in women. He certainly drives Lydia Glasher to acts of desperate folly. (He uses the word 'madwoman' about both her and Gwendolen: to their faces, naturally.) His sneering at Gwendolen about one of her claims to superiority, her music, goes parallel to his sneering at her manners, her other point of confidence. If he wishes her to feel like killing him, he succeeds. What he does not realise is that she means to do it. This is one of the two fatal mistakes, based on his own limitations, that he makes about Gwendolen; the other is that he cannot grasp that her conscience is torturing her about her usurpation of Lydia's rights. His would not, and neither is he a killer; he does not need to be.

Gwendolen does not push Grandcourt overboard. Chapter 54 ends like the instalment of a thriller with his saying, 'I shall put about', a manoeuvre about which experts at the quay have already warned him because of a likely change in the wind. The next thing we see, through Deronda's eyes, is Gwendolen being brought back without Grandcourt who has been drowned, and we learn from her later confession to Deronda that it was while her husband was turning the sail that there was a gust and he was struck. We are clearly meant to believe her, and therefore to believe her subsequent admission that she did not throw him the rope when he called for it, but stood there with the rope in her hand wishing him to die.

[48] Ibid., ch. 35.   [49] Ibid., ch. 48.

She insists on this wish to kill so eloquently – as eloquently as Tina did – that Deronda is bound to accept its validity, especially as it is the culmination of her dark hints over many months. But the results of her withholding of the rope he is afraid to accept.

> If it were true that he could swim, he must have been seized with cramp. With your quickest, utmost effort, it seems impossible that you could have done anything to save him. That momentary muderous will cannot, I think, have altered the course of events.[50]

And indeed Gwendolen's destructive intentions have been so violent as conceivably to blind even herself as to what really happened. In this, too, she resembles Tina: they are both exhibitionists with a taste for parading their sins, in the same way that they could not help parading their feelings for the men they loved, against all notions of propriety and pride.

It is at this point that George Eliot employs a technical device which is completely out of character. She frequently and legitimately withholds important information in the working out of her plots – Hetty's pregnancy, Dunsey Cass's death – until the time when it can be most effectively told. But Gwendolen's revelation to Daniel that, having planned to murder Grandcourt since her early bridal days, she has put a dagger aside on purpose, is a different sort of surprise, a shock which would have delighted Catherine Morland but may well jar on readers who feel safe with George Eliot's usual methods. The information has never been hinted or guessed at (it is not difficult to imagine from the first that Hetty may become pregnant or that Dunsey Cass may come to a bad end); it leads to no action, remains a secret except to Daniel and seems meant simply as a sign of Gwendolen's fluctuating passions, but they have been so well described that we need nothing more to help our imaginations.

> I did one act – and I never undid it – it is still there – as long ago as when we were at Ryelands. There it was – something my fingers longed for among the beautiful toys in the cabinet in my boudoir – small and sharp, like a long willow leaf in a silver sheath. I locked it in the drawer of my dressing-case. I was continually haunted with it, and

50 Ibid., ch. 57.

how I should use it. I fancied myself putting it under my pillow. But I never did. I never looked at it again. I dared not unlock the drawer: it had a key all to itself; and not long ago, when we were in the yacht I dropped the key into the deep water. It was my wish to drop it and deliver myself. After that I began to think how I could open the drawer without the key: and when I found we were to stay at Genoa, it came into my mind that I could get it opened privately at the hotel.[51]

It is hardly surprising that Daniel prefers to marry Mirah, a girl who, in desperation, turned her violence against herself. Had he married Gwendolen he would have been constantly looking under her pillow.

The girls we have spoken of so far never come to trial (it is just conceivable that Gwendolen might have, if the fishermen who were near enough to rescue her had been prepared to testify to her withholding of the rope); they are left to their consciences if any. The convicted murderess, Hetty Sorrel in *Adam Bede*, is possibly the one we think of last in this connection. Her character, as established by George Eliot in the first three-quarters of the book, is not that of a potential killer. She is cold-hearted and has fixed views of what she wants of life, which is to be a lady and wear fine clothes. But her inability to love is not accompanied by a desire to kill and the only person who can frustrate her wish to be a lady is the man who could make her one by marriage, so to kill him would be of little avail. After her flight from Hayslope, which her advancing pregnancy seems to her to make essential, she is in a state of diminished responsibility, which in a more medically informed age would have acquitted her completely. Her death-cell account to Dinah of how it all happened is the story of a nightmare, comparable with Gwendolen's outpourings to Deronda after Grandcourt's death. She was clearly out of her mind – she heard the baby crying long after it was dead – and equally clearly she neither killed it nor meant to. She wanted it to go away, in order that she might return home; she doorstepped it in the same spirit and hope that Antigonous abandoned Perdita – a hope which in Perdita's case came true. In the course of the book Hetty passes from

[51] Ibid., ch. 68.

dream world to nightmare with no intervening period of wakefulness and though perhaps we cannot join Adam in putting the blame entirely on Arthur Donnithorne, to hang Hetty as a murderess seems as inappropriate as executing a cat for killing its kitten.

Whatever else George Eliot's women characters are to her, and to us, they are central. Deprived, downtrodden, uncreative, murderous, at least they steal the show, from the first moment when in *Scenes of Clerical Life* the clerics walk into the background while their wives and sweethearts imposingly come forward. Victorian critics did not like this and several of them, Leslie Stephen for example, tried to get out of it by advancing the theory that many of the male characters – he mentions Tito, Daniel Deronda, Philip Wakem and Mr Lyon – were simply women in disguise, which would make their subordinate position in the novels more easily tolerated. This is an argument which cannot be sustained in our bisexual days. The fact must be faced that George Eliot's heroines are exceptional women who are more interesting, whatever their failings, than her heroes.

They may not be happier. At times George Eliot seems to be feeling as Yeats felt about the Gore-Booth girls: that if they had stayed in their silk kimonos and not gone into politics it would have been better for them. She sees very clearly the attendant difficulties of rarity. Even one of the most obtuse of her men characters, Mr Tulliver, sees it:

'I knew well enough what she'd be, before now – it's nothing new to me. But it's a pity she isn't made o' commoner stuff – she'll be thrown away, I doubt: there'll be nobody to marry her as is fit for her.' And Maggie's graces of mind and body fed his gloom.[52]

And when a woman comes to grief the waters close over her, either literally or metaphorically, with frightening speed and completeness. The dead hand of Casaubon is as tyrannical and not much colder than his living hand has been. So is Grandcourt's. But when Hetty is transported, within two years the Harvest Supper is being merrily celebrated at the Poysers' farm and Adam is courting Dinah. We hear nothing of Hetty's experiences as a convict – they hardly bear imagining when we think of, for example, Magwitch in

[52] *The Mill on the Floss*, bk. 4, ch. 3.

Great Expectations, and we are not encouraged to imagine them – and she is disposed of before she can return to embarrass everybody, with no more than a stilted comment from Dinah: 'The death of the poor wanderer, when she was coming back to us, has been sorrow upon sorrow,' and regret from Arthur Donnithorne that he cannot salve his conscience with some sort of handout.[53]

It is not just that George Eliot's male characters are less significant than her female characters. They are unsympathetic, in a collective way which underlines their differing superficial characteristics. They are particularly unsympathetic in their attitude to women, and on this point the warm-hearted Sir James Chettam and the cold-hearted Mr Casaubon are basically in agreement. They say scathing things about them, and the goodies and the baddies speak in the same voice. The comments of the noble-minded Felix Holt and the mean-minded Harold Transome on women are interchangeable as to content; Felix's style is more vigorous.

It doesn't signify what they think – they are not called upon to judge or to act.[54]

The utmost stretch of their ideas will not place them on a level with the intelligent fleas.[55]

You've had to worry yourself about things that don't properly belong to a woman. You shall have nothing to do now but to be grandmamma on satin cushions.[56]

I should like to come and scold her every day and make her cry and cut her fine hair off.[57]

This stream of male depreciation, relegation and sadism, so much a feature of George Eliot's novels, is bad enough and can cause lasting damage, but it can be fought against. Esther does fight back and in fact succeeds in denting the assumptions of both Felix and Harold. But physical seduction is shown to be worse and it cannot always be beaten off. If Arthur Donnithorne had contented himself with merely undermining Hetty's morale, with flirtatious treatment of her as an enchanting little kitten (which incidentally is exactly honest Adam Bede's view of her as well), he would have

---

[53] *Adam Bede,* conclusion.   [54] *Felix Holt,* ch. 2.
[55] Ibid., ch. 5.   [56] Ibid., ch. 1.   [57] Ibid., ch. 5.

destroyed her peace of mind but not all her worldly prospects and eventually her life, as he does by seducing her. Hetty is not the spotless victim of Adam's imagination but she is unusually vulnerable, being protected by neither common sense nor the ability to love, and has no real chance of escape from a man like Donnithorne. George Eliot introduces the theme of the irreversible consequences of seduction as early as *Janet's Repentance*, with the retrospective story of Mr Tryan whose treatment of Lucy resulted in her turning to prostitution and at length to suicide: after he had lured her from her father's house and set her up in an establishment under his 'protection', he left her alone for long periods while he travelled abroad.

In every case, including Adam's, the man's unshakeable view of what he cannot do is the most damaging factor to the woman: Mr Tryan cannot take Lucy with him as she is socially inferior; Arthur cannot marry Hetty, for the same reason. It is easy for the reader to be hypnotised into forgetting that, in fact, they *could*. But more significant (and even more hypnotic; one seldom hears it questioned) is Adam's assumption that he cannot wait for the girl he loves, and whom he loudly declares to have been an innocent victim, to return from transportation. He automatically casts her off, apparently without any soul-searching at all.

George Eliot draws a clear and proper distinction between the stories of girls like Lucy and Hetty and the cases of Mrs Glasher and Mrs Transome – experienced married women who have extramarital relationships. Neither Jermyn nor Grandcourt is a seducer. It is made plain that the women knew what they were doing and that their subsequent bitterness is rather unreasonable.

The general impression that there is something collectively amiss with George Eliot's male characters is reinforced by the study of one individual hero. Will Ladislaw is not presented as the ideal husband for Dorothea, but he is meant to be reasonably worthy of her, and we are told that she never regrets her second choice. Yet some of George Eliot's most stinging satire is directed at him, and in fact what she gives us is a superb portrait of the work-shy, mock-modest amateur, who 'writes' or 'paints' or 'composes', no matter which, who abandons pursuit after pursuit as being unworthy of his genius, and who scorns the plodders of the world especially when they provide him with the necessary money. Except that he is less rich and more conceited, he really is very like what the young Mr Brooke must have been. If Dorothea's first marriage is to her father, the second is to her uncle.

The portrayal of Will starts with Mr Casaubon's account of him. Dorothea, even before her marriage coming to the rescue of the younger man, has mentioned the great care necessary in choosing such professions as law or medicine. Mr Casaubon replies:

> Doubtless; but I fear that my young relative Will Ladislaw is chiefly determined in his aversion to these callings by a dislike to steady application, and to that kind of acquirement which is needful instrumentally, but is not charming or immediately inviting to self-indulgent taste ... I have pointed to my own manuscript volumes, which represent the toil of years preparatory to a work not yet accomplished. But in vain. To careful reasoning of this kind he replies by calling himself Pegasus, and every form of prescribed work 'harness'.[58]

At first we hardly know what to think. Shrewd Celia is made to find the comment apt and amusing, but the doubts that George Eliot has already cast on Mr Casaubon's own achievements are bound to undermine his criticism, when he starts comparing Will's attitude with his own.

However, we are not left long in doubt. On the next page the author, in her own person, gives the measure of Will's arrogance. In going abroad

> he had declined to fix on any more precise destination than the entire area of Europe. Genius, he held, is necessarily intolerant of fetters: on the one hand it must have the utmost play for its spontaneity; on the other, it may confidently await those messages from the universe which summon it to its peculiar work, only placing itself in an attitude of receptivity towards all sublime chances.[59]

In Rome, the painter Naumann, very much the professional, establishes Will's lack of any specific talent. Will is making silly, pretentious remarks about the difference between painting and writing.

[58] *Middlemarch*, ch. 9.   [59] Ibid., ch. 10.

'Your painting and Plastik are poor stuff after all. They perturb and dull conceptions instead of raising them. Language is a finer medium.'

'Yes, for those who can't paint,' said Naumann. 'There you have perfect right. I did not recommend you to paint, my friend.'[60]

And nobody recommends him to write either.

Naumann's well-applied snub rankles. When Will, a little later, is airing his views to Dorothea and she hopefully construes one of his speeches as his decision to become a painter, he passes on the snub to her, saying, 'with some coldness':

No, oh no. I have quite made up my mind against it. It is too one-sided a life. I have been seeing a great deal of the German artists here: I travelled from Frankfort with one of them. Some are fine, even brilliant fellows – but I should not like to get in their way of looking at the world entirely from the studio point of view.[61]

Dorothea thinks this is splendid stuff. She is destined to marry into Pseuds' Corner.

In this same interview Will further alienates the readers, if not Dorothea, by attacking Mr Casaubon for his ignorance of German scholarship in his own field. In fact the attack is justified but not in a way that Will, who is hitting out blindly at a new snub, is in a position to realise.[62]

Young Mr. Ladislaw was not at all deep himself in German writers: but very little achievement is required in order to pity another man's shortcomings.

Back in England, and the protégé of Mr Brooke, who thinks of him as 'a sort of Burke with a leaven of Shelley', Will does not charm everybody. Mrs Cadwallader is not impressed, even when his patron pleads his cause.

'He is trying his wings. He is just the sort of young fellow to rise. I should be glad to give him an opportunity. He would make a good secretary, now, like Hobbes, Milton, Swift – that sort of man.'

[60] Ibid., ch. 19.   [61] Ibid., ch. 21.

[62] See W. J. Harvey's essay, 'The Intellectual Background of the Novel' in Barbara Hardy's *Middlemarch: Critical Approaches.*

'I understand,' said Mrs. Cadwallader. 'One who can write speeches.'[63]

George Eliot herself speaks even more sharply than the vicar's wife. Politics is for Will only another medium for his essential amateurism.

> He studied the political situation with as ardent an interest as he had ever given to poetic metres or medievalism. It is undeniable that but for the desire to be where Dorothea was and perhaps the want of knowing what else to do, Will would not at this time have been meditating on the needs of the English people or criticising English statesmanship: he would probably have been rambling in Italy sketching plans for several dramas, trying prose and finding it too jejune, trying verse and finding it too artificial, beginning to copy 'bits' from old pictures, leaving off because they were 'no good', and observing that, after all, self-culture was the principal point; while in politics he would have been sympathising warmly with liberty and progress in general.[64]

This could hardly be more scathing. George Eliot does speak more kindly immediately afterwards.

> Our sense of duty must often wait for some work which shall take the place of dilettantism and make us feel that the quality of our action is not a matter of indifference.

In the Finale, where nearly everything takes place offstage, we are allowed to think, if we wish, that Will does at last find his lifework in politics. But the account of his self-fulfilment is cursory and not very persuasive. There is more conviction in the author's comment on Will's son who sounds like his father all over again. On Mr Brooke's eventual death,

> his estate was inherited by Dorothea's son, who might have represented Middlemarch, but declined, thinking that his opinions had less chance of being stifled if he remained out of doors.

Will's good qualities – his buoyancy, his ready understanding – and George Eliot's techniques for trying to make us like him – her recurring association of him with light, for

---

[63] *Middlemarch*, ch. 34.   [64] Ibid., ch. 46.

example, and such charming scenes as the one where he crosses the fields to church, composing a song and looking forward to seeing Dorothea – all go down before the satire which it almost seems she cannot help.

Yet however inadequate and inferior men may be, it is to them that women turn, not ibid for the strong arm and the protective presence, but for spiritual and moral guidance; and the turning is a deliberate action, very different from a passive submission to influence. The word 'confessor' appeared in critical comment early on. Leslie Stephen observed:

> It is not hard to say which is George Eliot's favourite theme. We may call it the woman in need of a confessor.[65]

Henry James's Pulcheria remarked about Deronda: 'A lay father-confessor. Dreadful.'[66]

Many of the father-confessors in George Eliot's novels are professionals, of varying eminence: Savonarola, Mr Tryan, Mr Gilfil, and it is true that these three, although Savonarola eventually fails Romola, do interpret the part more gracefully than the laymen who assume the right to preach: Felix Holt, for example, whose self-appointed hectoring of Esther can seem so uncouth. Of course, the most egregious lay-confessor is the one on which Pulcheria rightly picks: Deronda. To do him justice his quasi-priestly function is half forced upon him, principally by Gwendolen, though also by Hans Meyrick.

> Without the aid of sacred ceremony or costume her feelings had turned this man, only a few years older than herself, into a priest.[67]

And at times he resents the situation.

> He was conscious of that peculiar irritation which will sometimes befall the man whom others are inclined to trust as a mentor – the irritation of perceiving that he is supposed to be entirely off the same plane of desire and temptation as those who confess to him.[68]

But on the whole he has only himself to thank and most of the time he appears to enjoy his rôle. He certainly makes

[65] *Cornhill Magazine*, Feb 1881.
[66] *Atlantic Monthly*, Dec 1876.
[67] *Daniel Deronda*, ch. 35. [68] Ibid., ch. 37.

no attempt to slough it off; unlike Casaubon, who seems to know he cannot sustain it: after his marriage he systematically refuses to listen to Dorothea's confidences. In fact his sustained refusal is fatal to the relationship. His wife would probably never have criticised him had he felt able to be her confessor,

> if she had been encouraged to pour forth her girlish and womanly feeling, if he would have held her hands between his and listened with the delight of tenderness and understanding to all the little histories which made up her experience.[69]

Nearly all George Eliot's confessors fail their penitents. This is partly because the heroines go to the wrong box, often when the right one is nearer. It would have been more natural and more convenient for Gwendolen to confide in her clergyman uncle, Mr Gascoigne, than in a comparative stranger whose conferences with her were bound to be socially compromising. Whether Mr Gascoigne could have helped her is another matter. But does Deronda? The advice he gives her in the course of the story amounts to little more than a few gnomic platitudes about matters he has not himself experienced. What she learns, she, like Dorothea, learns without a teacher. Deronda's influence over her might not in fact have long survived the revelation that he was a Jew. Her reassuring words when she hears the news: '*You* are just the same as if you were not a Jew',[70] are the expression of an anti-Semitism which must soon have weakened his sway.

It is not always in understanding that the confessors are unsatisfactory. Philip Wakem understands Maggie perfectly, as his last sensitive and generous letter to her makes clear. Deronda understands Gwendolen well enough, even if he is over-optimistic about her future development. They fail for a variety of reasons, for most of which they can hardly be blamed. Mr Tryan dies of consumption. Mr Gilfil cannot, in spite of his devotion, restore Tina to a necessary love of life. Philip with all his mental abilities lacks the unblemished physique which proves to be the ultimate, and fatal, attraction for Maggie. Felix Holt, the bullying confessor, meets his match. Esther may say 'I am weak – my husband must be greater and nobler than I am', but their last recorded conver-

[69] *Middlemarch*, ch. 20.　　　　[70] *Daniel Deronda*, ch. 69.

sation has the light-hearted equality of a Mirabell and a Millamant. Savonarola has his own spiritual crisis to resolve. So has Daniel Deronda.

In all the novels there is one confessor who does not fail: Herr Klesmer. He is a remarkable character and an exception to the rule that in novels men of creative gifts – poets, painters, musicians – never sound as if they were any good. He does. He is certainly not presented as a perfect character; he is capable of petulance and vanity. But he is a superior being all the same.

> Klesmer's personality, especially his way of glancing round him, immediately suggested vast areas and a multitudinous audience.[71]

He makes people and houses and furniture seem to shrink. His two main contributions to the plot are godlike. His wise judgement has already been established by his love of Catherine Arrowpoint, the one mature woman in the book, a delightful girl whose attractions are not appreciated by everybody. He now exercises his discernment on the two opposing women characters, Gwendolen and Mirah, of whose fates he is at crucial points the arbiter. Not only does he show Gwendolen, and the world, what she is not, but he shows what Mirah is. After Gwendolen has resentfully taken his opinion as to her unsuitability for the stage and has, as a consequence, married Grandcourt, Herr Klesmer disappears from the scene for so long that we think he has left the story; happily married and increasingly famous he could well do so. But when Mirah is at a crisis in her fortunes he makes another of his spectacular appearances, not only awarding the accolade to Mirah's talent but, even in his boldly omniscient way, picking out which of the Meyrick girls has musical interests. As befits a *deus*, his arrival on these two important occasions is heralded by the sound of his *machina* wheels. In weighing up T. H. Huxley's quip that George Eliot depicts not the superiority of women but the inferiority of men, we should do well to remember Julius Klesmer.

[71] Ibid., ch. 39.